The Global
Findex Database 2021

The Global Findex Database 2021

Financial Inclusion, Digital Payments, and Resilience in the Age of COVID-19

Asli Demirgüç-Kunt
Leora Klapper
Dorothe Singer
Saniya Ansar

WORLD BANK GROUP

Contents

Maps

Tables

Foreword

The technological revolution, and the accelerated adoption of digital solutions as a result of the COVID-19 pandemic, are transforming access to finance. As this edition of *The Global Findex Database* shows, 71 percent of adults in developing economies now have a formal financial account, compared to 42 percent a decade ago when the first edition of the database was published. And the gap in access to finance between men and women in developing economies has fallen from 9 percentage points to 6 percentage points.

This is an important transformation for development. Having a financial account makes it easier, safer, and cheaper to receive wage payments from employers, to send remittances to family members, and to pay for goods and services. Mobile money accounts also make it possible, even for the poor, to save and cope with adverse shocks. And individual accounts give women more say on their household finances.

Importantly, the digital revolution is a powerful tool to improve governance. Social programs can now channel transfers directly to their beneficiaries' mobile phones, reducing leakage and delays. This potential became a reality during the COVID-19 crisis, helping cushion its impact on livelihoods. Digitalization also increases transparency as money flows from a country's budgets to government agencies to people, reducing the scope for corruption.

This edition of *The Global Findex Database* shows clear advances under way. The share of adults making or receiving digital payments in developing economies grew from 35 percent in 2014 to 57 percent in 2021, outpacing growth in account ownership. In Sub-Saharan Africa, 39 percent of mobile money account holders now use their account to save. And more than one-third of adults in developing economies who paid a utility bill from an account did so for the first time after the start of the COVID-19 pandemic—evidence of the pandemic's impact on digital adoption.

It is critical to build on these encouraging trends, especially given the current headwinds. High inflation, slow economic growth, and food scarcity will affect the poor the most. Expanding their access to finance, reducing the cost of digital transactions, and channeling wage payments and social transfers through accounts will be critically important to mitigate the reversals in development from the ongoing turbulence.

Further supporting this transformation requires decisive action across three areas:

- **Creating an enabling policy environment.** Progress in access to finance depends on the mobile phone much more than the banking system. Ubiquitous and affordable internet access is therefore a prerequisite to further progress. More progress is also needed on the policy front. The lack of verifiable identity is one of the main reasons why adults remain excluded from financial services. India has pioneered a successful model for universal identity, paying due attention to safety and privacy. The interoperability of systems and the availability of a low-cost switch for financial transactions are equally important. Consumer protections and stable regulations are needed to foster safe and fair practices by financial and technology companies.

- **Promoting the digitalization of payments.** Global Findex 2021 data show that 865 million account owners in developing economies opened their first financial institution account for the purpose of receiving money from the government. This helped households directly and also helps build digital payment systems. It serves as a foundation to assemble credible social registers, identifying gaps and overlaps along the way. As digital payments become more common and the cost falls, many private businesses will be able to pay their workers and suppliers electronically—and should. The digital revolution offers a chance to increase formal sector employment without making compliance overburdening. At a time of tighter budget constraints, digital payments can help reduce tax avoidance and evasion, broadening the tax base.

- **Emphasizing access for women and the poor.** The gender gap in access to finance has narrowed, but it still exists. Women, along with the poor, are more likely to lack identification or a mobile phone, to live far from a bank branch, and to need support to open and effectively use a financial account. Policy makers will need to make additional efforts to include underserved population groups in the ongoing transformation. Financial education programs are among the tools to consider, and they are bound to be more effective if they involve peer-to-peer learning, for instance through women's self-help groups.

At the World Bank we are firmly committed to financial inclusion through digitalization. Through country engagements, we are supporting our counterparts in boosting mobile phone networks, removing regulatory barriers to foster access to finance. We are also helping with the adoption of e-government platforms and the modernization of social protection systems.

Improving the knowledge on financial inclusion is part of our contribution, and the Global Findex Database is one of its cornerstones.

David Malpass
President
The World Bank Group

Acknowledgments

The Global Findex Database 2021 was prepared by the Finance and Private Sector Development team of the Development Research Group in the World Bank's Development Economics Vice Presidency (DEC). The team, led by Leora Klapper, Dorothe Singer, and Saniya Ansar, comprised Raaga Akkineni, Pratyush Dubey, Paul Gubbins, Mansi Panchamia, and Jijun Wang. Miriam Sangallo Kalembo and B. Elaine Wylie provided administrative support. Overall guidance was provided by Aart Kraay, director of development policy in DEC and deputy chief economist of the World Bank; Deon Filmer, director of the Development Research Group in DEC; and Robert Cull, research manager in DEC.

Special thanks are extended to the senior leadership and managers in the World Bank's Equitable Growth, Finance, and Institutions Vice Presidency (EFI VP) for their partnership and guidance in preparing this report, including Jean Pesme, global director; and Mahesh Uttamchandani, practice manager, Finance, Competitiveness, and Innovation (FCI), EFI VP; as well as the FCI regional practice managers. The team is also grateful for the comments on early drafts provided by Denis Medvedev, Tim Ogden, and Sophie Sirtaine. The team is grateful to Oya Ardic, Jennifer Chien, Maria Teresa Chimienti, Eric Duflos, Seth Garz, Xavier Giné, Rafe Mazer, Harish Natarajan, Rachel Pizatella-Haswell, Matthew Saal, and Imtiaz Ul Haq, as well as to World Bank colleagues in the Development Economics and Equitable Growth, Finance, and Institutions Vice Presidencies and the International Finance Corporation's Financial Institutions Growth group and Sector Economics and Development Impact department for providing substantive comments at different stages of the project. Helpful substantive comments were also received from the Bill & Melinda Gates Foundation, Better Than Cash Alliance, Consultative Group to Assist the Poor, GSM Association, G20's Global Partnership for Financial Inclusion, Women's World Banking, Mastercard Center for Inclusive Growth, Visa Social Impact, and Office of the UN Secretary-General's Special Advocate for Inclusive Finance for Development (UNSGSA). The team appreciates as well the excellent survey execution and related support provided by Gallup, Inc., under the direction of Joe Daly and with the support of Cynthia English.

The team is grateful to the Bill & Melinda Gates Foundation, the Mastercard Foundation, and the World Bank's Development Economics and Equitable Growth, Finance, and Institutions Vice Presidencies for their financial support, which made the collection and dissemination of the data possible. The team is also grateful to Flourish Ventures for their financial support for and thought partnership in our financial well-being chapter.

Laura Starita provided developmental guidance in drafting the report and led a team at Forge & Refine that included Kate Marshall Dole and Sara Laws. The report was edited by Sabra Ledent and proofread by Gwenda Larsen. Gordon Schuit was the principal graphic designer, with additional images created by Loaded Pictures. Maps were created by Marlee Beers, under the guidance of Bruno Bonansea from the World Bank's Map Design Unit. The databank was set up by Hiroko Maeda, and interactive web visualizations were created by Divyanshi Wadhwa and Kevin William Conklin, under the guidance of Umar Serajuddin. An online data visualization tool was created by Manar Eliriqsousi and his team, led by Misun Kim. Anugraha Palan and Shane Romig developed the communications and engagement strategy. Mikael Reventar and Roula Yazigi provided web and online services and related guidance. Special thanks are extended to Stephen Pazdan, who coordinated and oversaw the formal production of the report; Patricia Katayama, who oversaw the overall publication process; and the World Bank's Formal Publishing Program.

Team members would also like to offer their gratitude to the over half-million adults around the world who took the time to participate in the Global Findex survey over the past decade.

About the Global Findex Database

Financial inclusion is a cornerstone of development, and since 2011, the Global Findex Database has been the definitive source of data on the ways in which adults around the world use financial services, from payments to savings and borrowing, and manage financial events such as a major expense or a loss of income. Results from the first survey were published in 2011 and have been followed by subsequent survey results from 2014 and in 2017. The 2021 edition, based on nationally representative surveys of about 128,000 adults in 123 economies during the COVID-19 pandemic, contains updated indicators on access to and use of formal and informal financial services, including on the use of cards, mobile phones, and the internet to make and receive digital payments—including the adoption of digital merchant and utility payments during the pandemic—and offers insights into the behaviors that enable financial resilience. The data also identify gaps in access to and usage of financial services by women and poor adults.

The survey results reflect a snapshot in time based on questions that respondents answer about their habits and experiences of the previous year. Comparing the current survey with results from the 2011, 2014, and 2017 editions reveals which trends endure, expand, and grow over extended periods of time. The report provides global averages as well as averages for high-income and developing economies. It also highlights findings for select economies to illustrate general patterns and interesting findings. Data for all economies for all figures are available on the Global Findex website.

The Global Findex Database has become a mainstay of global efforts to promote financial inclusion. In addition to being widely cited by policy makers, researchers, and development practitioners, Global Findex data are used to track progress toward the United Nations Sustainable Development Goals.

The database, the full text of the report, and the underlying economy-level data for all figures—along with the questionnaire, the survey methodology, and other relevant materials—are available at http://www.worldbank .org/globalfindex.

All regional and global averages presented in this publication are adult population weighted. Regional averages include only developing economies (low- and middle-income economies as classified by the World Bank). Income group classifications reflect the World Bank income group classifications from 2020.

The reference citation for *The Global Findex Database 2021* is as follows:

Demirgüç-Kunt, Asli, Leora Klapper, Dorothe Singer, and Saniya Ansar. 2022. *The Global Findex Database 2021: Financial Inclusion, Digital Payments, and Resilience in the Age of COVID-19*. Washington, DC: World Bank.

Executive Summary

Financial services such as payments, savings accounts, and credit are a cornerstone of development. Accounts—whether they are with a bank or regulated institution such as a credit union, microfinance institution, or a mobile money service provider—allow their owners to safely and affordably store, send, and receive money for everyday needs, plan for emergencies, and make productive investments for the future, such as in health, education, and businesses. People without an account, by contrast, must manage their money using informal mechanisms, including cash, that may be less safe, less reliable, and more expensive than formal methods.

Evidence shows that households and businesses that have access to financial services are better able to withstand financial shocks than those that do not.[1] In Chile low-income women who were members of microfinance institutions and received free savings accounts were able to reduce their reliance on debt and improve their ability to make ends meet during an economic emergency.[2] Digital financial services such as mobile money let users safely and inexpensively store funds and transfer them quickly and affordably across long distances, which led to higher remittances and consumption and more investments. In Kenya, for example, mobile money users who experienced an unexpected drop in income were able to receive money from a more geographically disbursed social network of family and friends and so did not have to reduce household spending.[3] In Bangladesh, very poor rural households with family members who had migrated to the city received higher remittance payments when they had a mobile money account, and so spent more on food and other items, were able to reduce borrowing, and were less likely to experience extreme poverty.[4]

For women, accounts can enable financial independence and strengthen economic empowerment. In the Philippines, women who used commitment savings products that encouraged regular deposits into a personal bank account increased their household decision-making power and shifted their spending to household goods relevant to their needs, such as washing machines.[5] In India, a government workfare program that reached over 100 million people showed that paying women their benefits directly into their own account (and not into the account of a male household head) increased women's financial control, influenced gender norms preventing women from working, and incentivized women to find employment, compared with those paid in cash.[6] In another study in Nepal, women-headed households spent 15 percent more on nutritious foods after receiving free savings accounts.[7]

The receipt of payments such as wages and government support directly into an account can help achieve development goals. For example, studies have found that workers who received their wages through direct deposit, which can encourage account holders to leave the money in the account as well as take advantage of auto-transfers to savings instruments, had higher savings than workers who were paid in cash.[8] In Bangladesh, factory workers who received their wages directly into an account also learned to use their account without assistance and avoid illicit withdrawal fees.[9] Moreover, digitalizing government payments can reduce administrative costs and leakage (payments that do not reach the intended beneficiaries).[10]

---

1. Moore et al. (2019).
2. Pomeranz and Kast (2022).
3. Jack and Suri (2014).
4. Lee et al. (2021).
5. Ashraf, Karlan, and Yin (2010).
6. Field et al. (2021).
7. Prina (2015).
8. Blumenstock, Callen, and Ghani (2018).
9. Breza, Kanz, and Klapper (2020).
10. Aker et al. (2016); Muralidharan, Niehaus, and Sukhtankar (2016).

Such evidence on the benefits of financial inclusion has spurred efforts to expand account ownership and productive usage. Since 2011, the Global Findex survey has documented growth—at times incremental and at times dramatic—in account ownership across more than 140 economies. The Global Findex 2021 survey was conducted during the COVID-19 pandemic—a crisis that further mobilized financial inclusion efforts across the world through several mechanisms, including the emergency relief payments that governments sent to accounts.[11] This and other factors have contributed to the following key findings.

Worldwide, account ownership has reached 76 percent of adults—and 71 percent of adults in developing economies

Globally, in 2021, 76 percent of adults had an account at a bank or regulated institution such as a credit union, microfinance institution, or mobile money service provider. Account ownership around the world increased by 50 percent in the 10 years spanning 2011 to 2021, from 51 percent of adults to 76 percent of adults. From 2017 to 2021, the average rate of account ownership in developing economies increased by 8 percentage points, from 63 percent of adults to 71 percent of adults. In Sub-Saharan Africa, this expansion largely stems from the adoption of mobile money.

Recent growth in account ownership has been widespread across dozens of developing economies. This geographic spread is in stark contrast to the growth seen from 2011 to 2017, which took place mostly in China or India.

Despite continued gaps in financial services for typically underserved adults, such as women, the poor, and the less educated, progress has been made. For example, the gender gap in account ownership across developing economies has fallen to 6 percentage points from 9 percentage points, where it hovered for many years.

Receiving payments into an account is a catalyst for using other financial services, such as relying on an account to save, borrow, and store money for cash management

In developing economies, the share of adults making or receiving digital payments grew from 35 percent in 2014 to 57 percent in 2021. In high-income economies, the share of adults making or receiving digital payments is nearly universal (95 percent). Receiving a payment directly into an account is a gateway to using other financial services. Indeed, 83 percent of adults in developing economies who received a digital payment also made a digital payment, up from 66 percent in 2014 and 70 percent in 2017. Almost two-thirds of digital payment recipients also used their account to store money for cash management; about 40 percent used their account for saving; and 40 percent of payment recipients borrowed formally.

Payments may pave the way for wider adoption of financial services when it is easier to leave transferred money in an account until it is needed and then make a payment directly. Similarly, once money is in an account it is relatively easier to keep it there for savings. Receiving a payment into an account—especially if the payment can be used to document a regular income stream over time—can also ease the process of borrowing money formally.

Mobile money has become an important enabler of financial inclusion in Sub-Saharan Africa—especially for women—as a driver of account ownership and of account usage through mobile payments, saving, and borrowing

In Sub-Saharan Africa in 2021, 55 percent of adults had an account, including 33 percent of adults who had a mobile money account—the largest share of any region in the world and more than three times larger than the 10 percent global average of mobile money account ownership. Sub-Saharan Africa is home to all 11 economies in which a larger share of adults had only a mobile money account rather than a bank or other financial institution account. The spread of mobile money accounts has created new opportunities to better serve women, poor

---

11.   Gentilini et al. (2020); GPFI (Global Partnership for Financial Inclusion) and World Bank (2021).

people, and other groups who traditionally have been excluded from the formal financial system. Indeed, there are some early signs that mobile money accounts may be helping to close the gender gap.

Although mobile money services were first launched so that people could send remittances to friends and family living elsewhere within the country, adoption and usage have spread beyond those origins. Such services are still a powerful tool for sending domestic remittances, but the Global Findex survey revealed that in 2021 about three in four mobile account owners in Sub-Saharan Africa used their mobile money account to make or receive at least one payment that was not person-to-person. Mobile money accounts have also become an important method to save in Sub-Saharan Africa, where 15 percent of adults—and 39 percent of mobile money account holders—used one to save—the same share that used a formal savings account at a bank or other financial institution. Seven percent of adults in Sub-Saharan Africa also borrowed using their mobile money account.

COVID-19 catalyzed growth in the use of digital payments

In developing economies in 2021, 18 percent of adults paid utility bills directly from an account. About one-third of these adults did so for the first time after the onset of the COVID-19 pandemic. The share of adults making a digital merchant payment also increased after the outbreak of COVID-19. For example, in India, 80 million adults made their first digital merchant payment during the pandemic. In China, 82 percent of adults made a digital merchant payment in 2021, including over 100 million adults (11 percent) who did so for the first time after the start of the pandemic. In developing economies, excluding China, 20 percent of adults made a digital merchant payment in 2021. Contained within that 20 percent are the 8 percent of adults, on average, who did so for the first time after the start of the pandemic, or about 40 percent of those who made a digital merchant payment. These data point to the role of the pandemic and social distancing restrictions in accelerating the adoption of digital payments.

Despite promising growth in account ownership and use, only about half of adults in developing economies could access extra funds within 30 days if faced with an unexpected expense, and about two-thirds of adults were very worried about at least one area of financial stress

Only 55 percent of adults in developing economies could access extra funds within 30 days without much difficulty. Friends and family were the first-line source of extra funds for 30 percent of adults in developing economies, but nearly half of those said the money would be hard to get. Furthermore, women and the poor were less likely than men and richer individuals to successfully raise extra funds and more likely to rely on friends and family as their go-to source.

About 50 percent of adults in developing economies were very worried, in particular, about covering health expenses in the event of a major illness or accident, and 36 percent said health care costs were their biggest worry. In Sub-Saharan Africa, worry over school fees was more common than in other regions; 54 percent of adults are very worried about them, and for 29 percent it is their biggest worry. Eighty-two percent of adults in developing economies were very worried (52 percent) or somewhat worried (30 percent) about the continued financial toll of the COVID-19 pandemic.

Governments, private employers, and financial service providers—including fintechs—could help expand financial access and usage among the unbanked by lowering barriers and improving infrastructure

Lack of money, distance to the nearest financial institution, and insufficient documentation were consistently cited by the 1.4 billion unbanked adults as some of the primary reasons they did not have an account. Yet there are clear opportunities to address some of these barriers. Enabling infrastructure has an important role to play. For example, global efforts to increase inclusive access to trusted identification systems and mobile phones could be leveraged to increase account ownership for hard-to-reach populations. The chief actors in this effort, such as governments, telecommunications providers, and financial services providers, must also invest in regulations and governance to ensure that safe, affordable, and convenient products and functionality are available and accessible to all adults in their economies.

Findings from the Global Findex 2021 survey likewise reveal new opportunities to drive financial inclusion by increasing account ownership among the unbanked and expanding the use of financial services among those who already have accounts—in particular, by leveraging digital payments. For example, hundreds of millions of unbanked adults received payments in cash—such as for wages, government transfers, or the sale of agricultural goods. Digitalizing some of these payments is a proven way to increase account ownership. In developing economies, 39 percent of adults—or 57 percent of those with a financial institution account (excluding mobile money)—opened their first account (excluding mobile money) at a financial institution, specifically to receive a wage payment or receive money from the government.

Financially inexperienced users may not be able to benefit from account ownership if they do not understand how to use financial services in a way that optimizes benefits and avoids consumer protection risks

About two-thirds of unbanked adults said that if they opened an account (excluding mobile money) at a financial institution, they could not use it without help. About one-third of mobile money account holders in Sub-Saharan Africa say they could not use their mobile money account without help from a family member or an agent. Women are 5 percentage points more likely than men to need help using their mobile money account. Inexperienced account owners who must ask a family member or a banking agent for help using an account may be more vulnerable to financial abuse. Also, one in five adults in developing economies who receive a wage payment into an account paid unexpected fees on the transaction. Together, these issues point to the fact that less experienced financial customers may be more vulnerable to fraud. Thus investments are needed in numeracy and financial literacy skills, product design that takes into account customer usage patterns and capabilities, as well as strong consumer safeguards to ensure that customers benefit from financial access and to build public trust in the financial system.

References

Aker, Jenny, Rachid Boumnijel, Amanada McClelland, and Niall Tierney. 2016. "Payment Mechanisms and Antipoverty Programs: Evidence from a Mobile Money Cash Transfer Experiment in Niger." *Economic Development and Cultural Change* 65 (1): 1–7.

Ashraf, Nava, Dean Karlan, and Wesley Yin. 2010. "Female Empowerment: Further Evidence from a Commitment Savings Product in the Philippines." *World Development* 38 (3): 333–44.

Blumenstock, Joshua, Michael Callen, and Tarek Ghani. 2018. "Why Do Defaults Affect Behavior? Experimental Evidence from Afghanistan." *American Economic Review* 108 (10): 2868–901.

Breza, Emily, Martin Kanz, and Leora Klapper. 2020. "Learning to Navigate a New Financial Technology: Evidence from Payroll Accounts." NBER Working Paper 28249, National Bureau of Economic Research, Cambridge, MA.

Field, Erica, Rohini Pande, Natalia Rigo, Simone Schaner, and Charity Troyer Moore. 2021. "On Her Own Account: How Strengthening Women's Financial Control Impacts Labor Supply and Gender Norms." *American Economic Review* 11 (7): 2342–75.

Gentilini, Ugo, Mohamed Almenfi, Ian Orton, and Pamela Dale. 2020. *Social Protection and Jobs Responses to COVID-19: A Real-Time Review of Country Measures.* Washington, DC: World Bank. https://socialprotection .org/discover/publications/social-protection-and-jobs-responses-covid-19-real-time-review-country.

GPFI (Global Partnership for Financial Inclusion) and World Bank. 2021. "The Impact of COVID-19 on Digital Financial Inclusion." https://www.gpfi.org/sites/gpfi/files/sites/default/files/5_WB%20Report_The%20 impact%20of%20COVID-19%20on%20digital%20financial%20inclusion.pdf.

Jack, William, and Tavneet Suri. 2014. "Risk Sharing and Transactions Costs: Evidence from Kenya's Mobile Money Revolution." *American Economic Review* 104 (1): 183–223.

Lee, Jean N., Jonathan Morduch, Saravana Ravindran, Abu Shonchoy, and Hassan Zaman. 2021. "Poverty and Migration in the Digital Age: Experimental Evidence on Mobile Banking in Bangladesh." *American Economic Journal: Applied Economics* 13 (1): 38–71.

Moore, Danielle, Zahra Niazi, Rebecca Rouse, and Berber Kramer. 2019. "Building Resilience through Financial Inclusion: A Review of Existing Evidence and Knowledge Gaps." Financial Inclusion Program, Innovations for Poverty Action, Washington, DC. https://www.poverty-action.org/publication/building-resilience-through -financial-inclusion-review existing-evidence-and-knowledge.

Muralidharan, Karthik, Paul Niehaus, and Sandip Sukhtankar. 2016. "Building State Capacity: Evidence from Biometric Smartcards in India." *American Economic Review* 106 (10): 2895–929.

Pomeranz, Dina, and Felipe Kast. 2022. "Savings Accounts to Borrow Less: Experimental Evidence from Chile." *Journal of Human Resources.* Published ahead of print, March 9, 2022. doi:10.3368/jhr.0619-10264R3.

Prina, Silvia. 2015. "Banking the Poor via Savings Accounts: Evidence from a Field Experiment." *Journal of Development Economics* 115 (July): 16–31.

Financial Access

Introduction

Account ownership, the fundamental measure of financial inclusion, is the gateway that equips men and women to use financial services in a way that facilitates development. Owners of accounts—whether those accounts are with a bank or regulated institution such as a credit union, microfinance institution, or mobile money service provider—are able to store, send, and receive money, enabling the owners to invest in health, education, and businesses.

Account holders are better able to avoid a slide into poverty because they find it easier to rely on savings or receive financial resources from friends or family in the event of a financial emergency, such as an income loss or crop failure. Evidence shows that households and businesses that have access to financial services such as payments, savings accounts, and credit are better able to withstand financial shocks than those that do not.[1] People without an account must, by contrast, manage their money using informal mechanisms that may be less safe, less reliable, and more expensive than formal methods.

Digital financial services such as mobile money accounts let users safely and inexpensively store funds and transfer them quickly across long distances, which leads to higher domestic remittances and consumption. For example, in Kenya researchers found that mobile money users who experienced an unexpected drop in income were able to receive money from a more geographically disbursed social network of family and friends and did not have to reduce household spending. By contrast, nonusers and users with poor access to the mobile money network reduced their purchases of food and other items by between 7 percent and 10 percent.[2] In Tanzania, a country in which many are dependent on agriculture, low rainfall resulted in lower consumption on average, but mobile money users were able to maintain consumption because of improved risk sharing.[3] Researchers in Uganda found that adopting mobile money services increased the total value of remittances by 36 percent and was associated with a 13 percent increase in per capita consumption.[4] In Bangladesh, investigators introduced mobile money accounts to very poor rural households and family members who had migrated to the city and found that mobile money increased remittance payments. As a result, rural households spent more on food and other items and reduced borrowing, and extreme poverty fell.[5] And another study in Kenya revealed that mobile money users spent more on health care and were more likely to use formal health services when experiencing a medical emergency.[6]

For women, studies show that accounts can enable financial independence and strengthen economic empowerment. In a field experiment in the Philippines, researchers found that women who used commitment savings products that encouraged regular deposits into a personal account with a rural bank increased their household decision-making power and shifted their spending to household goods relevant to their needs,

1. Moore et al. (2019).
2. Jack and Suri (2014).
3. Riley (2018).
4. Munyegera and Matsumoto (2016).
5. Lee et al. (2021).
6. Haseeb and Cowan (2021).

such as washing machines.[7] In Kenya, researchers compared women's development outcomes in areas where mobile money accounts spread rapidly with those in areas where mobile accounts were less widespread. They found that areas with high mobile money access had fewer women in poverty by 9 percentage points, and their consumption was higher by more than 18.5 percent compared with that in areas with limited mobile money access.[8] In another study, women-headed households spent 15 percent more on nutritious foods after receiving free savings accounts.[9] Access to mobile money–based savings tools also can reduce women's reliance on high-risk financial sources of income (such as transactional sex), according to a study of low-income women in urban and rural western Kenya.[10] Savings also plays a role in risk management. In Chile, a study of more than 3,500 low-income members of microfinance institutions found that women who received free savings accounts reduced their reliance on debt and improved their ability to make ends meet during an economic emergency.[11]

The COVID-19 pandemic further mobilized financial inclusion efforts across the world through several mechanisms, including the emergency relief payments that governments sent to bank accounts and debit cards.[12] A recent study found that during epidemics more people conduct transactions via the internet, mobile banking accounts, and ATMs (automated teller machines). These shifts do not always persist over time, however, and digital adoption tends to be concentrated among relatively younger and wealthier people.[13] Although the longer-term impacts of the COVID-19 pandemic on financial inclusion efforts remain to be seen, initial research findings suggest an acceleration in the adoption of accounts and digital payments.

Account ownership is needed to use financial services, but ownership alone is not enough to drive development outcomes. An experimental study to test the impact of expanding access to basic bank accounts in Chile, Malawi, and Uganda, for example, found that giving free bank accounts to previously unbanked adults had no impact on savings or welfare.[14] This finding suggests that efforts directed only at expanding access to basic accounts are unlikely to lead to development outcomes unless policies, products, and incentives to increase the use of accounts for payments, savings, and credit are adopted (usage is discussed in chapter 2).

Given the range of the potential benefits of financial access, there is plenty to celebrate in the Global Findex 2021 findings on account ownership as described in section 1.1. But first a word is needed on methods. The Global Findex 2021 data collected in 2021 cover 123 economies. Findex has traditionally collected data through face-to-face interviews in most developing economies, but that method was not possible in some of these economies in 2021 because of the ongoing COVID-19 restrictions on mobility. Thus data were collected for some economies through phone-based surveys, which have some advantages for representation and some disadvantages (see the Findex methodology in appendix A for details on the survey methods and a list of the countries where phone-based methods were used).

---

7.   Ashraf, Karlan, and Yin (2010).
8.   Suri and Jack (2016).
9.   Prina (2015).
10. Jones and Gong (2021).
11. Pomeranz and Kast (2022).
12. Gentilini et al. (2021); GPFI and World Bank (2021).
13. Saka, Eichengreen, and Aksoy (2021).
14. Dupas et al. (2018).

Global Findex 2021 survey headline findings on account ownership

The Global Findex 2021 survey revealed growth in account ownership. The key findings are as follows:

Account ownership

- Worldwide, account ownership increased by 50 percent in the 10 years spanning 2011 to 2021, to reach 76 percent of the global adult population.

- From 2017 to 2021, the average rate of account ownership in developing economies increased by 8 percentage points, from 63 percent to 71 percent.

- Mobile money is driving growth in account ownership, particularly in Sub-Saharan Africa, where 33 percent of adults have a mobile money account.

- Recent growth in account ownership has been widespread across dozens of developing economies. This geographic spread is in stark contrast to that from 2011 to 2017, when most of the newly banked adults lived in China or India.

- The gender gap in account ownership across developing economies has fallen to 6 percentage points from 9 percentage points, where it hovered for many years.

Opportunities to increase account ownership

- Despite these areas of progress, there continue to be gaps in financial access for typically underserved adults. Women, the poor, the young, and those outside the workforce all continue to have lower account ownership rates on average than men and adults who are higher-income, older, and in the workforce.

- Lack of money, distance to the nearest financial institution, and insufficient documentation are consistently cited by unbanked adults as some of the primary reasons they do not have an account.

- Lack of a mobile phone is a common reason cited in Sub-Saharan Africa by 35 percent of unbanked adults for not having a mobile money account.

- Global efforts for inclusive access to digital identification and mobile phones could be used to increase the account ownership of hard-to-reach populations.

This chapter presents detailed Global Findex 2021 data on the trends in financial access at the global and regional levels and offers examples from specific economies that exemplify, or cut against, the trends. Section 1.1 describes the global growth in financial access, the impact of mobile money on that growth, and the degree to which growth has been equitable for women, the poor, the young, and the less educated. Section 1.2 presents data on those who remain unbanked and the reasons they give for not having an account. The section also points out opportunities to expand financial access.

1.1 Account ownership

1.1 ACCOUNT OWNERSHIP

Accounts are a safe way to store money and build savings for the future. They also make it easier to pay bills, access credit, make purchases, and send or receive remittances. Around 76 percent of people worldwide have an account either at a bank or similarly regulated deposit-taking financial institution, including a mobile money service provider. Yet a regional or economy-level view of account ownership shows wide variation (map 1.1.1). Among the 123 surveyed economies, account ownership ranges from just 6 percent in South Sudan to universal ownership in high-income economies such as Canada, Germany, and the United Kingdom.

How do we define account ownership?

The Global Findex 2021 defines account ownership as ownership of an individual or jointly owned account at a regulated institution, such as a bank, credit union, microfinance institution, post office, or mobile money service provider. Data on adults with an account also include an additional 3 percent of respondents who reported having a debit card in their own name; receiving wages, government transfers, a public sector pension, or payments for the sale of agricultural products into a financial institution account or mobile money account in the past 12 months; or paying utility bills from a financial institution account in the past 12 months.

Financial institution refers to banks and other financial institutions in a specific country that offer a transaction account and that fall under prudential regulation by a government body (excluding mobile money accounts). The definition does not include nonbank financial institutions such as pension funds, retirement accounts, insurance companies, or equity holdings such as stocks. Data on adults with a mobile money account only include respondents who personally used a mobile money service to make payments, buy things, or to send or receive money in the past 12 months.

MAP 1.1.1

Account ownership rates vary across the world

Adults with an account (%), 2021

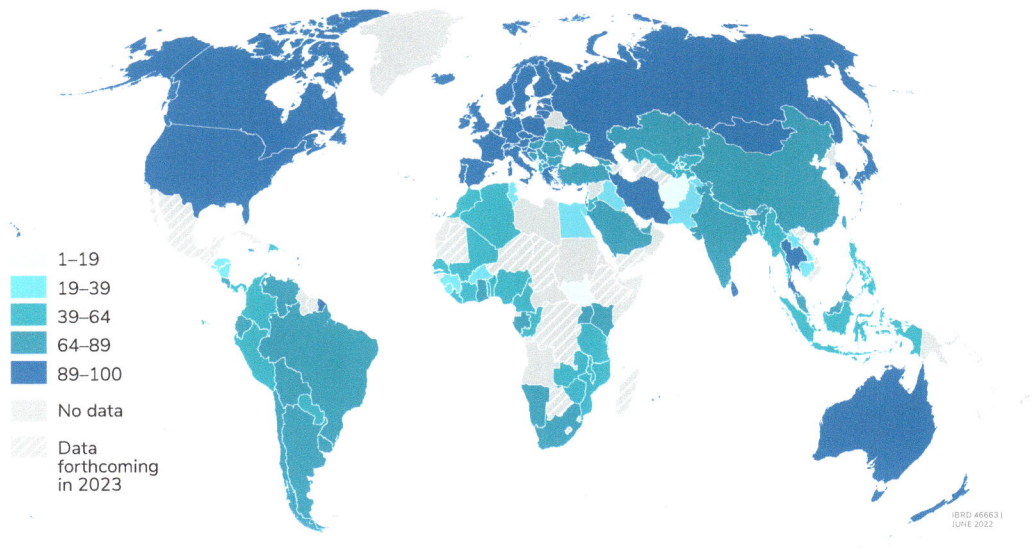

Source: Global Findex Database 2021.

FIGURE 1.1.1

Account ownership differs significantly even within income groups

Adults with an account (%), 2021

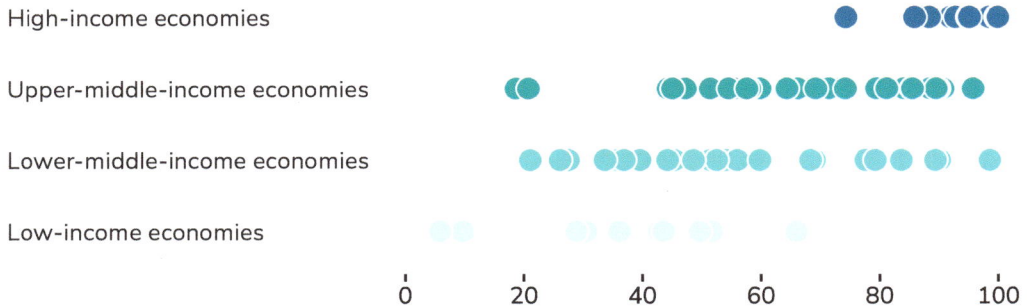

Source: Global Findex Database 2021.

The data also show significant differences in account ownership rates across economies in the same income group (figure 1.1.1). For example, among low-income economies account ownership varies from 6 percent in South Sudan to 66 percent in Uganda. Among high-income economies, Uruguay has the lowest account ownership rate, at 74 percent, and 10 high-income economies have 100 percent account ownership. Thailand boasts the highest account ownership rate among upper-middle-income economies, at 96 percent. And in lower-middle-income economies, account ownership ranges from 21 percent in Pakistan to 98 percent in Mongolia.[15]

Worldwide, account ownership grew by 50 percent over the past decade

The 76 percent global account ownership rate in 2021 represents a 50 percent increase from the worldwide average of 51 percent reported in 2011, a decade ago (figure 1.1.2). Although account ownership increased on average in both high-income and developing economies, the average rate of growth in developing economies was steeper. Overall, account ownership in developing economies grew by 30 percentage points, from 42 percent in 2011 to 71 percent in 2021—a more than 70 percent increase.

Individual economies saw different rates of growth over the past decade (figure 1.1.3). Between 2011 and 2021, economies such as Peru, South Africa, and Uganda drove up the average with account ownership increases of 25 percentage points or more. Uganda, in fact, saw its rate more than triple, from 20 percent to 66 percent. In India, account ownership more than doubled in the past decade, from 35 percent in 2011 to 78 percent in 2021. This outcome stemmed in part from an Indian government policy launched in 2014 that leveraged biometric identification cards to boost account ownership among unbanked adults. Other economies saw much smaller increases over longer periods. Pakistan, for example, grew by just 11 percentage points over the past decade, from 10 percent in 2011 to 21 percent in 2021. The Arab Republic of Egypt and Nigeria increased ownership by 18 percentage points and 16 percentage points, respectively—from 10 percent to 27 percent in Egypt, and from 30 percent to 45 percent in Nigeria.

The sources of global growth in account ownership have also changed and expanded in recent years. Between 2017 and 2021, account ownership grew by more than 5 percentage points in 62 out of 123 economies, including by more than 10 percentage points in 34 economies. That finding contrasts with the concentrated growth that occurred between 2014 and 2017, driven by India, when account ownership increased by 27 percentage points. During the same period, account ownership in developing economies grew by 8 percentage points, from

---

15. The high account ownership rate in Mongolia is driven by the Child Money Programme (CMP). A monthly allowance of Tog 20,000 (about US$7) is paid directly into a bank account by the Mongolian government for every child under the age of 18. Government payments into accounts are discussed further in chapter 2.

FIGURE 1.1.2

Global account ownership increased from 51 percent to 76 percent between 2011 and 2021

Adults with an account (%), 2011–21

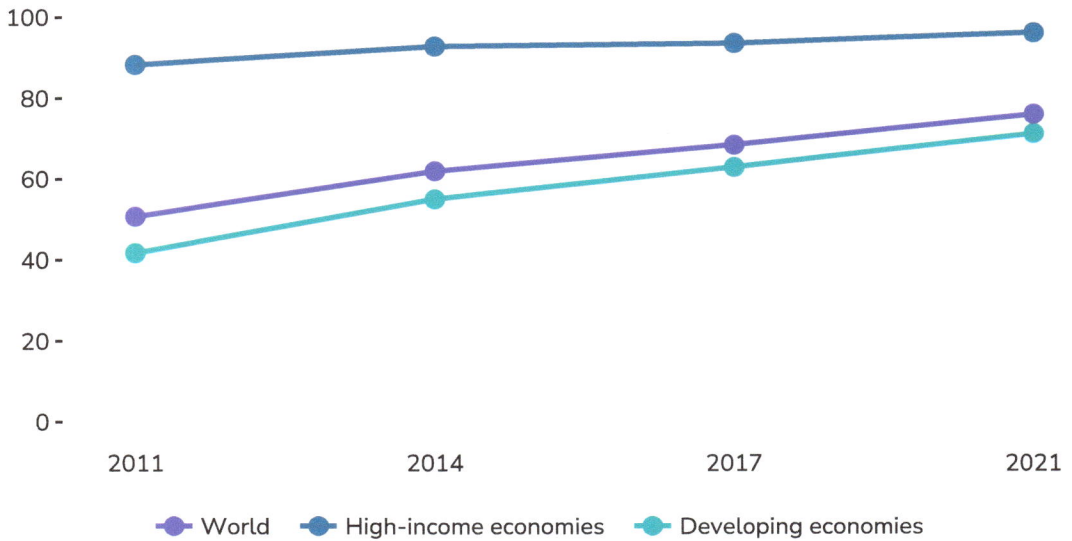

Source: Global Findex Database 2021.

55 percent in 2014 to 63 percent in 2017. If India is excluded, account ownership grew by just 3 percentage points, from 55 percent in 2014 to 58 percent in 2017. Put another way, in 2017, of the 467 million newly banked adults in developing economies, 186 million lived outside of India, whereas in 2021, of the 567 million newly banked adults in developing economies, 527 million lived outside of India. Of this recent growth, 284 million was contributed by 17 developing economies.

Among the economies experiencing significant growth just since 2017 are Brazil, Ghana, Morocco, and South Africa, each of which has seen double-digit growth in account ownership. Myanmar saw a 22 percentage point increase in account ownership, from 26 percent in 2017 to 48 percent in 2021.

Despite near-universal account ownership in many high-income economies since 2011, average ownership nonetheless increased by 8 percentage points over the past decade, from 88 percent in 2011 to 96 percent in 2021. Italy and Poland each saw overall account ownership increase by 26 percentage points since 2011, from 71 percent to 97 percent in Italy and from 70 percent to 96 percent in Poland.

Mobile money helped increase account ownership, especially in Sub-Saharan Africa

In addition to asking about accounts with formal financial institutions, since 2014 the Global Findex survey has asked respondents about their use of mobile money services. The 2014 data revealed that 2 percent of adults worldwide had a mobile money account, although 12 percent of adults in Sub-Saharan Africa had one. The 2021 data reflect continued global leadership by Sub-Saharan Africa in mobile money account ownership, with 33 percent of adults in the region having a mobile money account, compared with 10 percent of adults globally (figure 1.1.4).

The quick and sustained growth of mobile money accounts throughout the region can be attributed to the wide availability of mobile money services. Sub-Saharan Africa is home to all 11 of the world's economies in which more adults have only a mobile money account than have a financial institution account. They are Benin,

FIGURE 1.1.3

Developing economies grew account ownership overall, but at different rates

Adults with an account (%), 2011–21

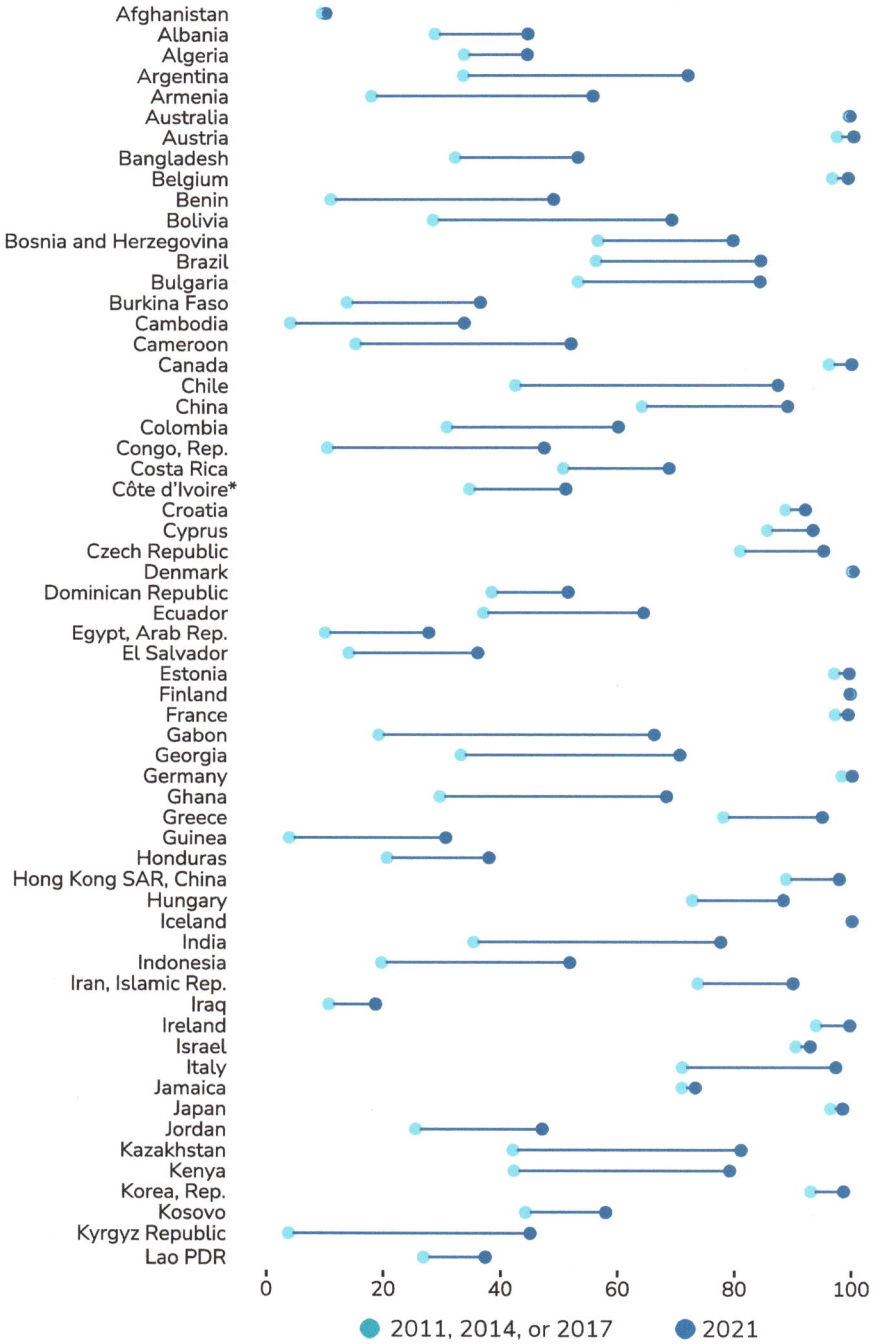

● 2011, 2014, or 2017   ● 2021

(figure continues on next page)

FIGURE 1.1.3 *(continued from previous page)*

Developing economies grew account ownership overall, but at different rates

Adults with an account (%), 2011–21

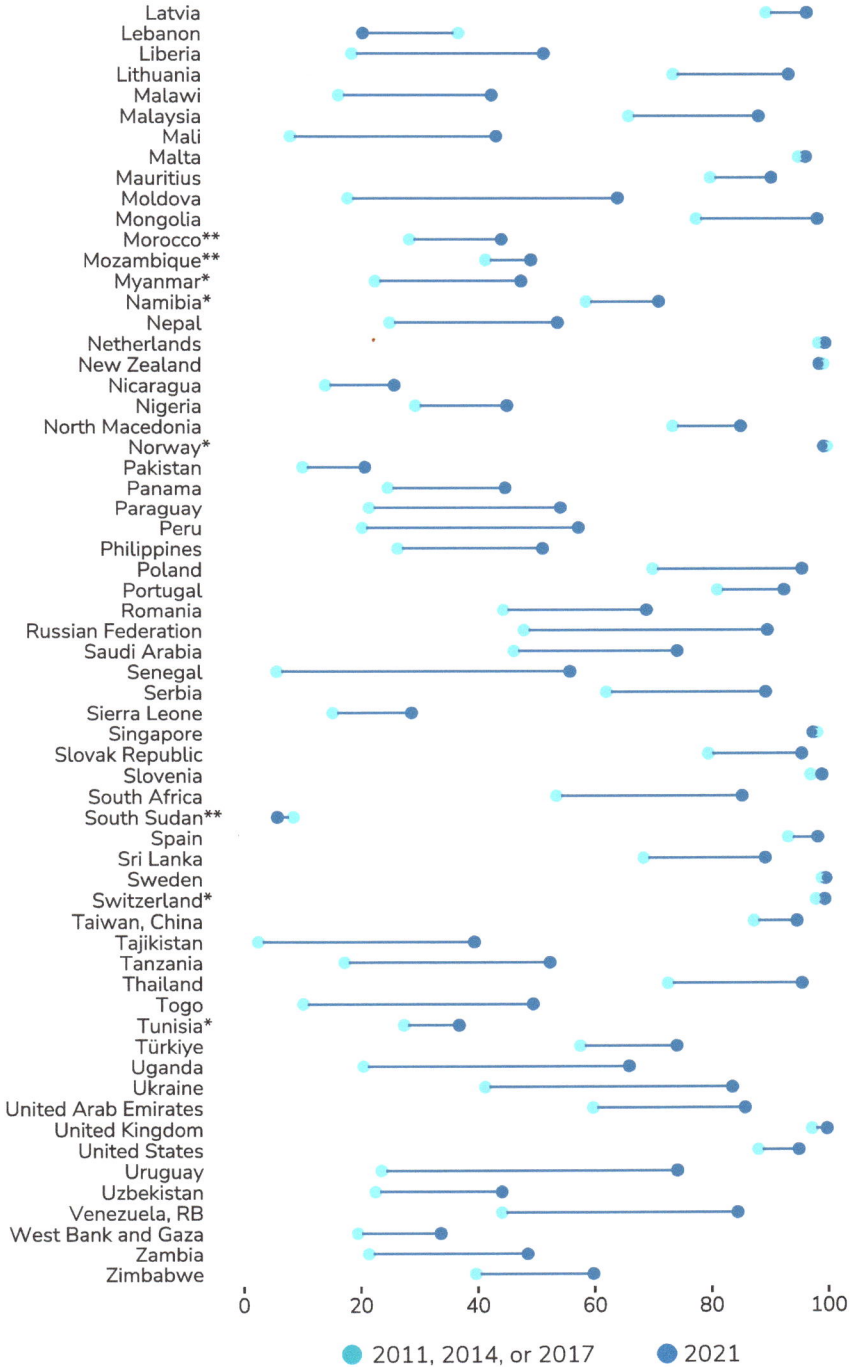

● 2011, 2014, or 2017   ● 2021

Source: Global Findex Database 2021.

Note: An asterisk (*) indicates that 2014 is the first year of available account ownership data for that economy. A double asterisk (**) indicates that 2017 is the first year of available account ownership data for that economy.

FIGURE 1.1.4

Mobile money accounts contributed to an 8 percentage point increase in account ownership in developing economies from 2014 to 2021

Adults with an account (%), 2014–21

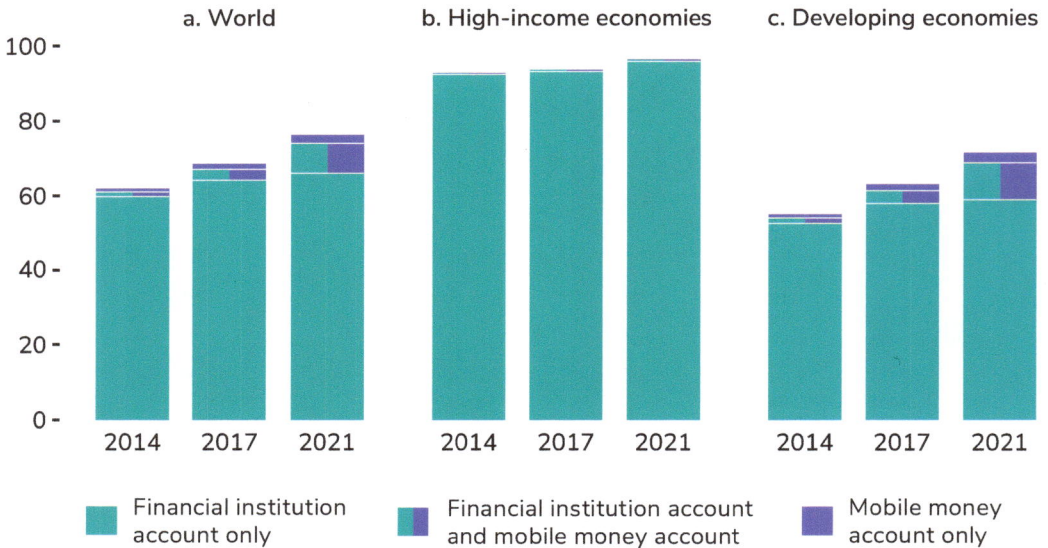

Source: Global Findex Database 2021.

Cameroon, the Republic of Congo, Côte d'Ivoire, Gabon, Guinea, Malawi, Sierra Leone, Tanzania, Zambia, and Zimbabwe. In 2014, mobile money accounts were concentrated in East Africa. Since then, these accounts have spread to West Africa and beyond, with mobile money account ownership in Gabon (Central Africa) increasing from just 7 percent in 2014 to 57 percent in 2021 and in Uganda (East Africa) from 35 percent in 2014 to 54 percent in 2021 (map 1.1.2).

In economies such as Benin and Cameroon, mobile money account ownership has more than doubled just since 2017, from 18 percent to 37 percent in Benin and from 15 percent to 42 percent in Cameroon (figure 1.1.5). Economies outside Sub-Saharan Africa—such as Bangladesh, Brazil, and Paraguay—also saw increases in mobile money account ownership.

Mobile money accounts are not just an addition for those people who already own an account. Many economies in Sub-Saharan Africa saw growth in mobile money accounts accompanied by a decline in financial institution accounts. For example, account ownership in Benin increased overall, from 38 percent in 2017 to 49 percent in 2021. During that time, the share of adults with a mobile money account doubled, from 18 percent in 2017 to 37 percent in 2021, and the share of adults with a financial institution account decreased by 8 percentage points, from 32 percent to 24 percent. In another example, financial institution account ownership in Ghana remained mostly stagnant after 2017, and yet mobile money account ownership increased by 21 percentage points, from 39 percent to 60 percent, boosting overall account ownership by 11 percentage points. Meanwhile, in Zambia overall account ownership remained mostly stagnant from 2017 to 2021: financial institution account ownership decreased by 12 percentage points, from 36 percent to 24 percent, and mobile money account ownership increased by 14 percentage points, from 28 percent to 42 percent.

The COVID-19 pandemic drove increases in the adoption of mobile money as people embraced the ease of using mobile phones for financial transactions. Benin, Cameroon, the Republic of Congo, Gabon, Ghana, Malawi, Togo, and Zambia each saw double-digit growth in mobile money accounts.

MAP 1.1.2

Mobile money accounts both grew and spread across Sub-Saharan Africa from 2014 to 2021

Adults with a mobile money account (%), 2014–21

a. 2014   b. 2017   c. 2021

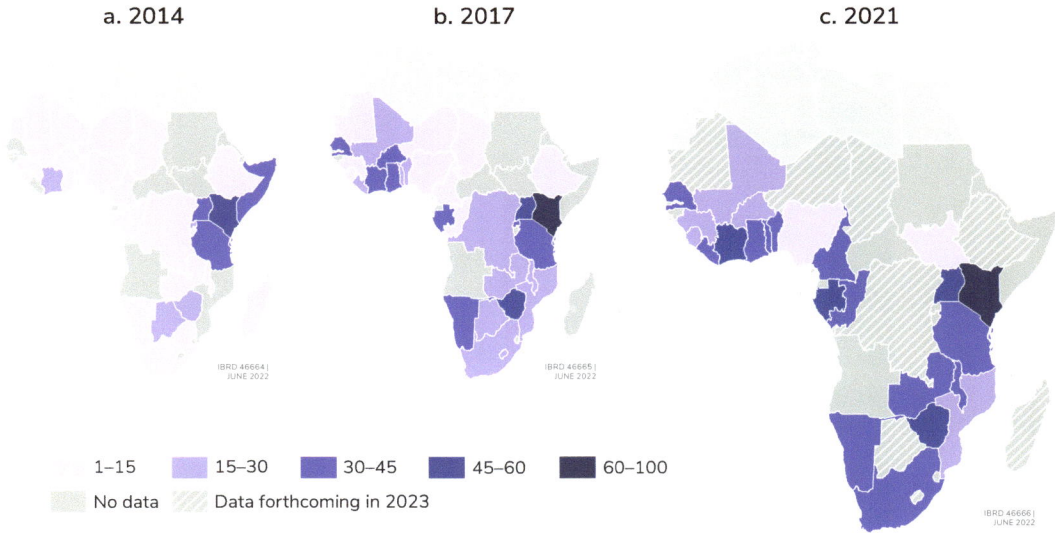

1–15   15–30   30–45   45–60   60–100

No data   Data forthcoming in 2023

Source: Global Findex Database 2021.

Fragile and conflict-affected economies such as Cameroon and the Republic of Congo saw almost 30 percentage point growth in the share of adults with a mobile money account. In parallel, most of the fragile and conflict-affected economies saw either stagnation or a decrease in the share of adults with a financial institution account.

Some economies in Sub-Saharan Africa showed an increase in both financial institution and mobile money accounts. For example, in Côte d'Ivoire overall account ownership increased by 9 percentage points, from 41 percent in 2017 to 51 percent in 2021. The increase was driven by 6 percentage point growth in both financial institution and mobile money accounts. South Africa saw a 16 percentage point increase in account ownership from 2017 to 2021, also led by both financial institution and mobile money accounts.

Account access gaps are narrowing overall, but not everywhere or for everyone

The growth in account ownership since 2011 has not benefited all groups equally. There has been some progress, although women, the poor, and the less educated remain less likely than men, the rich, and the educated to have an account (figure 1.1.6).

Documenting the gender gap in account ownership

Globally, 78 percent of men and 74 percent of women have an account—a gender gap of 4 percentage points. Developing economies have a wider average gap, 6 percentage points, a decrease from 9 percentage points after many years of remaining unchanged (figure 1.1.7). In 2021, 74 percent of men but only 68 percent of women in developing economies had an account.

FIGURE 1.1.5

Economies saw increases, decreases, and substitutions between mobile money and financial institution accounts

Adults with an account (%), 2014–21

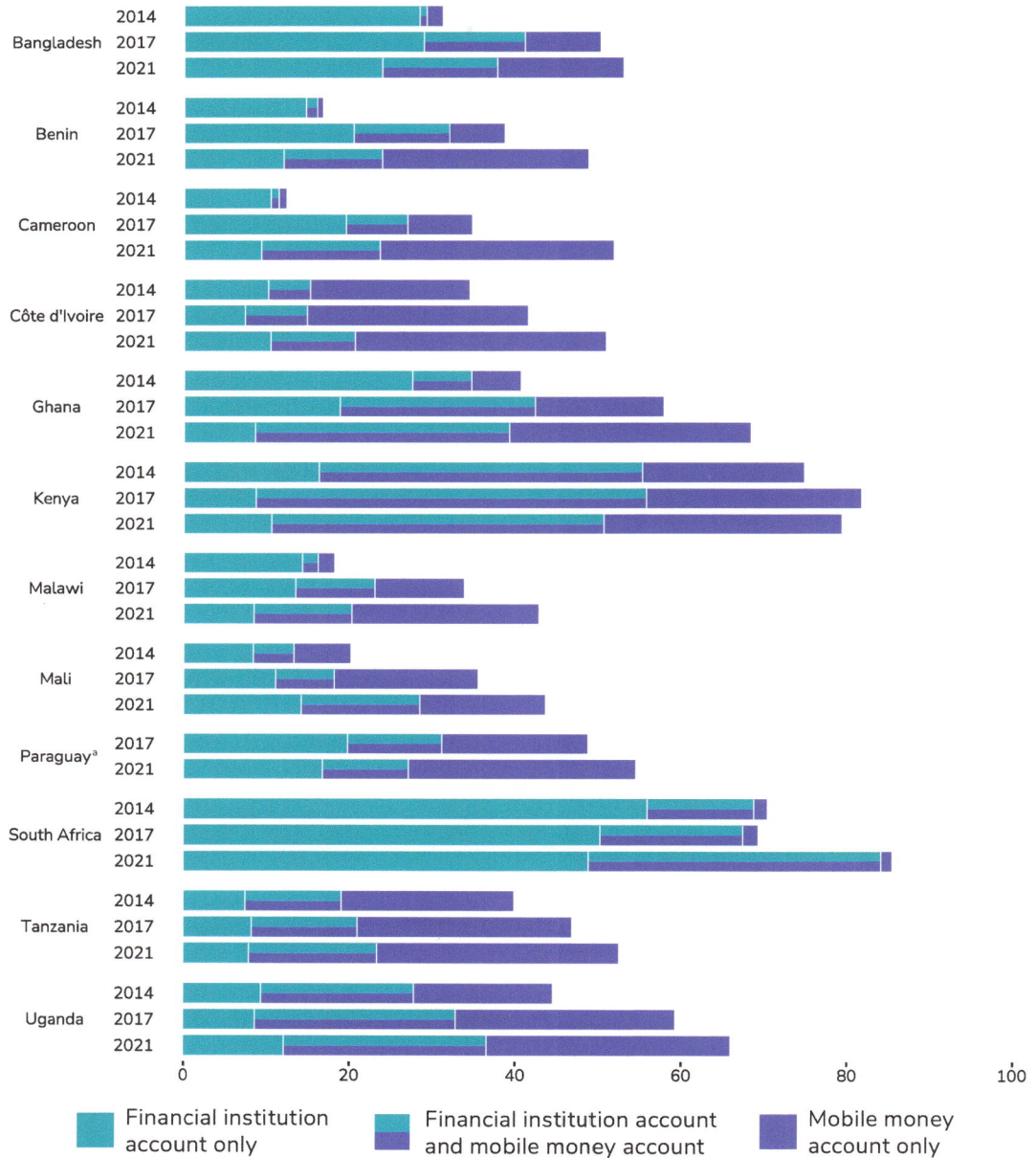

Financial institution account only

Financial institution account and mobile money account

Mobile money account only

Source: Global Findex Database 2021.
a. Paraguay was not surveyed in 2014.

FIGURE 1.1.6

Gender, income, age, education, and workforce gaps remain in every region around the world

Adults with an account (%), 2021

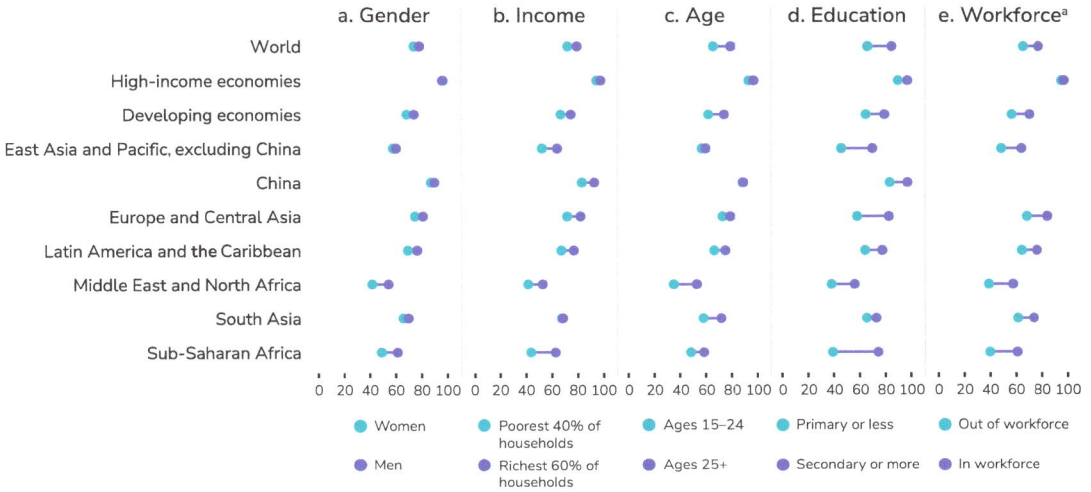

Source: Global Findex Database 2021.

a. Employment status for adults in China is not available.

FIGURE 1.1.7

Efforts to narrow the gender gap in account ownership have paid off since 2017

Adults with an account (%), 2011–21

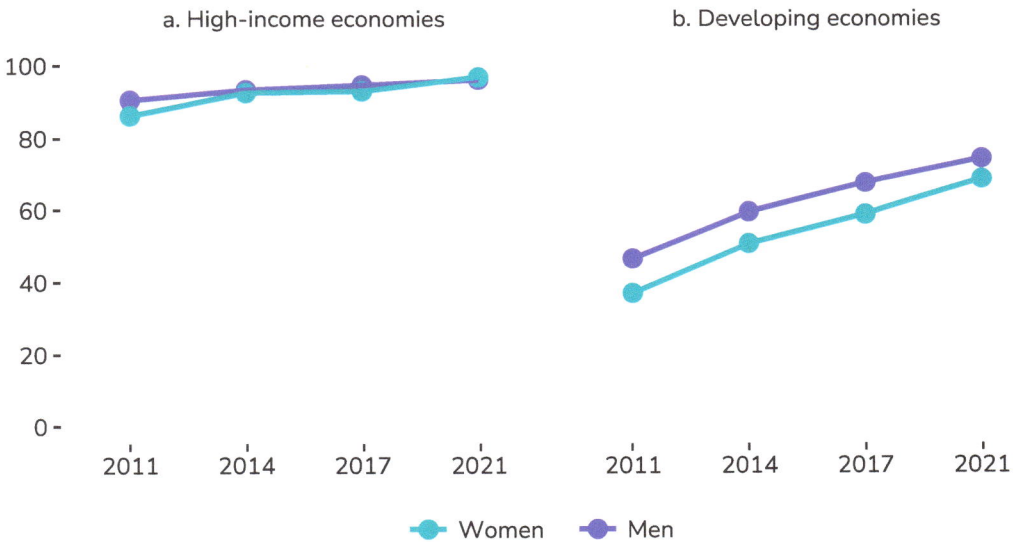

Source: Global Findex Database 2021.

Sub-Saharan Africa and the Middle East and North Africa reported 12 and 13 percentage point gender gaps, respectively—twice as large as the developing economy average and three times larger than the global average. By contrast, the gender gap in account ownership in East Asia and Pacific is insignificant at 3 percentage points. In Latin America and the Caribbean, women are 7 percentage points less likely than men to have an account.

On average, developing economies that had no gender gap in 2017—such as Indonesia, Mongolia, Myanmar, the Russian Federation, Serbia, Sri Lanka, and South Africa—still do not have a gap. Even within regions, there are appreciable differences. For example, in Sub-Saharan Africa the gender gap ranges from insignificant in Uganda to 27 percentage points in Côte d'Ivoire. In the East Asia and Pacific region, the differences range from virtually no gender gap in account ownership in Indonesia and Mongolia, to an 8 percentage point gap in the Philippines.

The growth or decline of the gender gap adheres to different patterns, depending on the economy. No single set of circumstances drives gender equity in relation to account growth overall. In some economies, the gender gap has narrowed as overall account ownership has increased. For example, Uganda saw significant growth in account ownership among women, thereby removing any gender gap. Large growth in account ownership in India likewise reduced the gender gap from 17 percentage points in 2011 to insignificant in 2021. Türkiye saw a modest decline in the gender gap from 29 percentage points in 2017 to 23 percentage points in 2021, accompanied by growth in account ownership. In Mali and Peru, the gender gap fell significantly after 2017 as account ownership for women increased by almost 60 percent (figure 1.1.8).

In other economies, however, gender gaps have decreased despite the lack of growth in overall account ownership. Bangladesh, for example, showed no growth in overall account ownership between 2017 and 2021, although the growth in mobile money accounts for women narrowed the gender gap to 19 percentage points. Similarly, Pakistan saw its gender gap narrow from 28 percentage points to 15 percentage points, despite flat overall account ownership.

FIGURE 1.1.8

Developing economies have varied widely in how effectively they tackle the gender gap

Adults with an account (%), 2017–21

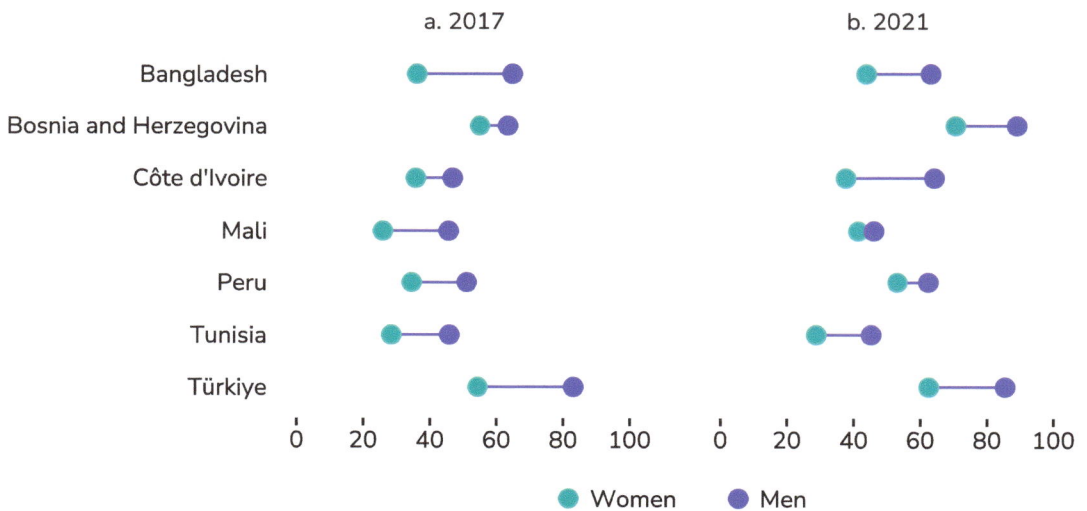

Source: Global Findex Database 2021.

Other developing economies that saw growth in account ownership over the past decade missed the opportunity for greater progress because of lack of inclusive growth. In Brazil and Colombia, for example, account ownership grew by about 15 percentage points, but the gender gap remained unchanged at around 7 percentage points. In Côte d'Ivoire, account ownership grew by 9 percentage points from 2017 to 2021, but the gender gap between women and men more than doubled during the same time, from 11 percentage points to 27 percentage points. In Bosnia and Herzegovina, account ownership grew by 20 percentage points after 2017, but the gender gap doubled from 8 percentage points to 18 percentage points.

Mobile money has enabled more equal access to accounts in some regions

In some regions, the spread of mobile money accounts has created new opportunities to better serve women, poor people, and other groups who traditionally have been excluded from the formal financial system. Indeed, there are some early signs that mobile money accounts may be helping to close the gender gap.

In Sub-Saharan Africa, technology is helping to drive inclusive access to finance, especially for women. In the 15 economies (up from eight in 2017) in which 20 percent or more of adults have only a mobile money account, all but Uganda have a statistically significant gender gap for account ownership overall, including both financial institution and mobile money accounts. The 15 economies are Benin, Cameroon, the Republic of Congo, Côte d'Ivoire, Gabon, Ghana, Kenya, Liberia, Malawi, Senegal, Tanzania, Togo, Uganda, Zambia, and Zimbabwe. Yet in seven of these 15—Cameroon, Gabon, Ghana, Kenya, Liberia, Tanzania, and Uganda—women were equally or more likely than men to only have a mobile money account in 2021. In Gabon, women are 5 percentage points more likely than men to have only a mobile money account. In Kenya, men and women are equally likely to have only a financial institution account, and men are 9 percentage points more likely to have both accounts, while women are 4 percentage points more likely to have only a mobile money account.

These results are encouraging, but many more years of data and research are needed to understand the connections among mobile money accounts, formal financial services, and gender inequality in account ownership. Meanwhile, the distinction between types of accounts may begin to blur as more financial institutions design services tailored to the needs of poor people and as more mobile money operators enter partnerships with financial institutions.

The income gap in account ownership has halved in the past decade

Poorer adults worldwide are less likely than wealthier ones to have an account. Among adults in the richest 60 percent of households, 79 percent have an account, while only 72 percent of the poorest 40 percent of households do, resulting in an income gap in account ownership of 7 percentage points. This gap has halved since 2011. In developing economies, the income gap is 8 percentage points, a decrease from 20 percentage points in 2011 (figure 1.1.9).

In many developing economies, however, the income gap in account ownership is still in double digits. In Kenya, where account ownership is 79 percent, wealthier adults are about 20 percentage points more likely than poor adults to have an account. In economies such as Mozambique, Myanmar, Nigeria, Uganda, and Zambia, where account ownership ranges from 45 percent to 66 percent, the gap is more than 20 percentage points. In the Philippines and Türkiye, account ownership grew significantly over the past decade, but the income gap remained stagnant at more than 20 percentage points.

A few developing economies do not have a significant income gap. In Brazil, for example, account ownership among richer adults stood at 85 percent in 2021, compared with 82 percent among poorer adults. Mongolia and Thailand have achieved near-universal account ownership, with almost equal coverage of richer and poorer adults.

FIGURE 1.1.9

The income gap in financial access has narrowed by 6 percentage points since 2017

Adults with an account (%), 2011–21

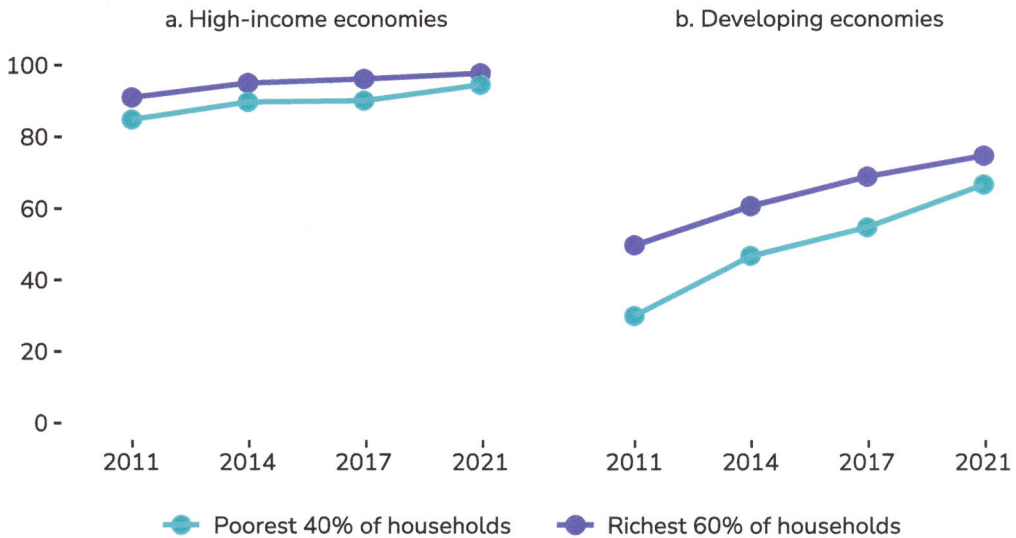

a. High-income economies   b. Developing economies

Poorest 40% of households   Richest 60% of households

Source: Global Findex Database 2021.

On average, high-income economies do not have a large gap in account ownership between richer and poorer adults because account ownership is nearly universal in these economies. There are, however, some exceptions. Croatia, Hungary, and Uruguay all have a double-digit account ownership gap between adults in the richest 60 percent of households and those in the poorest 40 percent. The income gap in account ownership in the United States is 6 percentage points, down from 13 percentage points in 2017.

Gender and income are not the only individual characteristics that appear to matter for the likelihood of owning an account. Age, educational level, employment status, and rural residency are all associated with significant differences in account ownership.

Account access differs by age group

Account ownership is higher among older adults—that is, those 25 and up—than among young adults—those between the ages of 15 and 24.[16] Worldwide, this gap narrowed marginally by 4 percentage points, from 17 percentage points in 2011 to 14 percentage points in 2021. In 2021, 79 percent of adults worldwide age 25 and older had an account, while 66 percent of those ages 15–24 did. The trend is similar for both high-income and developing economies.

The age gap varies among developing economies. In the West Bank and Gaza, older adults are more than twice as likely as younger adults to have an account. In Algeria and Egypt, the age gap in account ownership is almost 25 percentage points. In Jordan, Morocco, and Tunisia, the age gap is not as high, yet it is still in double digits. In other economies such as Peru and the Philippines, the age gap is about 15 percentage points, similar to the global age gap. Yet in China and Türkiye, the data show no major difference in account ownership between the age groups. And in Myanmar, younger adults are 11 percentage points more likely than older ones to have an account.

---

16. Some countries restrict account ownership to ages 21 and above.

In Sub-Saharan Africa, technology-enabled mobile money accounts are also helping drive inclusive access to finance for younger women. The gender gap for financial institution accounts increases as women age, but it remains small for men and women who have only mobile money accounts (figure 1.1.10). Among economies in Sub-Saharan Africa with more than 20 percent of adults with a mobile money account, young adult men are 6 percentage points more likely than young adult women to have a financial institution account. As adults grow older, this gap increases to 9 percentage points between men and women ages 25–50 and 15 percentage points between men and woman age 51 and older.

By contrast, there is no gender gap in mobile money account ownership as adults age. Twenty-three percent of young women have only a mobile money account, and 24 percent of the men do; the age gap for mobile money accounts remains insignificant as adults age.

Mobile money account ownership is lower among older age groups, however, and the take-up of mobile money accounts is lower for older women, compared with younger women. Among economies with more than 20 percentage point mobile money account ownership, women age 51 and older are 7 percentage points less likely than young women ages 15–24 to use only a mobile money account. Technology can create barriers for older consumers who may prefer traditional methods of making transactions, or for those who may lack the familiarity, confidence, or digital literacy to engage with digital financial services.[17]

FIGURE 1.1.10

In Sub-Saharan Africa, a gender gap barely exists for young adults who have only a mobile money account

Adults with an account (%), 2021

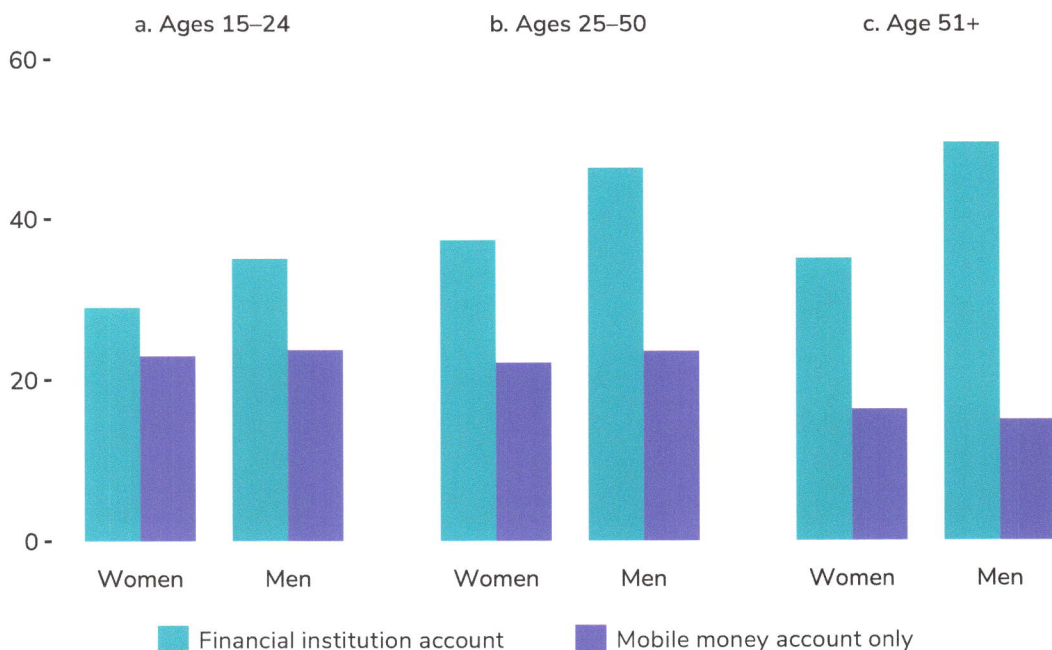

Source: Global Findex Database 2021.
Note: Data are shown for economies in Sub-Saharan Africa in which the share of adults with a mobile money account is greater than 20 percent.

17. GPFI and OECD (n.d.).

Education also drives account ownership

Account ownership continues to be low among less educated adults—that is, those who have a primary education or less. In developing economies, these adults are 14 percentage points less likely to have an account than their counterparts with at least a secondary education. Less educated adults are also likely to be poorer, which may help explain the gap. Less educated adults are more likely as well to be vulnerable to fraud and to falling into poverty, which makes it challenging to increase account ownership in this group.

In Europe and Central Asia, in economies such as Romania and Ukraine, account ownership rates among more educated adults are almost twice those of less educated adults. In Bosnia and Herzegovina, less educated adults are 32 percentage points less likely than their more educated counterparts to have an account. In Sub-Saharan Africa, although there are wide variations in the education gap in account ownership, more educated adults continue to have greater account ownership. In South Africa, for example, more educated adults are 13 percentage points more likely than their less educated counterparts to have an account. This gap is 39 percentage points in Nigeria and 45 percentage points in Mozambique.

Working—or looking for work—correlates with having a financial account

Adults who are active in the labor force—whether employed or seeking work—are more likely to have an account than those who are out of the labor force. Working adults have many needs for financial services, such as receiving wages from an employer or saving their earnings from a business.

Globally, excluding China (its employment status for adults is unavailable), 77 percent of adults who are active in the labor force have an account, whereas only 65 percent of those out of the labor force have an account, leaving a gap of 12 percentage points. The gap is similar in developing economies and smaller in high-income ones. Most developing economies have a gap in account ownership between the active and inactive groups. In Nigeria and Pakistan, adults who are active in the labor force are roughly twice as likely to have an account as those who are not. In other regions such as Europe and Central Asia and the Middle East and North Africa, this gap is about 16 percentage points. On the other hand, developing economies such as Argentina and Myanmar show no account ownership gap between adults based on their labor force participation.

In some regions, the gap in labor force participation is accentuated by the gender gap. For example, in the East Asia and Pacific region, excluding China, men out of the labor force are 8 percentage points more likely than women out of the labor force to have an account. By contrast, the gender gap for adults in the labor force is insignificant. This pattern is the same in all regions except Sub-Saharan Africa, where both groups have a substantial gender gap. In Türkiye, the gender gap among adults who are out of the labor force is high, 31 percentage points. Among adults in the labor force, it shrinks to 9 percentage points.

The rural gap exists, but it is not clear how big it is

In developing economies, account ownership tends to be lower in rural areas than in urban areas. But precisely quantifying the urban-rural gap is difficult. Defining what makes an area rural is complex—should the distinction be based on population density, on the availability of certain services and infrastructure, or on the subjective judgment of the interviewer or of the respondent? These definitional issues become more challenging when applied across economies—what might be considered rural in Bangladesh or India, for example, might be considered urban in less populous economies. The Gallup World Poll—the survey to which the Global Findex questionnaire is added—uses different approaches in different economies to account for these variables, thereby making it difficult to produce a consistent definition of the urban-rural divide at the global and regional levels. Another challenge is that the estimates of account ownership for urban populations are often imprecise.

Recently, Gallup distinguished between rural and urban based on population grids[18] (not administrative units) that directly capture the spatial concentration of people, instead of relying on the perception respondents have of the urbanicity of their residence. The Global Findex 2021 database uses this estimate and provides account ownership averages for adults living in rural and urban areas. These averages are available only for those economies in which face-to-face surveys were conducted and are not compared with the 2011, 2014, and 2017 data, nor with regional or global averages.

The data on the relationship between rural and urban residency and account ownership are mixed (figure 1.1.11). In the Lao People's Democratic Republic, adults in urban areas are 39 percentage points more likely to have an account than adults in rural areas, where only 30 percent of adults have an account. In Cambodia and Zambia, adults in urban areas are almost twice as likely to have an account as adults in rural areas. There are also double-digit differences in account ownership between adults in urban areas and those in rural areas in Côte d'Ivoire (12 percentage points), Kenya (14 percentage points), Nigeria (20 percentage points), Tanzania (13 percentage points), and Uganda (12 percentage points). By contrast, in developing economies such as Bangladesh, India, and Malaysia, there is virtually no difference in account ownership between adults living in urban and rural areas.

FIGURE 1.1.11

The rural-urban account ownership gap varies widely by economy

Adults with an account (%), 2021

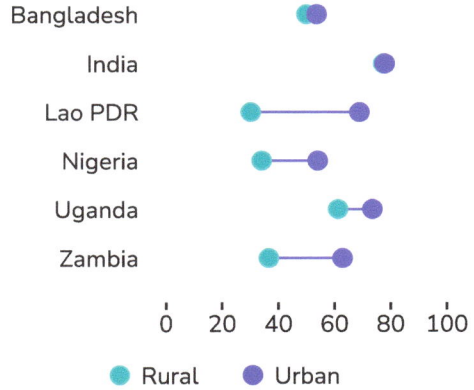

Source: Global Findex Database 2021.

---

18.   For additional information, see OECD and EC (2020).

1.2 Opportunities to increase account ownership through an enabling environment

1.2 OPPORTUNITIES TO INCREASE ACCOUNT OWNERSHIP THROUGH AN ENABLING ENVIRONMENT

Globally, about 1.4 billion adults are still unbanked—that is, they do not have an account at a financial institution or through a mobile money provider (map 1.2.1). This number has declined from 2.5 billion in 2011 and 1.7 billion in 2017. Because account ownership is nearly universal in high-income economies, virtually all unbanked adults live in developing economies. Indeed, 54 percent of the unbanked—740 million people—live in only seven economies. Meanwhile, despite having relatively high rates of account ownership, China and India claim large shares of the global unbanked population (130 million and 230 million, respectively) because of their size (figure 1.2.1). Pakistan, with 115 million unbanked adults, and Indonesia, with 100 million, have the next-largest populations of unbanked. These four economies, together with Bangladesh, Egypt, and Nigeria—are home to more than half of the world's unbanked population. The top five economies hosting the largest share of the world's unbanked were the same in 2017 and 2021.

Women, poor adults, the less educated, and those outside the labor market continue to be underserved

As account ownership continues to grow, women, poor adults, and less educated adults continue to make up the majority of people excluded from the formal financial sector. Improving financial access for these groups will involve building an enabling, inclusive infrastructure for financial services.

MAP 1.2.1

Globally, 1.4 billion adults are unbanked

Adults with no account, 2021

- • 1 million
- • 10 million
- ● 100 million
- ⬤ 200 million

IBRD 46659 |
JUNE 2022

Source: Global Findex Database 2021.

Note: Data are not displayed for economies in which the share of adults without an account is 5 percent or less or for economies for which no data were available.

FIGURE 1.2.1

More than half of the world's unbanked adults live in seven economies

Adults with no account (%), 2021

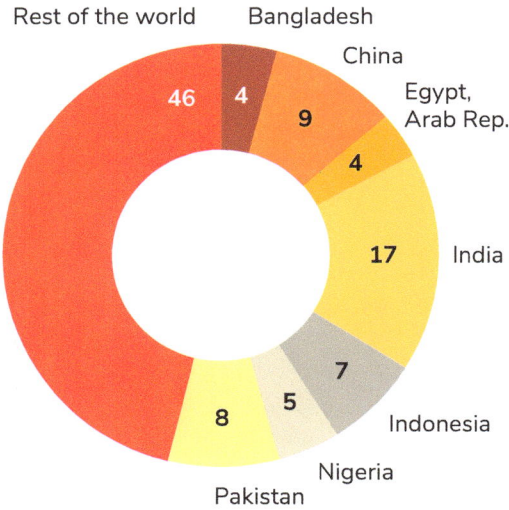

Source: Global Findex Database 2021.

FIGURE 1.2.2

The majority of unbanked adults worldwide are women

All adults with and without an account (%), 2021

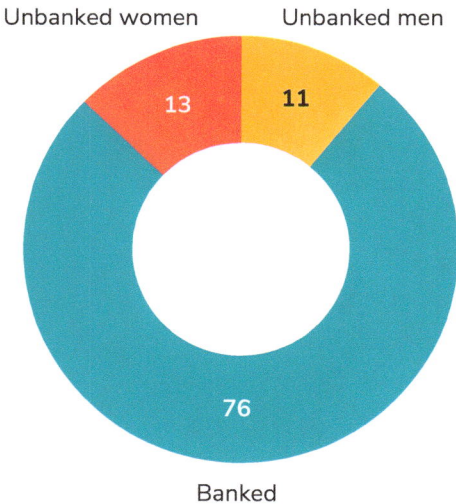

Source: Global Findex Database 2021.

Women are more likely than men to be unbanked. About 740 million women (13 percent of all adults globally and 54 percent of the unbanked) do not have an account (figure 1.2.2). The majority of unbanked adults continue to be women even in economies that have successfully increased account ownership and have a small share of unbanked adults. In Türkiye, for example, about a quarter of adults are unbanked, and yet 71 percent of those unbanked adults are women. Brazil, China, Kenya, Russia, and Thailand also have relatively high rates of account ownership, compared with their developing economy peers, and yet a majority of those who are still unbanked are women. Things are not much different in economies in which less than half the population is banked. For example, in Egypt, Guinea, and Pakistan women make up more than half of the unbanked population. Why? As explained later in this chapter, women are often excluded from formal banking services because they lack official forms of identification, do not own a mobile phone or other form of technology, and have lower financial capability.

In the developing world, vulnerable adults continue to be those more likely unbanked, with some regional variations in the groups representing large shares of the unbanked. In the East Asia and Pacific region, 53 percent of unbanked adults are in the poorest 40 percent of households. In China, only 11 percent of adults are unbanked—and yet 60 percent of them are in the poorest 40 percent of households. Globally, the poorest 40 percent of households make up nearly half of all the unbanked.

In the Middle East and North Africa, 70 percent of the unbanked adults are unemployed or out of the workforce. For example, in Egypt 73 percent of adults are unbanked, and, of those, 65 percent are unemployed or out of the workforce. Some of these numbers obscure gender inequality in labor force participation among unbanked adults: in the same region, women are 12 percentage points more likely than men to be out of the labor force. Globally, 64 percent of unbanked adults have a primary education or less. In Sub-Saharan Africa, 74 percent of the unbanked have only a primary education or less. The share of unbanked adults with low educational attainment is even higher in some economies, such as Mozambique, where 90 percent of unbanked adults have a primary education or less, as well as Côte d'Ivoire (83 percent) and Tanzania (88 percent). In Kenya, where 79 percent of adults have an account, 62 percent of the remaining unbanked adults have a primary education or less.

Adults living in rural areas also represent a higher share of the unbanked in certain economies, particularly in Sub-Saharan Africa, where 62 percent of unbanked adults are rural dwellers. In Tanzania, of the 48 percent of unbanked adults, 71 percent live in rural areas. In Uganda and Zambia, 70 percent and 67 percent of unbanked adults, respectively, live in rural areas.

As for account ownership and a person's age, in Sub-Saharan Africa, for example, young adults (ages 15–24) make up almost 40 percent of the unbanked. Adults in this age range, who may be entering the workforce as wage workers or as self-employed professionals, could benefit from having a safe place to save money and build a credit history. By contrast, in some Europe and Central Asian countries, older adults are more likely to be unbanked. In Bulgaria and Ukraine, about a third of unbanked adults are 65 years and older. One reason is that older adults may be reluctant to adopt new ways of making financial transactions, particularly if these new methods require technologies with which they are unfamiliar.

These trends related to the unbanked suggest that further efforts to expand access must consider the needs and existing skills of the population to ensure that increased access provides key benefits while protecting users from financial abuse.

Lack of money, perceived cost of accounts, and distance to financial institutions are the top reasons people remain unbanked

Globally, 24 percent of adults are unbanked. To help shed light on why people do not have an account, the Global Findex 2021 survey asked unbanked adults why they did not have one—either a financial institution account (as queried by Findex since its inception) or a mobile money account (as queried by Findex for the first time in the 2021 survey).

Respondents could offer more than one reason, and most, on average, gave more than two reasons for not having a financial institution account. Sixty-two percent of the unbanked cited "lack of money" as one of multiple responses (figure 1.2.3). In other words, people typically replied that they do not have enough money, and then included another barrier, such as financial services are too expensive to use or too far away. These answers suggest that people would open an account if banking costs were lower or if the banks were located more conveniently. Only 12 percent of adults reported not having enough money as their only barrier. All other barriers were reported as the only reason by fewer than 4 percent of unbanked adults.

Worldwide, 36 percent of unbanked adults said that financial services are too expensive. This share was almost twice as high (60 percent) in Latin America and the Caribbean. In Brazil, Colombia, Honduras, Nicaragua, Panama, Paraguay, and Peru, more than 60 percent of unbanked adults cited cost as a barrier.

Distance is a barrier for 31 percent of unbanked adults. In some economies, the share was higher, with 53 percent of unbanked adults in Liberia saying that financial institutions were too far away. Other economies in which a higher share of unbanked adults cited distance as a barrier were Bolivia (47 percent), India (43 percent), Lao PDR (45 percent), and Uganda (41 percent).

Globally, 30 percent of unbanked adults said that they do not have an account because a family member already has one. In some economies, this reason is more likely to be reported by women than by men. Among the unbanked in Türkiye, 39 percent of women mentioned this reason and 25 percent of men. The data reveal significant gender gaps in Algeria, Bolivia, Nepal, Pakistan, and Tunisia, where women are more likely than men to report this reason. Most of these countries also had significant gender gaps in account ownership. By contrast, in China and India men and women were equally likely to say they do not have an account because a family member already has one.

FIGURE 1.2.3

Lack of money, among other reasons, is often a barrier for not having a financial institution account

Adults with no account (%) citing a given barrier as a reason for having no financial institution account, 2021

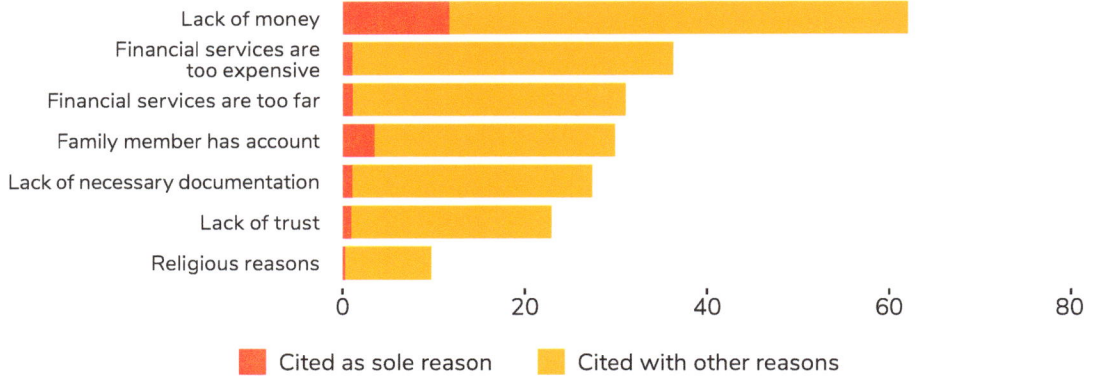

Source: Global Findex Database 2021.

Note: Respondents could choose more than one reason.

Documentation requirements may also hamper account ownership. Twenty-seven percent of the unbanked reported lacking the documentation needed to open an account. Unbanked adults were more likely to cite these barriers in economies such as Colombia (43 percent), Tanzania (50 percent), and Uganda (50 percent). Opportunities to address documentation requirements are discussed in more detail later in this chapter.

Distrust of the financial system is a greater barrier in some regions, and globally it was cited by 23 percent of unbanked adults. In Europe and Central Asia and in Latin America and the Caribbean, about a third of unbanked adults said they do not have an account because they distrust the banking system. In Ukraine, 54 percent of unbanked adults listed distrust in the financial system as one of the reasons for their lack of an account. More than one in three unbanked adults cited the same barrier in Argentina, Bolivia, Bulgaria, Colombia, Jamaica, and Russia, among others.

Finally, only 10 percent of the unbanked adults globally cited religion as a barrier. In the Middle East and North Africa, where adults might prefer Sharia-compliant banking services, 24 percent and 19 percent of the unbanked in Iraq and Morocco, respectively, cited religion as a barrier.

In Sub-Saharan Africa, mobile phone ownership and identification documents are important barriers to mobile money accounts, especially for women

As discussed in section 1.1 of this chapter, Sub-Saharan Africa continues to be the global leader in mobile money account ownership, with 33 percent of adults reporting having a mobile money account, compared with only 10 percent of the global population. In the context of such growing mobile adoption, the Global Findex 2021 survey asked unbanked adults why they do not have a mobile money account. Respondents could give more than one reason, though most gave fewer than two for not having a mobile money account.

The most cited barrier to getting a mobile money account was lack of money, which is consistent with the reasons cited for why unbanked adults do not have a financial institution account. Nearly 60 percent of unbanked adults said they do not have enough money to open one, but this was the sole barrier cited by only about 14 percent of unbanked adults (figure 1.2.4).

FIGURE 1.2.4

In Sub-Saharan Africa, the top barrier to having a mobile money account mirrors the top barrier to having a financial institution account

Adults with no account (%) citing a given barrier as a reason for having no mobile money account, 2021

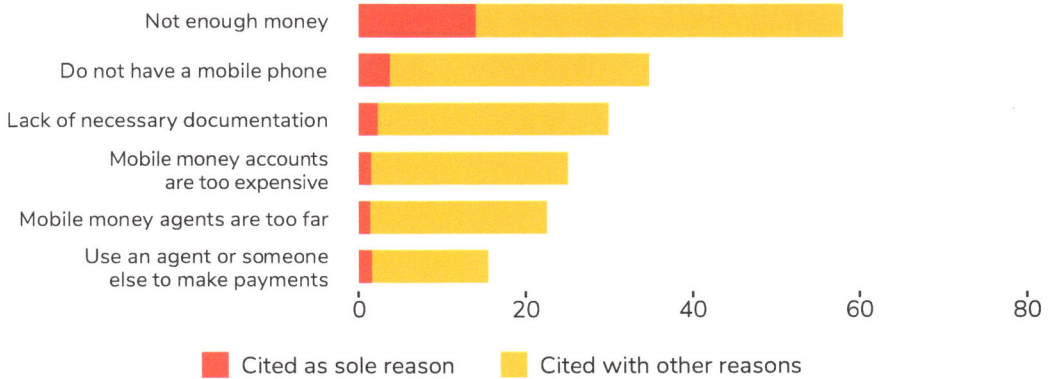

Source: Global Findex Database 2021.
Note: Respondents could choose more than one reason.

The second most cited reason for not having a mobile money account was lack of a mobile phone—35 percent of unbanked adults in Sub-Saharan Africa reported this as one of the reasons. In Liberia, Malawi, Mozambique, and South Sudan, more than half of unbanked adults cited the lack of a mobile phone as a barrier to mobile money account ownership. Across Sub-Saharan Africa, unbanked women are 7 percentage points more likely than unbanked men to cite lack of a mobile phone as one reason they do not have an account. This gap increases to 14 percentage points in Nigeria, where women are almost twice as likely as men to cite lack of a mobile phone as a barrier to account ownership. Ghana reported a double-digit gap (10 percentage points) between women and men citing mobile phone ownership as a barrier.

Another barrier is lack of identification. Thirty percent of unbanked adults in the Sub-Saharan region reported they do not have the documentation needed to open a mobile money account. In Liberia, Mozambique, South Sudan, and Tanzania more than 40 percent of unbanked adults cited lack of documentation as a barrier. Benin, Burkina Faso, Côte d'Ivoire, Nigeria, Senegal, and South Sudan all have significant gender gaps corresponding to this barrier.

Finally, 16 percent of unbanked adults use an agent or someone else, such as a family member or friends, to make payments and thus do not open an account. Even in an economy such as Ghana, where 60 percent of adults have a mobile money account, 26 percent of unbanked adults say they do not have an account because they use an intermediary to make payments.

Opportunities exist to expand financial inclusion through better access to formal identification and mobile phones

Providing adults with identification could help increase account ownership

Identification is almost always a requirement for opening an account. In addition, identification is typically required to purchase and activate the registered SIM card needed to run a mobile phone—and these registered SIM cards are also required to open a mobile money account. Widespread identification documentation is therefore necessary for the success of national strategies to expand financial inclusion, especially among women, rural dwellers, and poor adults. Policies around identification have already proven to be successful at driving account ownership. In India, for example, the introduction of a widely accessible digital identifier (Aadhar number) contributed to a significant increase in financial inclusion, driving account ownership up to 80 percent of adults in 2017 from 35 percent in 2011.

In 83 percent of economies in Sub-Saharan Africa, commercial banks require a government-issued identification document.[19] This requirement appears to be a barrier for adults across the region—37 percent of unbanked adults say lack of documentation is one reason they do not have a financial institution account, and 30 percent of adults say it is a barrier to opening a mobile money account. In Liberia, Mozambique, South Sudan, and Tanzania more than 40 percent of unbanked adults say lack of documentation is one reason they do not have a financial institution account.

New data collected in partnership with the World Bank's Identification for Development (ID4D) initiative reveal fresh insights into the relationship between account ownership and access to identification (ID), such as a national

MAP 1.2.2

More than 100 million unbanked adults in Sub-Saharan Africa have no ID

Adults with no account and no ID, 2021

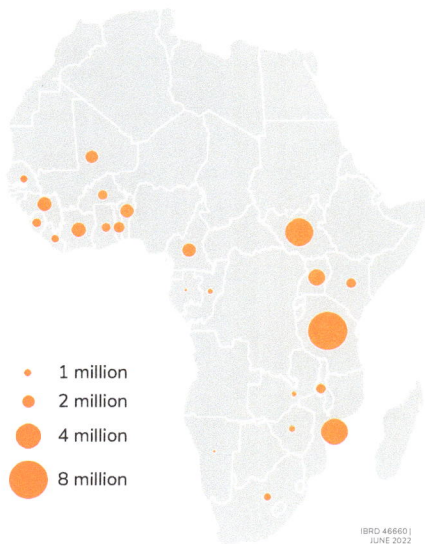

Legend:
- 1 million
- 2 million
- 4 million
- 8 million

IBRO 46660 | JUNE 2022

Sources: Global Findex Database 2021; ID4D-Findex series.
Note: Data are not displayed for economies for which no data were available.

ID document or other legally recognized ID credential.[20] In Sub-Saharan Africa, 105 million adults (16 percent of adults) are unbanked and have no ID (map 1.2.2). In South Sudan, 83 percent of the unbanked (5 million adults) have no ID. Other economies with large shares of adults who are unbanked and have no ID are Mozambique (5 million adults, or 58 percent of the unbanked) and Tanzania (8 million adults, or 48 percent of the unbanked). Women in the region are 5 percentage points more likely than men to be unbanked and have no ID. Larger gender gaps among the unbanked with no ID are observed in Benin, Côte d'Ivoire, and Liberia (13 percentage points in each economy), among others.

Improving access to identification is often not enough to increase account ownership because national ID does not always satisfy the KYC ("know your customer") requirements when opening an account. People often need to show local documentation as well—such as a utility bill with a home address—and this may be difficult to produce. For example, within the sample of adults who report documentation as a barrier, almost half of adults do have an ID. In Guinea and Tanzania, about half of the unbanked adults have an ID, and this share is greater than two-thirds in 12 Sub-Saharan Africa economies, including Cameroon, Côte d'Ivoire, and Mali (figure 1.2.5). The majority of unbanked adults in Kenya, Namibia, and South Africa have ID. Outside of Sub-Saharan Africa, more than 80 percent of the unbanked adult populations in developing economies have national ID, except for the unbanked in Armenia, the Islamic Republic of Iran, Jamaica, Lao PDR, and Nepal.

---

19. World Bank Group (2017).

20. The survey asks respondents whether they personally possessed the economy's foundational ID. For each economy, the survey used the actual term for the foundational ID in the local language. A foundational ID system is primarily created to manage identity information for the general population and provide credentials that serve as proof of identity for a wide variety of public and private sector transactions and services. For more details, see World Bank (forthcoming).

FIGURE 1.2.5

In some economies in Sub-Saharan Africa, greater access to ID could drive account access

Adults with no account (%), 2021

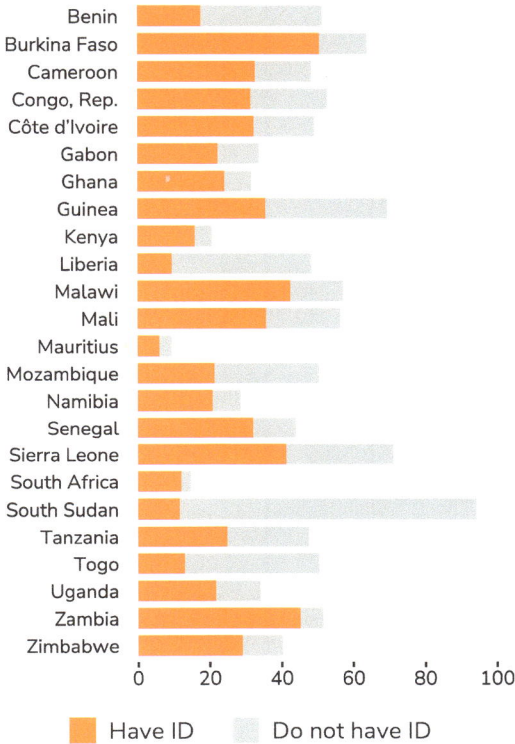

Have ID   Do not have ID

Sources: Global Findex Database 2021; ID4D-Findex series.

MAP 1.2.3

More than half of unbanked adults in South Asia have a mobile phone

Adults with no account but with a mobile phone, 2021

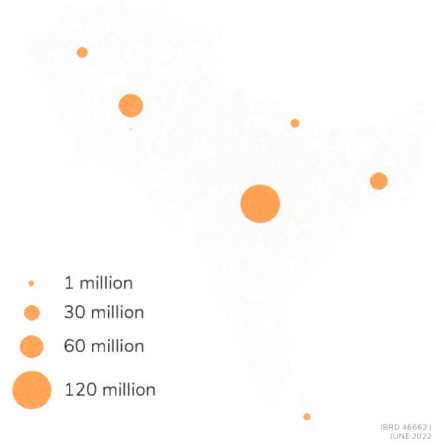

- 1 million
- 30 million
- 60 million
- 120 million

Sources: Global Findex Database 2021; Gallup World Poll.
Note: Data are not displayed for economies for which no data were available.

Leveraging mobile phones could increase financial account ownership

In many high-income economies, debit and credit cards used at point-of-sale terminals dominate the digital payments landscape. By contrast, in most developing economies fewer adults have such cards. The growing presence of mobile phones in developing economies could allow these economies to leapfrog directly to mobile payments and thereby increase account ownership.

The Gallup World Poll collects data on mobile phone ownership in countries surveyed face-to-face. In South Asia, for example, 240 million unbanked adults have a mobile phone—that is, more than half of the 430 million unbanked in the region (map 1.2.3). More specifically, 56 percent of all unbanked adults in the region have a mobile phone, including 51 percent of unbanked adults in India and 55 percent of unbanked adults in Pakistan. In Bangladesh, 69 percent of unbanked adults have a mobile phone; in Nepal, 73 percent (figure 1.2.6).

Similarly, in Sub-Saharan Africa 165 million adults without an account (56 percent of the unbanked) have a mobile phone. Although the data show variations from economy to economy, in most Sub-Saharan African economies surveyed, the majority of unbanked adults have mobile phones. For example, in Côte d'Ivoire, where 49 percent of adults are unbanked, 72 percent of unbanked adults have a mobile phone. In Guinea, where 70 percent of adults are unbanked, 74 percent of them have a mobile phone. However, in Mozambique and Zambia, only 36 percent and 40 percent of unbanked adults, respectively, have a phone (map 1.2.4 and figure 1.2.7).

FIGURE 1.2.6

In some South Asian economies, over half of unbanked adults have a mobile phone

Adults with no account (%), 2021

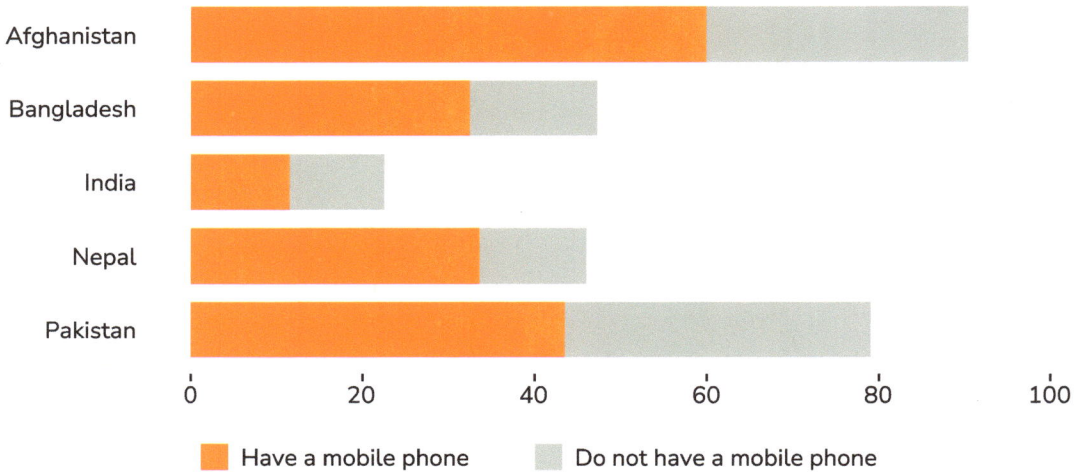

Afghanistan
Bangladesh
India
Nepal
Pakistan

0   20   40   60   80   100

■ Have a mobile phone   ■ Do not have a mobile phone

Sources: Global Findex Database 2021; Gallup World Poll.

Note: Sri Lanka is not included in the figure because data on mobile phone ownership were not available.

Data suggest that mobile phones could overcome some of the barriers that unbanked adults say prevent them from accessing financial services. For example, digital financial services could mitigate the problem of physical distance between financial institutions and their customers. Confirmation may be the fact that unbanked adults in developing economies who cited distance as a barrier have high rates of mobile phone ownership. The share is even higher in some economies with remote areas or remote islands where digital financial services could be especially effective. In Indonesia, for example, 36 percent of unbanked adults cited distance as a barrier, and 55 percent of this group reported having a mobile phone. In Cambodia, 35 percent of unbanked adults cited distance as a barrier, and yet 75 percent of them also reported owning a mobile phone.

The gender gap in mobile access must be addressed to ensure equitable progress on financial inclusion

Leveraging mobile phone ownership to expand financial inclusion could also narrow the gender gap in economies where women are as likely as men to own a mobile phone. But that is not the

MAP 1.2.4

More than half of unbanked adults in Sub-Saharan Africa have a mobile phone

Adults with no account but with a mobile phone, 2021

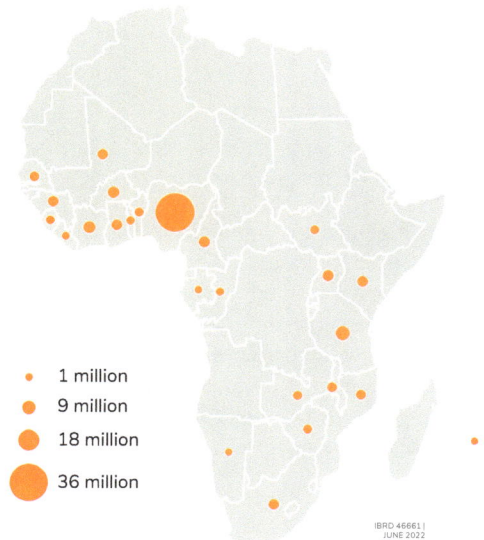

• 1 million
• 9 million
● 18 million
● 36 million

IBRD 46661 | JUNE 2022

Sources: Global Findex Database 2021; Gallup World Poll.

Note: Data are not displayed for economies for which no data were available.

FIGURE 1.2.7

In most economies in Sub-Saharan Africa, most unbanked adults have a mobile phone

Adults with no account (%), 2021

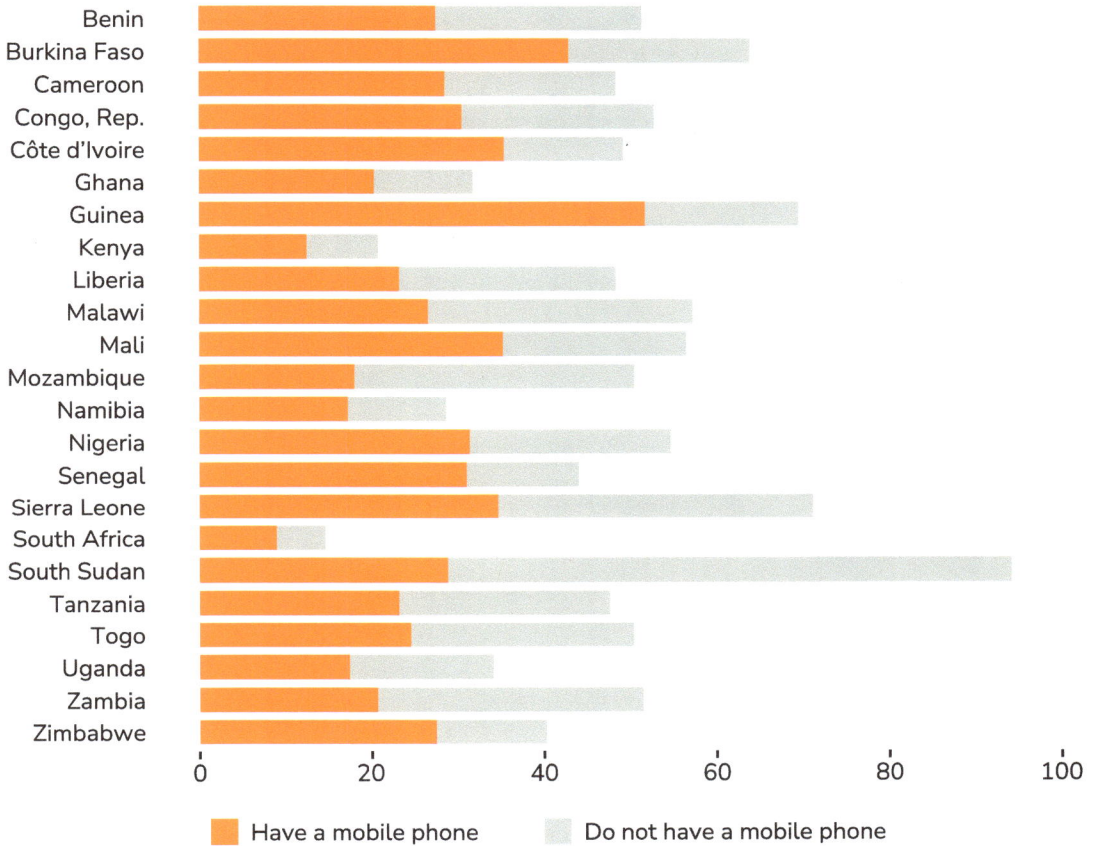

Sources: Global Findex Database 2021; Gallup World Poll.

Note: Gabon and Mauritius are not included in the figure because data on mobile phone ownership were not available.

case everywhere. In South Asia, for example, women are 18 percentage points less likely than men to have a mobile phone. India and Bangladesh are near the South Asian average, with gaps in mobile ownership of 19 and 17 percentage points, respectively. In Pakistan, women are half as likely as men to have a mobile phone (figure 1.2.8).

Mobile phones in Sub-Saharan Africa are central to account ownership in the economies in this region. Future progress, however, depends in part on ensuring that women have access to this crucial technology. Among adults in Sub-Saharan Africa, 86 percent of men have a mobile phone, compared with 77 percent of women—a gender gap of 8 percentage points. Yet in several economies, including Cameroon and Zambia, women are almost as likely as men to own a mobile phone (figure 1.2.9). In some economies, such as Zimbabwe, women are more likely than men to have a mobile phone.

FIGURE 1.2.8

The gender gap persists in mobile phone access in South Asia

Adults with a mobile phone (%), 2021

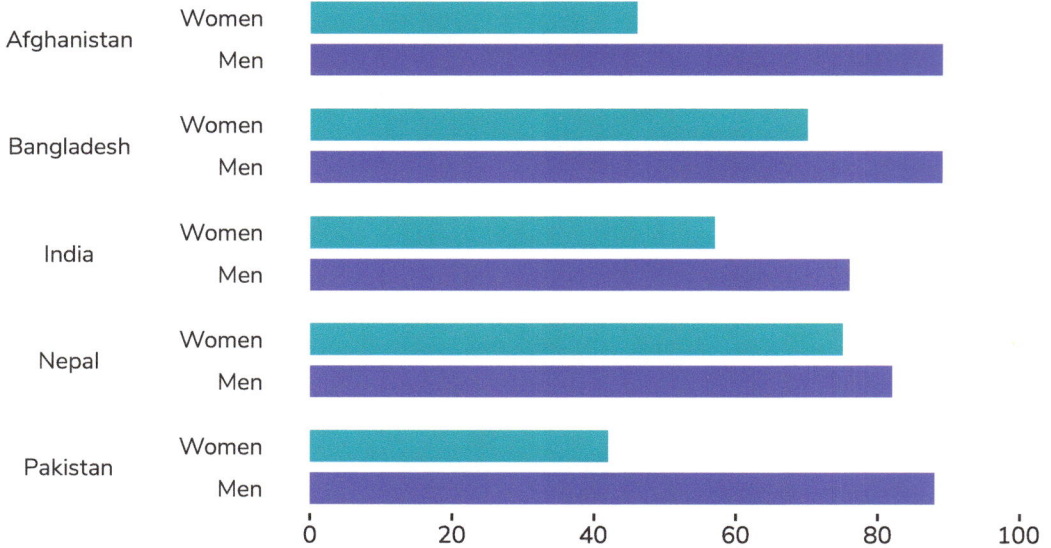

Source: Gallup World Poll.

Note: Sri Lanka is not included in the figure because data on mobile phone ownership were not available.

Unbanked adults express insecurity about managing an account on their own

To understand both whether unbanked adults are comfortable using an account at a financial institution and how receptive populations might be to digitalization, the Global Findex 2021 survey asked unbanked adults whether they would be able to use an account without help if they opened one.

The responses revealed much insecurity. In developing economies, 64 percent of unbanked adults said they could not use an account at a financial institution without help, and in some economies the proportion was even larger. In Pakistan, for example, more than four out of five unbanked adults said they could not use an account at a financial institution without help. In Egypt and South Sudan, 65 percent and 79 percent of unbanked adults, respectively, said they would need help using an account at a financial institution (figure 1.2.10).

Disadvantaged populations are even less likely to be able to use banking services confidently. In developing economies, unbanked women are 10 percentage points more likely than unbanked men to say they would need help using an account at a financial institution. In Brazil, unbanked women are 31 percentage points more likely than unbanked men to say they would need help; in Nigeria, they are twice as likely.

Thus new account holders, especially those opening their first account to receive a payment, must be able to understand the fee structure for the account and receive ongoing support in using it. Financial service providers play a role in ensuring that staff and agents provide complete and accurate information, and governments must define and enforce consumer protection regulations.

FIGURE 1.2.9

A gender gap in mobile access exists in some economies in Sub-Saharan Africa, but not all

Adults with a mobile phone (%), 2021

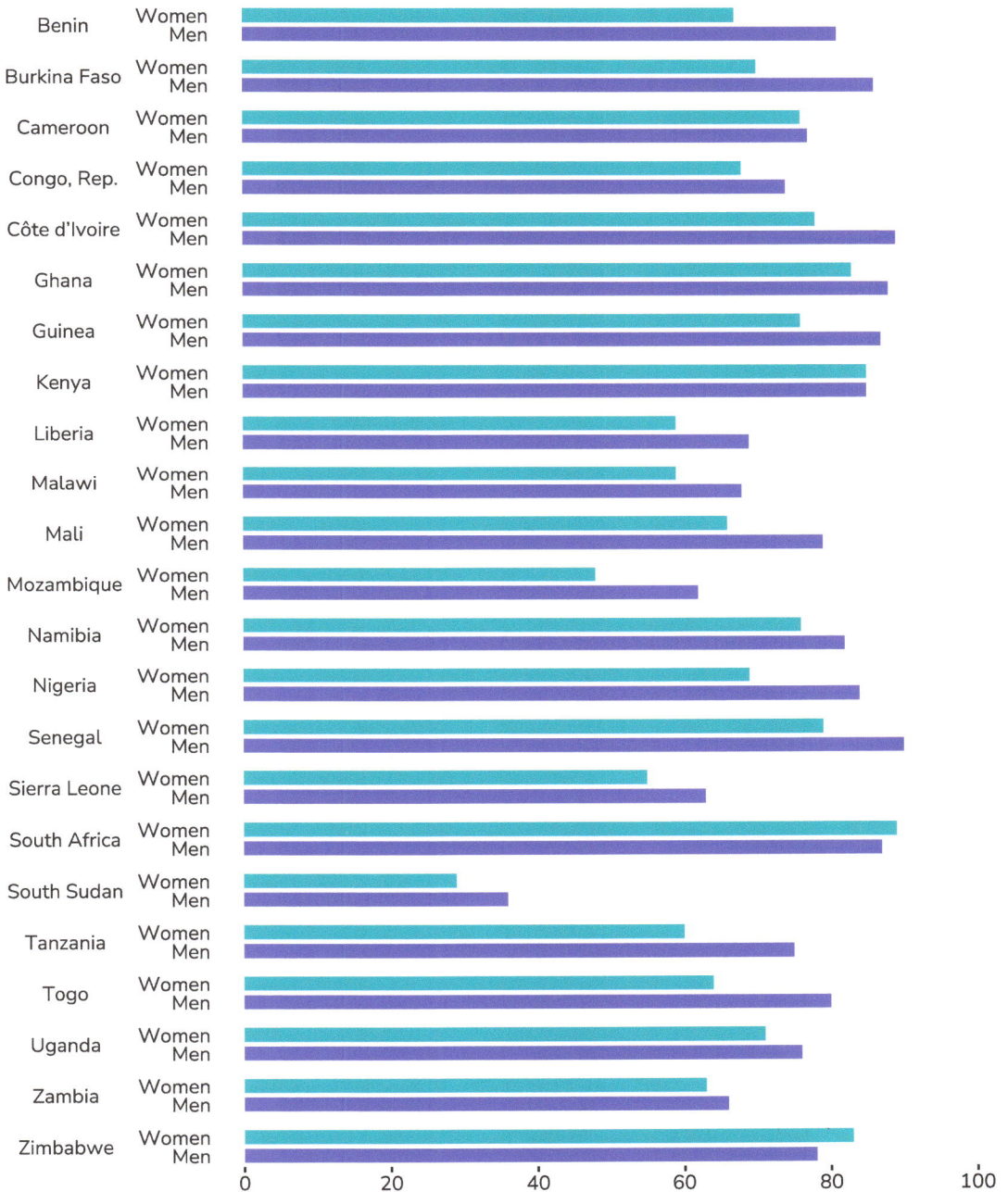

FIGURE 1.2.10

Unbanked adults lack the confidence to manage an account by themselves

Adults with no account who said they could not use a financial institution account without help (%), 2021

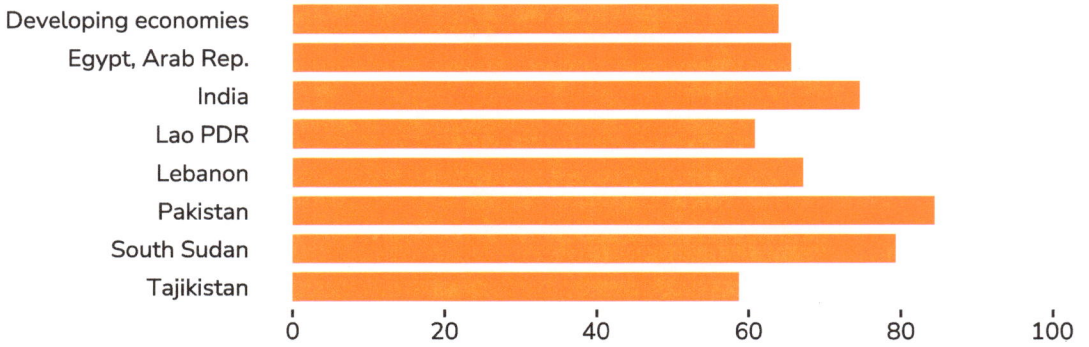

Source: Global Findex Database 2021.

References

Ashraf, Nava, Dean Karlan, and Wesley Yin. 2010. "Female Empowerment: Impact of a Commitment Savings Product in the Philippines." *World Development* 38 (3): 333–44.

Dupas, Pascaline, Dean Karlan, Jonathan Robinson, and Diego Ubfal. 2018. "Banking the Unbanked? Evidence from Three Countries." *American Economic Journal: Applied Economics* 10 (2): 257–97.

Gallup World Poll. 2021. Gallup Organization. Washington DC. https://www.gallup.com/analytics/318875 /global-research.aspx.

Gentilini, Ugo, Mohamed Almenfi, John Blomquist, Pamela Dale, Luciana De la Flor Giuffra, Vyjayanti Desai, Maria Belen Fontenez, et al. 2021. "Social Protection and Jobs Responses to COVID-19: A Real-Time Review of Country Measures." "Living paper" version 15, May 14. https://documents1.worldbank.org/curated /en/281531621024684216/pdf/Social-Protection-and-Jobs-Responses-to-COVID-19-A-Real-Time -Review-of-Country-Measures-May-14-2021.pdf.

GPFI (Global Partnership for Financial Inclusion) and OECD (Organisation for Economic Co-operation and Development). No date. "G20 Fukuoka Policy Priorities on Aging and Financial Inclusion: 8 Key Steps to Design a Better Future." https://www.oecd.org/g20/summits/osaka/G20-Fukuoka-Policy-Priorities-on -Aging.pdf.

GPFI (Global Partnership for Financial Inclusion) and World Bank. 2021. "The Impact of COVID-19 on Digital Financial Inclusion." https://www.gpfi.org/sites/gpfi/files/sites/default/files/5_WB%20Report_The%20 impact%20of%20COVID-19%20on%20digital%20financial%20inclusion.pdf.

Haseeb, Ahmned, and Benjamin Cowan. 2021. "Mobile Money and Healthcare Use: Evidence from East Africa." *World Development* 141: 105392.

IMF (International Monetary Fund). 2021. "2021 Financial Access Survey Trends and Development." IMF, Washington, DC.

Jack, William, and Tavneet Suri. 2014. "Risk Sharing and Transactions Costs: Evidence from Kenya's Mobile Money Revolution." *American Economic Review* 104 (1): 183–223.

Jones, Kelly, and Erick Gong. 2021. "Precautionary Savings and Shock-Coping Behaviors: The Effects of Promoting Mobile Bank Savings on Transactional Sex in Kenya." *Journal of Health Economics* 78 (July).

Lee, Jean N., Jonathan Morduch, Saravana Ravindran, Abu S. Shonchoy, and Hassan Zaman. 2021. "Poverty and Migration in the Digital Age: Experimental Evidence on Mobile Banking in Bangladesh." *American Economic Journal: Applied Economics* 13 (1): 38–71.

Moore, Danielle, Zahra Niazi, Rebecca Rouse, and Berber Kramer. 2019. "Building Resilience through Financial Inclusion: A Review of Existing Evidence and Knowledge Gaps." Brief, Innovations for Poverty Action, Washington, DC. https://www.poverty-action.org/publication/building-resilience-through-financial-inclusion -review-existing-evidence-and-knowledge.

Munyegera, Ggombe Kasim, and Tomoya Matsumoto. 2016. "Mobile Money, Remittances, and Household Welfare: Panel Evidence from Rural Uganda." *World Development* 79: 127–37.

OECD (Organisation for Economic Co-operation and Development) and EC (European Commission). 2020. "Cities in the World: A New Perspective on Urbanisation." https://doi.org/10.1787/d0efcbda-en.

Pomeranz, Dina, and Felipe Kast. 2022. "Savings Accounts to Borrow Less: Experimental Evidence from Chile." *Journal of Human Resources*. Published ahead of print, March 9, 2022. doi:10.3368/jhr.0619-10264R3.

Prina, Silvia. 2015. "Banking the Poor via Savings Accounts: Evidence from a Field Experiment." *Journal of Development Economics* 115: 16–31.

Riley, Emma. 2018. "Mobile Money and Risk Sharing against Village Shocks." *Journal of Development Economics* 135 (November): 43–58.

Saka, Orkun, Barry Eichengreen, and Cevat Giray Aksoy. 2021. "Epidemic Exposure, Fintech Adoption, and the Digital Divide." NBER Working Paper 29006, National Bureau of Economic Research, Cambridge, MA.

Suri, Tavneet, and William Jack. 2016. "The Long-Run Poverty and Gender Impacts of Mobile Money." *Science* 354 (6317): 1288–92.

World Bank. Forthcoming. "Global ID Coverage Estimates: 2021 Update." World Bank, Washington, DC. https://id4d.worldbank.org/global-dataset.

World Bank Group. 2017. *Global Financial Inclusion and Consumer Protection Survey, 2017 Report*. Washington, DC: World Bank. https://openknowledge.worldbank.org/handle/10986/28998.

CHAPTER 2

Use of Financial Services

Introduction

The increases in formal financial account ownership and the narrowing of equity gaps documented in chapter 1 are good news. The goal of financial inclusion, however, is for account owners to benefit from the use of accounts for digital payments, savings, and appropriate credit because such uses provide a range of positive benefits, which extend far beyond convenience. Among those benefits, account holders, and especially women, enjoy greater security and greater privacy for their transactions. In other benefits, a field experiment in Bangladesh found that factory workers saved more when they received their wages through direct deposit—but there was no such effect for the control groups paid in cash.[1] Likewise, workers in Afghanistan who automatically deposited part of their salary into a mobile savings account had higher savings and financial security than workers who did not adopt automatic deposits.[2]

For recipients, digital payments can also be cheaper than receiving payments in cash. In Liberia, for example, by receiving their salaries as digital deposits teachers saw the cost of collecting their money (including bus fare) fall by 92 percent, from $25 per paycheck to $2, and they were able to spend more time in the classroom because they no longer had to take time off to travel into town to collect their wages.[3] Teachers were also able to avoid traveling with cash in their pockets, a safety benefit confirmed by research that associates digital payments with reductions in crime.[4]

Government payments are one category of digital payments known to produce benefits for both the sender and the recipient. In India, internal fraud and leakage from pension payments dropped by 47 percent when the country transitioned from cash to sending payments to biometric smart cards. Recipients also spent less time collecting payments, and they received more money because of reductions in fraud. The government saved millions of dollars annually in administrative costs—more than enough to cover the cost of the new system.[5]

Also in India, a government workfare program that reached over 100 million people found that women who received benefits paid directly into their own account in a financial institution (and not into the account of a male household head) were more likely to find employment than those paid in cash. Women whose husbands had been most opposed to their working saw the biggest impact. These patterns suggest that gender norms can be influenced by giving women greater control over their income, which can increase household bargaining power.[6]

Beyond South Asia, a study of safety net payments made primarily to women after a drought in Niger found that social benefits paid through mobile phones instead of in cash offered women greater privacy and greater

---

1. Breza, Kanz, and Klapper (2020).
2. Blumenstock, Callen, and Ghani (2018).
3. Dusza (2016).
4. An analysis of 20 years of crime data from the US state of Missouri and nearby areas found that the introduction of digital safety net payments reduced burglary, assault, and larceny, lowering overall crime rates by about 9 percent (Wright et al. 2017).
5. Muralidharan, Niehaus, and Sukhtankar (2016).
6. Field et al. (2021).

control over their funds, and it boosted their spending on nutritious food. The administrative costs for the social benefits program were 20 percent less for mobile transfers than for cash payments.[7] Digital payments can also speed up the collection of social benefits payments. A recent study in Bangladesh on the impact of moving education subsidies from cash to digital channels found that nearly 80 percent of mothers preferred the digital payments, largely because receiving the subsidies digitally did away with the need to travel and wait for cash disbursements and instead allowed mothers to draw down money securely and at their convenience.[8]

Digital payments can also expand financial inclusion among farmers—and encourage the use of additional formal financial services such as credit and insurance. Farmers in Malawi whose earnings were deposited into savings accounts spent 13 percent more on farming equipment and increased their crop value by 15 percent.[9] A large-scale coffee buyer in Uganda worked to digitize payments to 7,000 smallholder coffee farmers, which saved time and money and reduced risk.[10]

Beyond payments, using financial accounts helps people build savings and access credit, which leads to higher income-generating investments, such as in new equipment or in a business. Business owners are given a gateway to the digital economy, where they can connect with more buyers, suppliers, and service providers than is possible through analog networks. For women in low- and middle-income countries, savings, credit, and payment services can serve as a critical link to the formal economy and a gateway to greater economic security and personal empowerment. Meanwhile, an emerging body of evidence indicates that access to these services also pays dividends for their families in the form of better health and education.[11] Unfortunately, the converse is also true—in India, a reduction in microfinance was associated with significant decreases in wages, income, and consumption.[12]

However, the introduction of digital payments to low-income adults is accompanied by risks to consumers, such as fraud and phishing scams targeting accounts, overindebtedness in digital credit, and customers receiving incomplete or incorrect information on the fees and costs of financial products.[13] Chapter 3 discusses opportunities to identify consumer issues and improve consumer use and trust of new financial technology.

7. Aker et al. (2016).
8. Gelb et al. (2019).
9. Lasse et al. (2016).
10. Kvaran and Peters (2017).
11. See chapter 1 for a review of the literature on ways that the use of formal financial services can increase savings and income and lead to achievement of development goals such as greater spending on health care, education, and nutritious food.
12. Breza and Kinnan (2021).
13. For a review of studies on consumer protection, see Innovations for Poverty Action, "Consumer Protection Initiative: Research Initiatives" (dashboard), https://www.poverty-action.org/program-area/financial-inclusion/consumer-protection-initiative.

Global Findex 2021 survey headline findings on the use of financial services

Like the growth found in account ownership, the Global Findex 2021 survey revealed growth in the use of accounts to make digital payments, as well as to save and borrow, and highlights the ways in which these financial services overlap in the broader financial ecosystem. The key findings are as follows:

Digital payments

- The share of adults making or receiving digital payments in developing economies grew from 35 percent in 2014 to 57 percent in 2021—an increase that outpaces growth in account ownership over the same period.

- Thirty-nine percent of adults in developing economies—or 57 percent of those with a financial institution account—opened their first account at a financial institution specifically to receive a wage payment or money from the government.

- Twenty percent of adults living in developing economies, excluding China, made a merchant payment using a card, mobile phone, or the internet—and about 40 percent of them did so for the first time after the start of the pandemic. About one-third of adults in developing economies who paid a utility bill directly from an account did so for the first time after the start of the COVID-19 pandemic—evidence of the role of the pandemic in accelerating digital adoption.

Savings

- Twenty-five percent of adults in developing economies saved using an account, and an even higher share, 39 percent, used an account to store money for cash management purposes.

- More than half of the people in developing economies who saved any money did so in a formal account in 2021—the first year that formal methods were the most common method of saving.

- Mobile money accounts are an important method of saving in Sub-Saharan Africa, where 15 percent of adults—and 39 percent of mobile money account holders—used one to save. Equal shares of adults in Sub-Saharan Africa used a mobile money account and a formal savings account at a financial institution.

Borrowing

- About 50 percent of adults in developing economies borrowed money, although fewer than half used formal means such as taking out a loan from a financial institution, using a credit card, or borrowing through their mobile money account.

- Credit cards were the dominant form of borrowing in high-income economies and in some developing economies such as Argentina, Brazil, China, the Russian Federation, Türkiye, and Ukraine.

- Borrowing only from family and friends is as common in developing economies as borrowing formally, although in some developing economies it far outstripped formal mechanisms.

The financial ecosystem

- In both high-income and developing economies the most common use for an account is to make or receive a payment, followed by saving and borrowing.

- In developing economies, 36 percent of adults received a payment into an account. Of those, 83 percent also reported that they made a digital payment. Almost two-thirds of payment recipients used their account to store money, about 40 percent to save money, and about 40 percent to borrow money. This finding suggests that digital inflows can pave the way for wider use of financial services.

Opportunities to improve financial inclusion by leveraging specific services

These findings reveal new opportunities to drive financial inclusion by increasing account ownership among the unbanked and expanding the use of financial services among those who already have accounts, in particular by leveraging digital payments:

- Hundreds of millions of unbanked adults receive payments in cash—such as wages, government transfers, or proceeds from the sale of agricultural goods. Shifting these payments to financial institution or mobile money accounts could create an entry point for increasing account ownership among the unbanked.

- About 620 million adults with an account pay their utility bills in cash. Promoting digital payments could expand the use of financial services among adults who already have an account and increase investment in pay-as-you-go sustainable electrification.

- Digitalizing merchant payments could also help expand the use of accounts among adults who already have an account and help business owners build alternative credit information histories and promote formalization. In developing economies, 1.6 billion adults with an account made merchant payments in cash only.

- Enabling actors such as governments, telecommunications providers, and financial services providers must create an environment in which safe, affordable, and convenient products and functionality are more appealing than cash.

This chapter presents detailed Global Findex 2021 data on the trends in the use of financial services at the global and regional levels and offers examples from specific economies that exemplify, or contradict, the trends. Sections 2.1, 2.2, and 2.3 describe the trends in payments adoption, savings, and borrowing, respectively, and section 2.4 explores the ways in which account owners leverage all three within the broader financial ecosystem. Sections 2.5 and 2.6 in turn explore opportunities to expand financial services adoption by banked and unbanked adults.

2.1 Digital payments

2.1 DIGITAL PAYMENTS

In developing economies, growth in digital payments outpaced growth in account ownership

In the Global Findex 2021 survey, 64 percent of adults around the world—or 84 percent of account owners—made or received at least one digital payment. In high-income economies, 95 percent of adults (98 percent of account owners) did so, compared with 57 percent (80 percent of account owners) of adults in developing economies (figure 2.1.1). As defined, digital payments include the use of a mobile money account, a debit or credit card, or a mobile phone or the internet to make a payment from an account, or the use of a mobile phone or the internet to send money to relatives or friends or to pay bills. Digital payments also include in-store or online merchant payments; paying utility bills; sending or receiving domestic remittances; receiving payments for agricultural products; or receiving wages, government transfers, or a public pension directly from or into an account. Survey respondents were prompted to answer based on their experience during the past year.

In high-income economies, the use of digital payments has been virtually universal since 2014, when such data were first collected as part of the Global Findex survey (figure 2.1.1, panel a). In developing economies (panel b), the share of adults making or receiving digital payments has grown rapidly in recent years and rose by 13 percentage points between 2017 and 2021, from 44 percent to 57 percent. In 2014, the share was 35 percent. Indeed, growth in the use of digital payments outpaced growth in account ownership in developing economies: the share of account owners making or receiving a digital payment increased to 80 percent in 2021, up from 69 percent in 2017 and 63 percent in 2014.

FIGURE 2.1.1

In developing economies, the share of account owners using digital payments has grown rapidly in recent years

Adults with an account (%), 2014–21

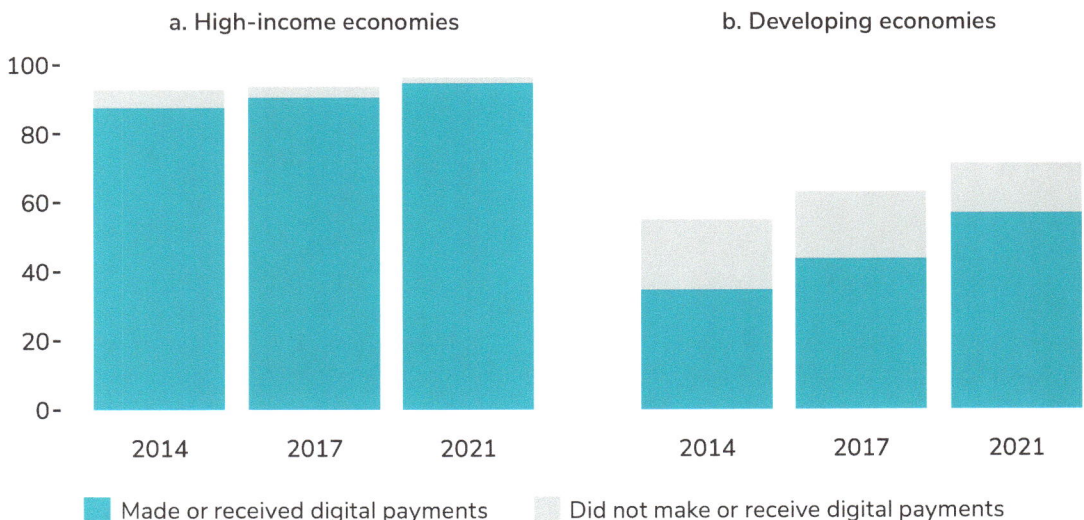

a. High-income economies   b. Developing economies

Made or received digital payments   Did not make or receive digital payments

Source: Global Findex Database 2021.

FIGURE 2.1.2

The largest share of digital payment users both made and received payments (versus only made or only received)

Adults with an account (%), 2014–21

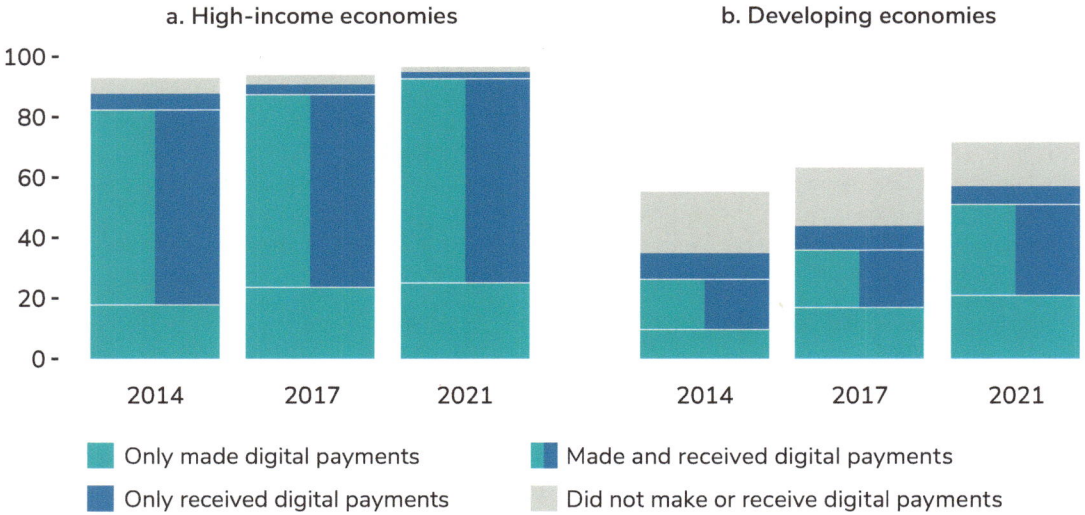

a. High-income economies   b. Developing economies

- Only made digital payments
- Only received digital payments
- Made and received digital payments
- Did not make or receive digital payments

Source: Global Findex Database 2021.

People who use digital payments most commonly both make and receive payments, compared with only making or only receiving digital payments (figure 2.1.2). Between 2014 and 2021, the share of adults making a digital payment in developing economies doubled from 26 percent to 51 percent, while the share of account owners doing so increased from about half to over two-thirds. The share of adults receiving a digital payment increased from 25 percent in 2014 to 36 percent in 2021 in developing economies, but remained steady for account owners, half of whom received a digital payment in 2021. The share of adults receiving digital payments increased in parallel with account ownership from 2014 to 2021. However, adults receiving a digital payment are now more likely to make a digital payment than ever before. Among those who received a digital payment in developing economies, 83 percent made a digital payment in 2021, up from 70 percent in 2017 and 66 percent in 2014. The overlap in the use of financial services is discussed in greater detail in section 2.4.

Some developing economies have a gender gap in the use of digital payments

Women are less likely to have an account than men, as discussed in chapter 1, but does the gender gap also apply to how women use their account? Among account owners in high-income economies, the use of digital payments is nearly universal for both women and men. In developing economies, however, men with an account are, on average, 6 percentage points more likely than women with an account to use digital payments. This gender gap in the use of digital payments among account owners has remained virtually unchanged since 2014, despite the overall increase in digital payments.

The gender gap in the use of digital payments among account owners varies substantially across developing economies. In six economies, including four in South Asia, it reaches double digits. In India and Sri Lanka—countries with no gender gap in account ownership—it is 17 percentage points and 18 percentage points, respectively. Bangladesh and Nigeria have similarly large gender gaps in the use of digital payments at 15 percentage points and 16 percentage points, respectively, on top of a gender gap in account ownership of about 20 percentage points. The Arab Republic of Egypt and Nepal have double-digit gaps in the use of digital payments among account owners (12 percentage points and 14 percentage points, respectively), even though their gender gaps in account ownership are smaller. In many other economies, there is no payments gender gap, including in some economies with double-digit gaps in account ownership. In Pakistan, for example, men and women account owners are equally likely to use their account for digital payments and most do (84 percent), despite low overall account ownership and an ownership gender gap of 15 percentage points.

Not surprisingly, there are also differences in digital payment adoption between account owners with incomes in the poorest 40 percent of an economy's households and those with incomes in the richest 60 percent. In high-income economies, poorer and richer account owners are equally likely to use digital payments. In developing economies, by contrast, 83 percent of richer account owners use digital payments, and 74 percent of poorer account owners do—a 9 percentage point gap. In those economies, the gap between poorer and richer in the use of accounts for digital payments has narrowed substantially since 2014, when it was 15 percentage points, and 2017, when it was 13 percentage points.

The remainder of this chapter explores the different types of payments that people receive or make. In developing economies, the survey collected data on all types of payments discussed here. In most high-income economies, however, the survey did not collect data on some types of payments because of the time limits on phone-based interviews.[14]

The chapter distinguishes mainly between payments using an account and payments made only in cash.[15] For domestic remittances, it includes payments made using a money transfer service provider such as Western Union that transfers money on behalf of the sender and recipient. Some people who reported sending or receiving a payment, when asked about the payment channel used, responded with "no," "don't know," or "refuse" to all possible options. These respondents, typically representing only a small share of adults in any economy, are reported as "using other method." This category could include people making or receiving payments by check.

Receiving payments

Government payments were mostly paid into accounts in both high-income and developing economies

Globally, 28 percent of adults received at least one payment from the government, whether it came in the form of public sector wages, a public sector pension, or government transfer payments. Government transfer payments include any kind of social benefits such as subsidies, unemployment benefits, or payments for educational or medical expenses. Not surprisingly, the share of adults receiving government payments is more than twice as high in high-income economies (52 percent) as in developing economies (22 percent)—see figure 2.1.3. In high-income economies, the overwhelming majority (84 percent) of those receiving government payments do so into an account. Another 13 percent received such payments in some other way than into an account or in cash, probably in the form of either checks or vouchers. Similarly, adults in developing economies most often receive government payments into an account: on average, 67 percent of those receiving government payments do so into an account, ranging from 78 percent in upper-middle-income economies to just over half in lower-middle-income and lower-income economies.

---

14. Gallup, Inc., imposes a time limit on phone interviews collected in high-income economies, where phone interviews are the typical survey method. This restriction limits the number of Global Findex survey questions that can be added to the Gallup World Poll core questionnaire. In 14 high-income economies included in the Global Findex 2021 database, however, Gallup, Inc., typically conducts face-to-face rather than phone interviews. In these economies, data were collected for all types of payments. In one developing economy included in the database, Gallup, Inc., also typically conducts phone interviews, similarly limiting the number of questions that could be asked in this economy.

15. Payments are considered to have been received into an account if the respondent reported receiving them directly into an account at a financial institution; into a card, which is assumed to be linked to an account or to support a card-based account; or through a mobile phone. Payments are considered to have been sent from an account if the respondent reported sending them directly from a financial institution account or through a mobile phone. However, a payment to or from a mobile phone is considered a payment into or from an account only if the respondent lives in an economy where mobile money accounts are provided by a service that was in the GSM Association's Mobile Money for the Unbanked (GSMA MMU) database at the time of the survey.

Of the types of government payments in developing economies, 3 percent of adults, on average, received a public sector wage payment, and 20 percent received a government transfer or pension payment. The average share of adults receiving a government transfer or pension payment varies widely based on an economy's income level, from 7 percent in low-income economies, to 19 percent in lower-middle-income economies, to 23 percent in upper-middle-income economies (figure 2.1.4). Shares also vary by country, from 5 percent or less of adults receiving a government transfer or pension payment in Nigeria, South Sudan, and Tanzania to 87 percent receiving one in Mongolia. In high-income economies, 44 percent of adults reported having received such a government payment. Compared with 2017, the share of adults receiving government transfer and pension payments increased in lower-middle, upper-middle, and high-income economies. This expansion likely reflects the fact that many governments expanded government transfer payments in response to the economic impact of COVID-19.[16]

FIGURE 2.1.3

Most adults receiving government payments did so into an account

Adults receiving government payments in the past year (%), 2021

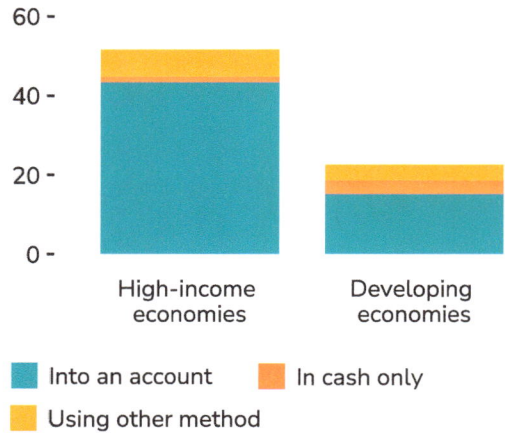

Into an account   In cash only

Using other method

Source: Global Findex Database 2021.

FIGURE 2.1.4

Most adults receiving government transfer or pension payments did so into an account

Adults receiving government transfer or pension payments in the past year (%), 2017–21

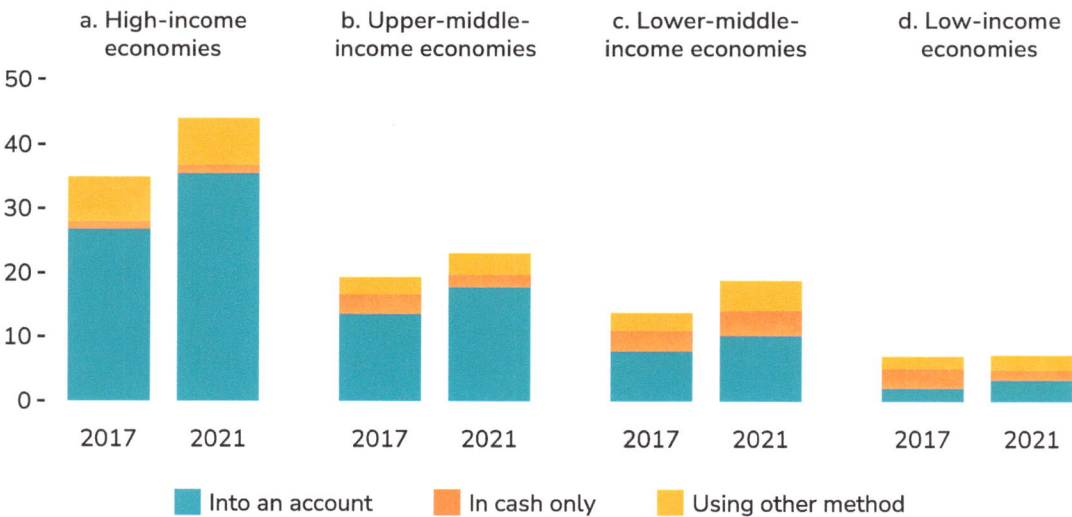

Into an account   In cash only   Using other method

Source: Global Findex Database 2021.

16. Gentilini et al. (2022).

Except in low-income economies, most adults receiving government transfer or pension payments received them into an account, and in both developing and high-income economies the share of adults receiving a public sector wage into an account is virtually universal. Over time, the share of adults receiving a public sector wage payment has remained steady in both high-income economies (13 percent in 2021) and developing economies (3 percent in 2021).

In many developing economies, including Brazil, Colombia, Ghana, Russia, and Uzbekistan, a higher share of government wage payments than government transfer and pension payments is paid into an account (figure 2.1.5). One explanation may be that wage payments are recurrent, whereas government transfer payments may be less frequent, and they are harder to digitize when issued to people living in more remote areas and so less likely to be served by financial institutions. Thus it is easier for governments to digitalize wage payments first.

FIGURE 2.1.5

Government wage payments were more likely than government transfer and pension payments to be paid into an account

Adults receiving public sector wages or government transfers or pensions in the past year (%), 2021

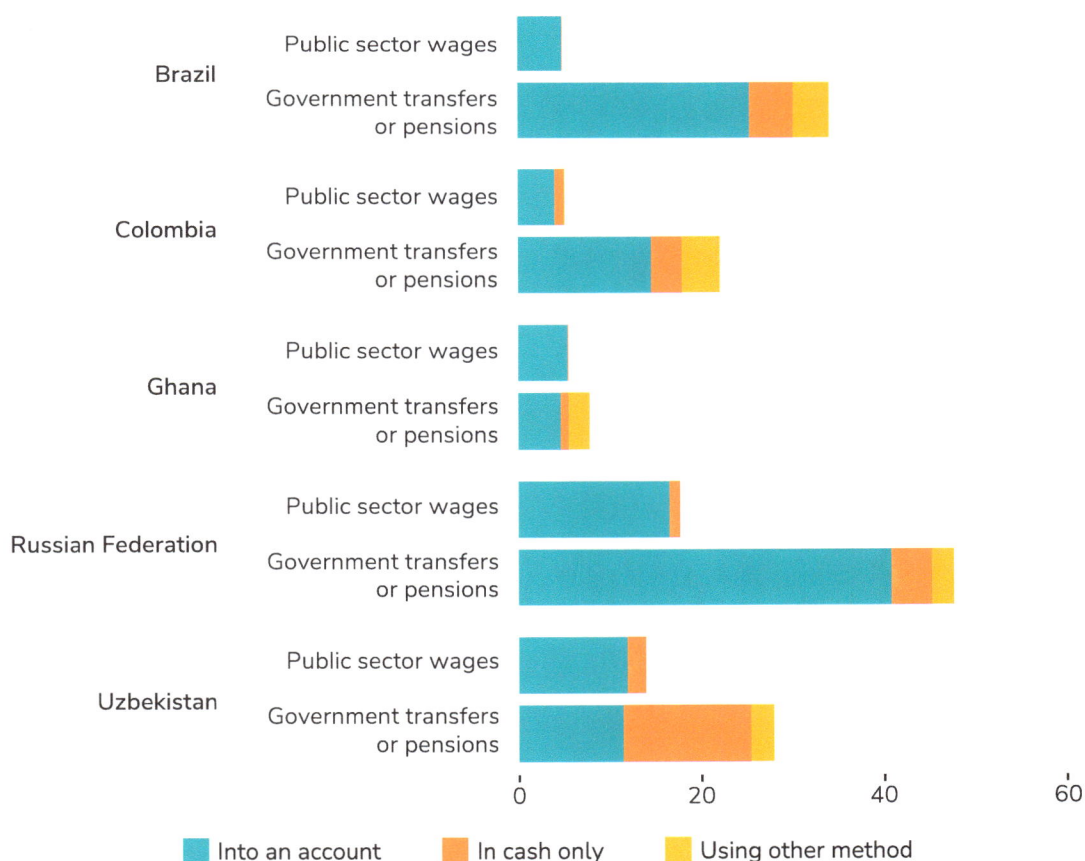

Source: Global Findex Database 2021.

In both high-income and developing economies, private sector wage payments were mostly paid into accounts

Globally, 31 percent of surveyed adults received at least one wage payment from a private sector employer—43 percent in high-income economies and 28 percent in developing economies. In high-income economies, 87 percent of wage earners received their wage payments into an account (a share that has remained steady over time), compared with 61 percent in developing economies—an increase from just 37 percent in 2014 and 45 percent in 2017 (figure 2.1.6).

These averages mask large variations among developing economies, both in the share of adults receiving private sector wage payments and in how they receive these payments. Although some economies have achieved levels of digitalization of private wage payments comparable to those in high-income economies, others still have room for growth. Consider economies in the East Asia and Pacific region. In China and Thailand, two upper-middle-income economies, about 45 percent of adults received a private sector wage payment, and the vast majority (about 80 percent) received it into an account. In Cambodia, Indonesia, the Lao People's Democratic Republic, and the Philippines, all lower-middle-income economies, about a quarter of adults received a private sector wage payment, with the share of wage earners receiving the payment into an account ranging between 17 percent in Lao PDR and 41 percent in the Philippines (figure 2.1.7).

Country income group does not necessarily predict the proportion of people who receive private sector wage payments into an account. In Mongolia, a lower-middle-income economy with nearly universal account ownership, the percentages of adults who received a private sector wage payment (about 40 percent) and who received that payment into an account (about 90 percent) are similar to those in Malaysia, an upper-middle-income economy. However, in Myanmar, a lower-middle-income economy like Mongolia and one in which a similar proportion of adults (about 40 percent) receive private sector wage payments, just about one-fifth of these adults received their wages in an account.

FIGURE 2.1.6

Most private sector wages were paid into an account

Adults receiving private sector wages in the past year (%), 2014–21

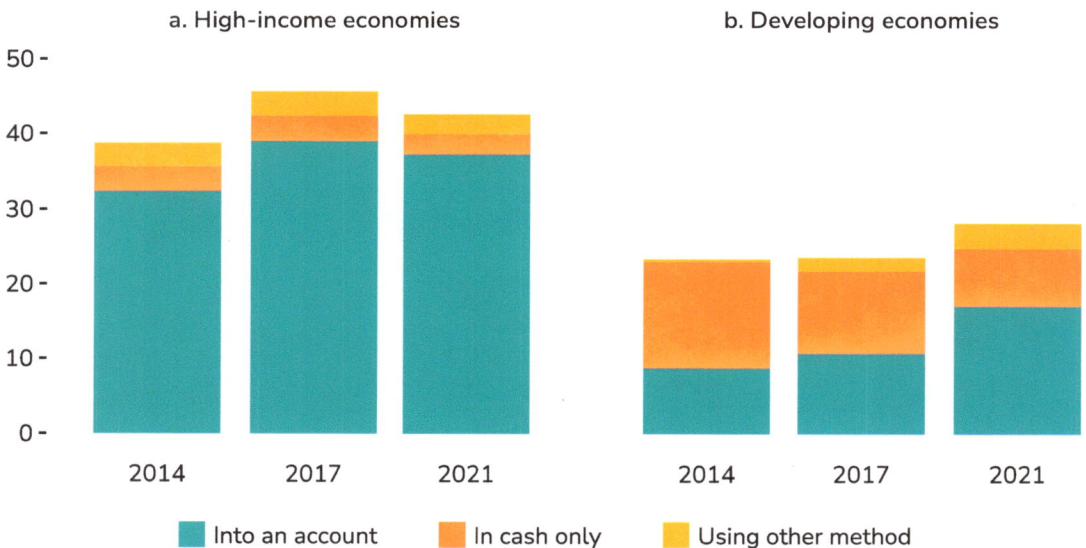

Source: Global Findex Database 2021.

FIGURE 2.1.7

Digitalization of private sector wage payments varied across economies in the East Asia and Pacific region

Adults receiving private sector wages in the past year (%), 2021

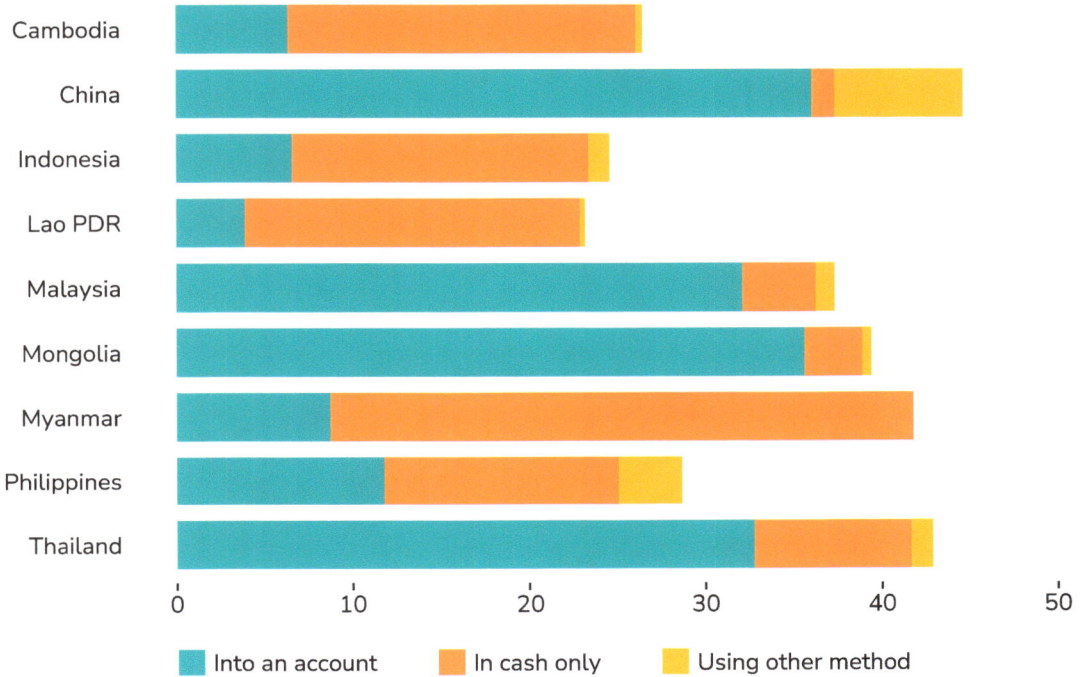

Source: Global Findex Database 2021.

Agricultural payments were received predominantly in cash, with some exceptions

In developing economies, 11 percent of surveyed adults received payments for the sale of agricultural products, and most of the payments were in cash. On average, across developing economies only one-fourth of recipients received such a payment into an account, which translates to 3 percent of adults receiving such a payment into an account in developing economies, including 2 percent in South Asia. However, in Sub-Saharan Africa, where the share of adults receiving agricultural payments is more than twice the developing economy average of 26 percent, some economies saw a much higher share of recipients receiving agricultural payments into accounts. Sixty-three percent in Kenya, 39 percent in Mali, and 35 percent in Uganda—more than 10 percent of all adults in each of these three countries—reported receiving agricultural payments into an account, most often into a mobile money account (figure 2.1.8). In Kenya and Uganda, the share of all adults who received an agricultural payment into an account remained at about the same level as in 2017. In Mali, the share of adults who did so in 2021 was more than double the share in 2017.

FIGURE 2.1.8

In Sub-Saharan African economies, payments for agricultural products were usually in cash, with notable exceptions

Adults receiving payments for agricultural products in the past year (%), 2021

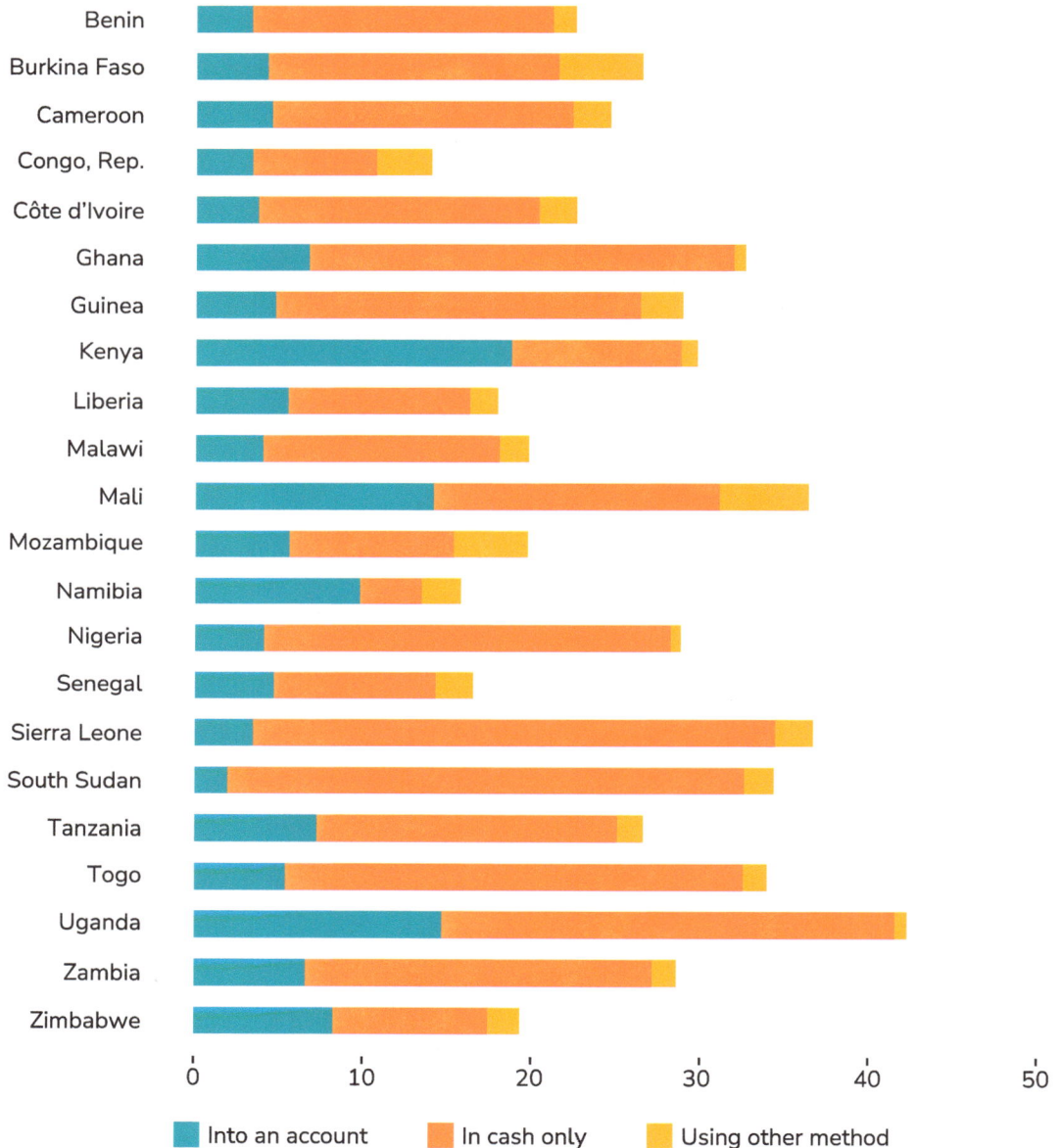

Source: Global Findex Database 2021.

Most domestic remittance payments were received and sent using an account

Domestic remittances are an important part of the economy in many places around the world.[17] In developing economies, 33 percent of adults sent or received a domestic remittance to or from a relative or friend living elsewhere in the country.[18] Domestic remittances are particularly important in Sub-Saharan Africa, where 53 percent of adults sent or received such payments.[19] Ghana has the highest share at 77 percent, with Cameroon, Gabon, Kenya, Namibia, Senegal, and Uganda in the 60–70 percent range (figure 2.1.9). The most common way of sending or receiving domestic remittances is through an account. On average, a little over two-thirds of adults in Sub-Saharan Africa who reported having sent or received domestic remittances said they used an account.

Other ways to send or receive domestic remittances include using cash or a money transfer service, such as Western Union. Financial institutions and mobile money operators also offer money transfer services for domestic remittances. Payments are classified as money transfers if the sender or recipient did not use an account but instead brought cash to a service provider, which transferred the funds electronically.

Outside of Sub-Saharan Africa, Thailand has the highest share of adults (67 percent) who sent or received domestic remittances (figure 2.1.10). About half of adults in Cambodia, Mongolia, the Philippines, Russia, and República Bolivariana de Venezuela sent or received them. Much like in Sub-Saharan Africa, the use of accounts for such payments dominated in Mongolia, Russia, and Thailand. By contrast, a money transfer service was more commonly used in Cambodia (71 percent). In the Philippines, both accounts and money transfer services were generally used for such payments.

FIGURE 2.1.9

In Sub-Saharan African economies, remittances were sent and received mainly using an account

Adults sending or receiving domestic remittances in the past year (%), 2021

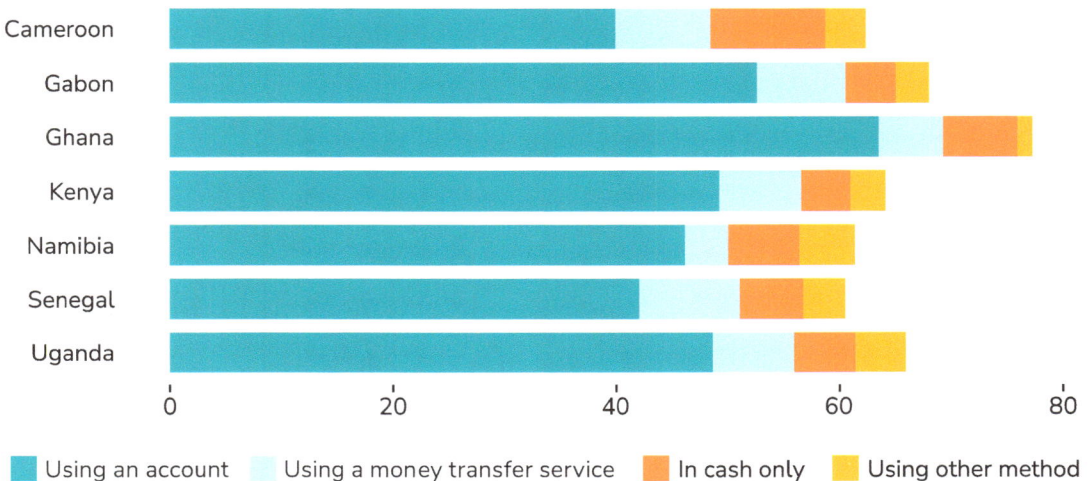

Using an account   Using a money transfer service   In cash only   Using other method

Source: Global Findex Database 2021.

---

17. The Global Findex 2021 survey did not cover international remittances. Although international remittances are economically important for some economies, the share of adults in developing economies who reported sending or receiving them is, on average, 4 percent (Gallup World Poll 2017, https://www.gallup.com/analytics/318875/global-research.aspx).

18. In developing economies, 21 percent of adults reported having sent domestic remittances in the past year; 25 percent reported having received them; and 13 percent reported having both sent and received them.

19. In Sub-Saharan Africa, 35 percent of adults reported having sent domestic remittances in the past year; 42 percent reported having received them; and 24 percent reported having both sent and received them.

FIGURE 2.1.10

Money transfer services play an important role in domestic remittance payments in some economies outside of Sub-Saharan Africa

Adults sending or receiving domestic remittances in the past year (%), 2021

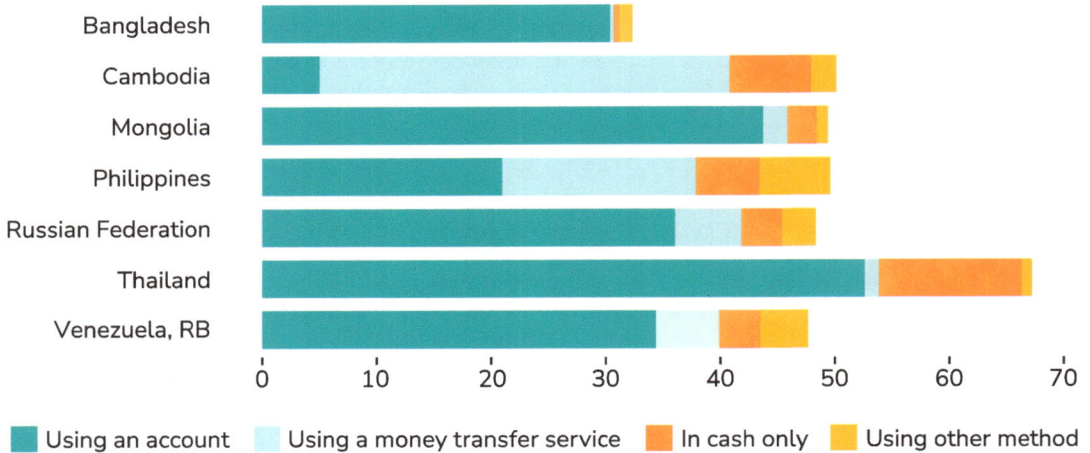

Source: Global Findex Database 2021.

Making payments

The share of adults paying utility bills from an account grew in developing economies, accelerated by COVID-19

Globally, 54 percent of adults made regular payments for water, electricity, or trash collection.[20] In high-income economies, 76 percent of adults reported making such payments, with the vast majority (83 percent) making payments directly from an account. In developing economies, about half of surveyed adults made a utility payment, with equal shares (about 40 percent) making payments directly from an account and in cash only (figure 2.1.11).

The share of adults in developing economies paying utility bills directly from an account has steadily increased, from 8 percent in 2014 to 18 percent in 2021 (figure 2.1.12). In 2021, more than a third of adults in developing economies who paid utility bills directly from an account did so for the first time after the outbreak of COVID-19. In high-income economies, the share of those paying utility bills from an account remained about steady over this

FIGURE 2.1.11

In developing economies, 4 in 10 people paying utility bills did so directly from an account

Adults paying utility bills in the past year (%), 2021

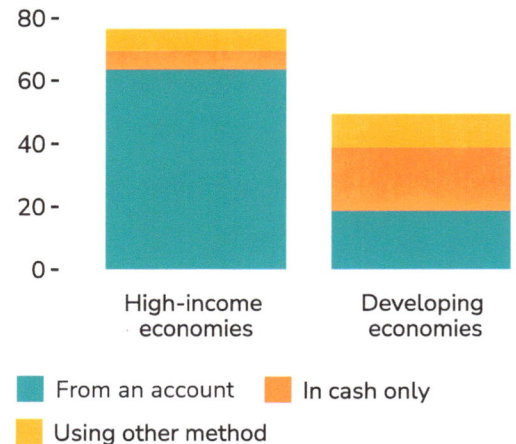

Source: Global Findex Database 2021.

20. The Global Findex 2021 survey asks whether the respondent personally, not the household, made such a payment.

FIGURE 2.1.12

In developing economies, more than a third of adults paying utility bills from an account did so for the first time after the start of the COVID-19 pandemic

Adults paying utility bills in the past year (%), 2014–21

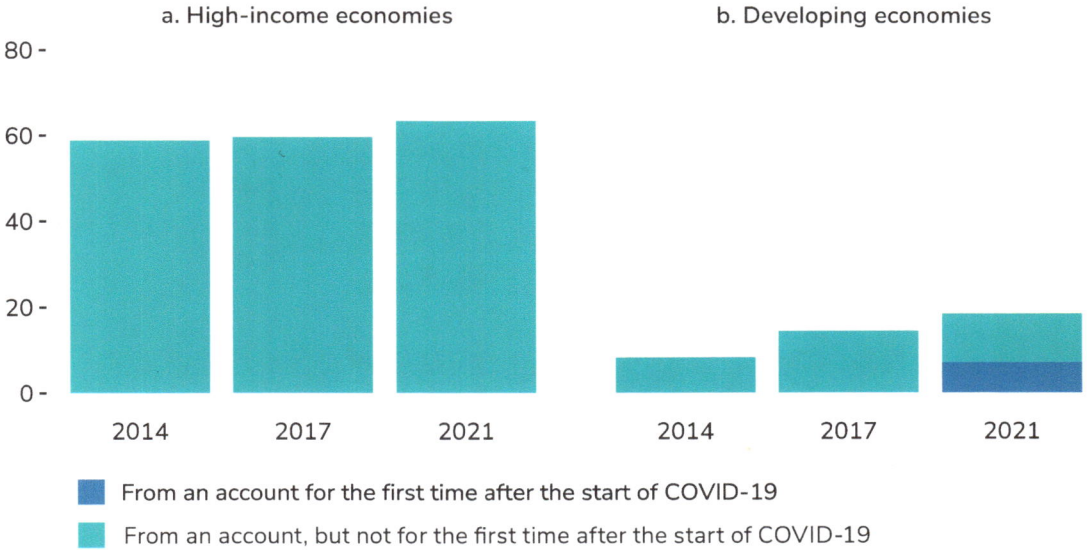

a. High-income economies   b. Developing economies

(Bar chart)

Legend:
- From an account for the first time after the start of COVID-19
- From an account, but not for the first time after the start of COVID-19

Source: Global Findex Database 2021.

Note: Data on making a payment from an account for the first time after the start of COVID-19 are available only for developing economies.

period (no data were collected in high-income economies on account usage for utility bill payment after the outbreak of COVID-19).

Across developing economies, utility bill payment practices vary widely. In Egypt, for example, virtually everyone who made utility payments did so in cash, as did more than 80 percent of those paying utility bills in Indonesia, Morocco, Myanmar, and Pakistan, among others (figure 2.1.13). But in many economies in Sub-Saharan Africa (including Kenya and Uganda) and in Brazil, the Islamic Republic of Iran, Malaysia, Mongolia, Russia, and Türkiye, among others, a majority of those paying utility bills did so directly from an account.

COVID-19 accelerated the digitalization of utility payments in some developing economies. The share of adults who made a utility payment from an account for the first time after the outbreak of COVID-19 was especially high in many economies in Latin America and the Caribbean. On average, 15 percent of adults in the region did so—almost twice the developing economy average. In Bolivia, for example, 23 percent of adults made their first utility payment from an account after the onset of the COVID-19 pandemic, accounting for about 80 percent of all those who reported having made a utility payment from an account (figure 2.1.13). In Colombia, Ecuador, Honduras, and Peru, about 15 percent of adults made such payments for the first time after COVID-19 emerged, representing two-thirds or more of all those who made a utility payment from an account. In Brazil, 18 percent of adults made such payments for the first time, almost doubling the share of adults making utility payments from an account.

FIGURE 2.1.13

The methods used by adults in developing economies to make utility payments varied widely

Adults paying utility bills in the past year (%), 2021

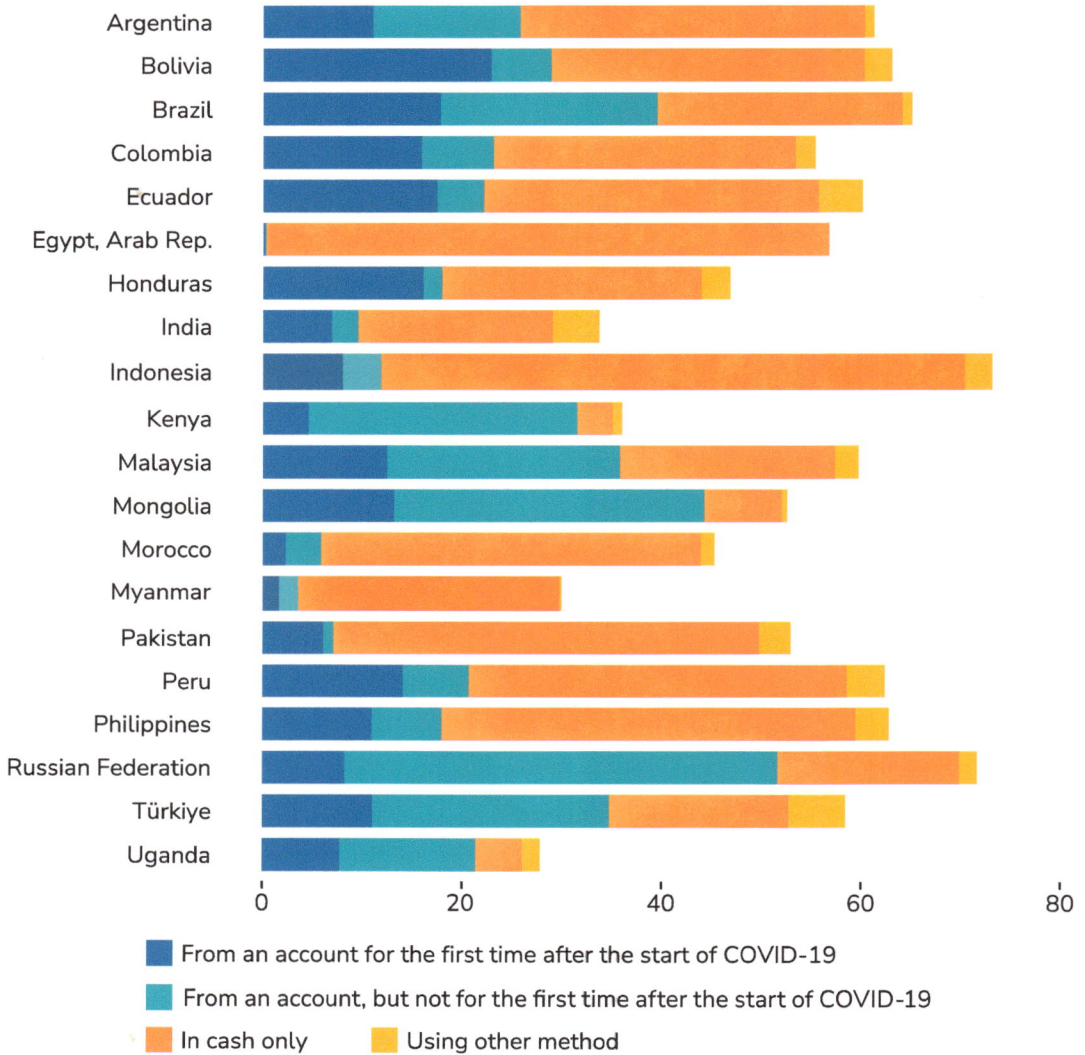

From an account for the first time after the start of COVID-19

From an account, but not for the first time after the start of COVID-19

In cash only   Using other method

Source: Global Findex Database 2021.

Note: Data on making a payment from an account for the first time after the start of COVID-19 are available only for developing economies.

The share of adults making digital merchant payments increased in developing economies after the outbreak of COVID-19

In 2021, for the first time, the Global Findex survey included an expanded module on digital merchant payments in developing economies, where 37 percent of adults made digital merchant payments (figure 2.1.14). This average is heavily skewed by the pervasive use of digital merchant payments in China (82 percent of adults). Excluding China, the average share of adults in developing economies making digital merchant payments is 20 percent. This percentage includes all respondents who made a purchase in a store using a debit or credit card or a mobile phone or the internet to pay directly from their account (digital in-store merchant payment). It also includes all respondents who made a purchase online and paid for it online directly from their account (digital online merchant payment).

The share of adults making a digital merchant payment increased after the outbreak of COVID-19. In developing economies, excluding China, 8 percent of adults, on average, made their first digital merchant payment after the start of the pandemic, accounting for about 40 percent of those who made a digital merchant payment.

The use of digital merchant payments varies considerably across developing economies. In Brazil, Mongolia, and South Africa, more than half of adults made a digital merchant payment (figure 2.1.15). About 20 percent of adults in these economies made a digital merchant payment for the first time after the onset of COVID-19. Social distancing and hygiene concerns during the pandemic may have accelerated the adoption of digital merchant payments in economies where a significant share of adults already made such payments pre–COVID-19 and where the infrastructure to accept these payments was in place.

By contrast, in India, only about 12 percent of adults—fewer than 20 percent of account owners—made a digital merchant payment. However, two-thirds of those who made a digital merchant payment did so for the first time after the onset of COVID-19, suggesting that the pandemic may have spurred the adoption of digital payments even in economies with low adoption of digital merchant payments.

FIGURE 2.1.14

In China, 8 in 10 adults made a digital merchant payment, whereas in other developing economies, 2 in 10 adults did so, including about 40 percent who did so for the first time after COVID-19 emerged

Adults with an account (%), 2021

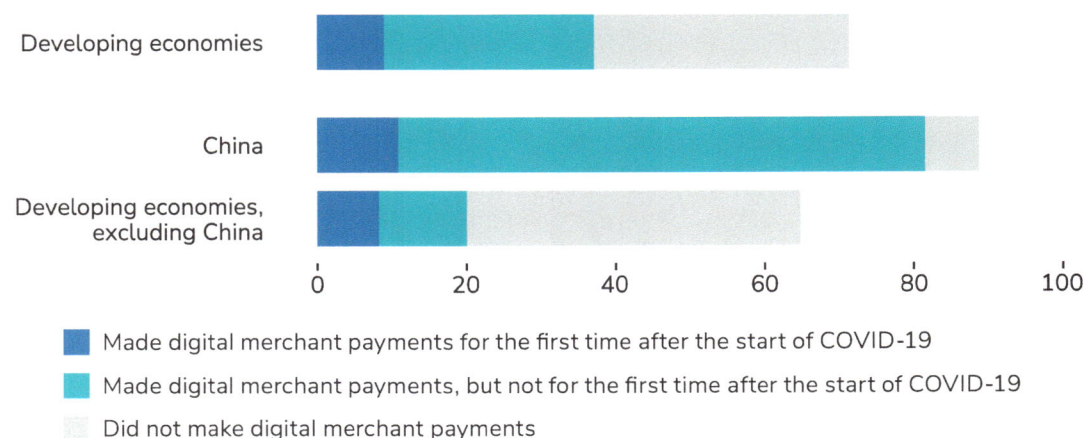

■ Made digital merchant payments for the first time after the start of COVID-19

■ Made digital merchant payments, but not for the first time after the start of COVID-19

Did not make digital merchant payments

Source: Global Findex Database 2021.

The use and adoption of digital merchant payments during COVID-19 varied across developing economies

Adults with an account (%), 2021

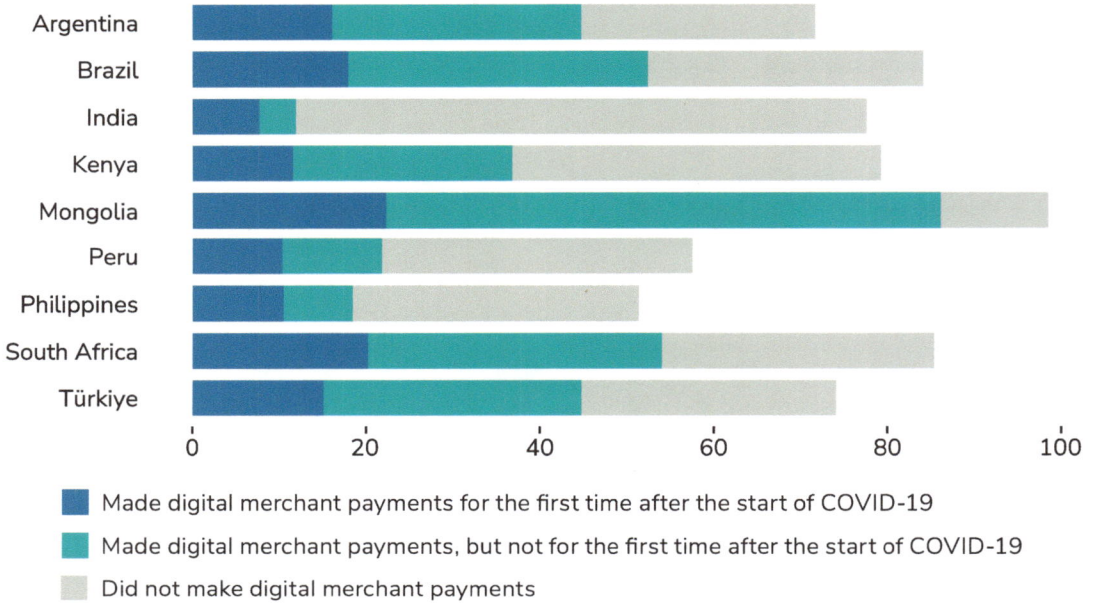

Made digital merchant payments for the first time after the start of COVID-19

Made digital merchant payments, but not for the first time after the start of COVID-19

Did not make digital merchant payments

Source: Global Findex Database 2021.

Digital in-store merchant payments

Nearly all adults in developing economies (96 percent) who made a digital merchant payment did so in-store. Much like overall digital merchant payments, 36 percent of adults in developing economies made a digital in-store payment, but this average is heavy skewed by the use of such payments in China (79 percent). In developing economies, excluding China, 19 percent of adults made a digital in-store merchant payment, with 7 percent of adults (about 40 percent of digital in-store merchant payment users) making their first such payment after the onset of the pandemic (figure 2.1.16).

FIGURE 2.1.16

In developing economies, excluding China, one in five adults made a digital in-store merchant payment

Adults with an account (%), 2021

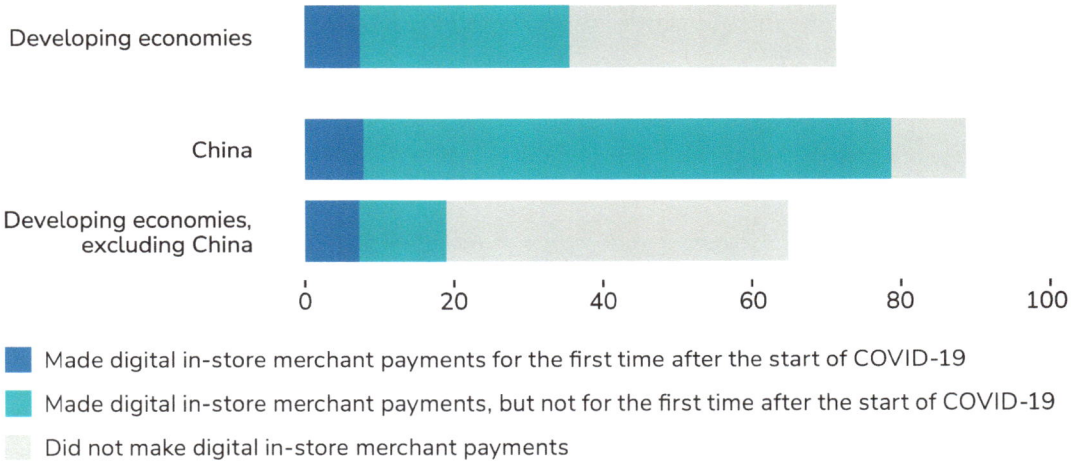

- Made digital in-store merchant payments for the first time after the start of COVID-19
- Made digital in-store merchant payments, but not for the first time after the start of COVID-19
- Did not make digital in-store merchant payments

Source: Global Findex Database 2021.

Digital online merchant payments

In developing economies, 26 percent of adults made a digital online merchant payment (figure 2.1.17). The widespread use of such payments in China (71 percent of adults) again drives this average. Four percent of adults in China made their first online merchant payment after the start of the pandemic. Excluding China, just 9 percent of adults in developing economies made a digital online merchant payment. Less than 2 percent of adults in developing economies, excluding China, made their first online payment after the outbreak of the pandemic. This finding highlights that online payments require a supportive infrastructure, including technology, security, and delivery logistics, which takes time to build.

Despite this generally low average number, digital online merchant payments were relevant in some economies. In Malaysia, Mongolia, Russia, and Thailand, more than one-third of adults made such a payment (figure 2.1.18).

FIGURE 2.1.17

In China, many adults made digital online merchant payments—but few did so in other developing economies

Adults with an account (%), 2021

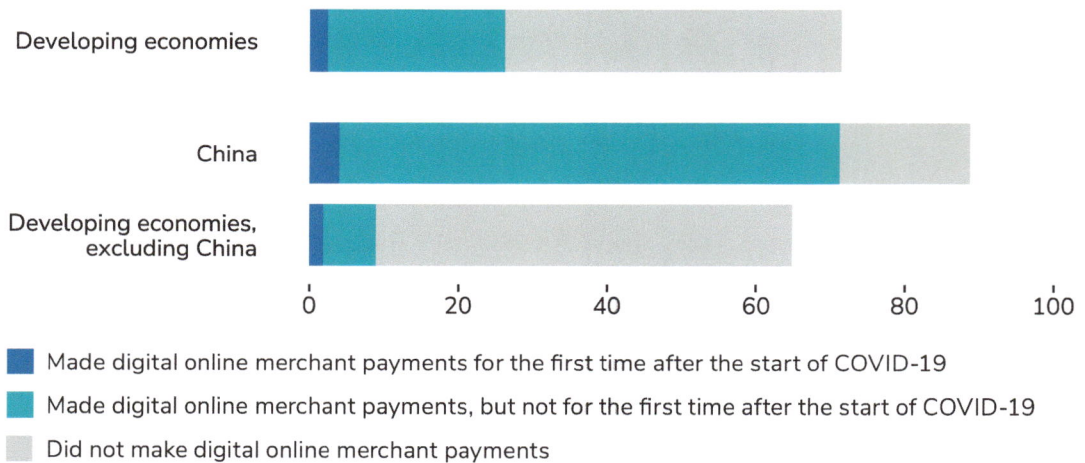

■ Made digital online merchant payments for the first time after the start of COVID-19

■ Made digital online merchant payments, but not for the first time after the start of COVID-19

■ Did not make digital online merchant payments

Source: Global Findex Database 2021.

FIGURE 2.1.18

The use and adoption of digital online merchant payments during COVID-19 varied across developing economies, but was typically small

Adults with an account (%), 2021

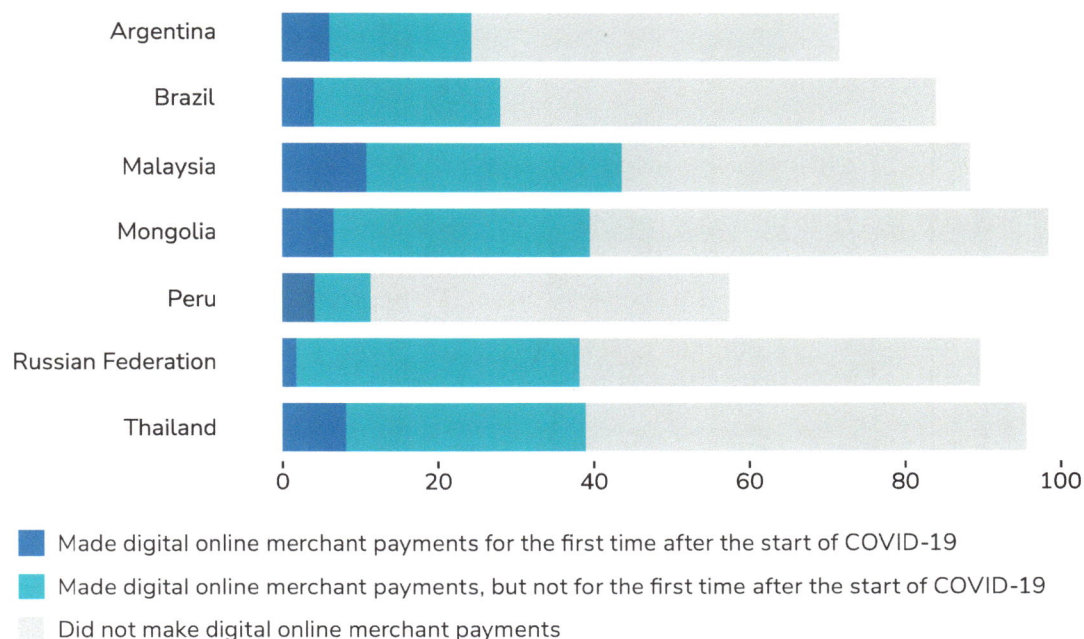

Made digital online merchant payments for the first time after the start of COVID-19

Made digital online merchant payments, but not for the first time after the start of COVID-19

Did not make digital online merchant payments

Source: Global Findex Database 2021.

The majority of adults making online purchases paid online

Not everyone who buys something online also pays for it online. In many developing economies, people can pay in cash on delivery for internet orders. To understand how common that practice is, the Global Findex 2017 survey asked for the first time how people in developing economies pay for their online purchases. The 2021 edition of the survey refined the question to include the additional option to answer "both" online and in cash.

In China, 80 percent of adults bought something online. Virtually all of these buyers also paid for their purchase online (94 percent, including 9 percent who answered "both"). Although the survey did not pose a question about payment platforms, it is likely that many online buyers used popular third-party online and mobile payment platforms such as Alipay and WeChat, which were developed specifically to facilitate online payments.

In developing economies, excluding China, 15 percent reported having bought something online (figure 2.1.19). About two-thirds of these buyers (including 15 percent who answered "both") also paid for their purchase online. In 2017, the majority (53 percent) of online shoppers in developing economies, excluding China, paid with cash on delivery. Thus the 2021 finding indicates a major shift toward online payments for adults making online purchases, which is a small share of the total adults in most developing economies. Indeed, in every economy surveyed in the Middle East and North Africa (excluding Iraq, where 21 percent of adults bought something online), South Asia, and Sub-Saharan Africa, the share of adults who bought something online was under 20 percent.[21]

---

21. In the Islamic Republic of Iran, 31 percent of adults bought something online; however, no question was posed on how those purchases were paid for.

FIGURE 2.1.19

In most developing economies, a majority of online shoppers have paid online

Adults using a mobile phone or the internet to buy something online in the past year (%), 2021

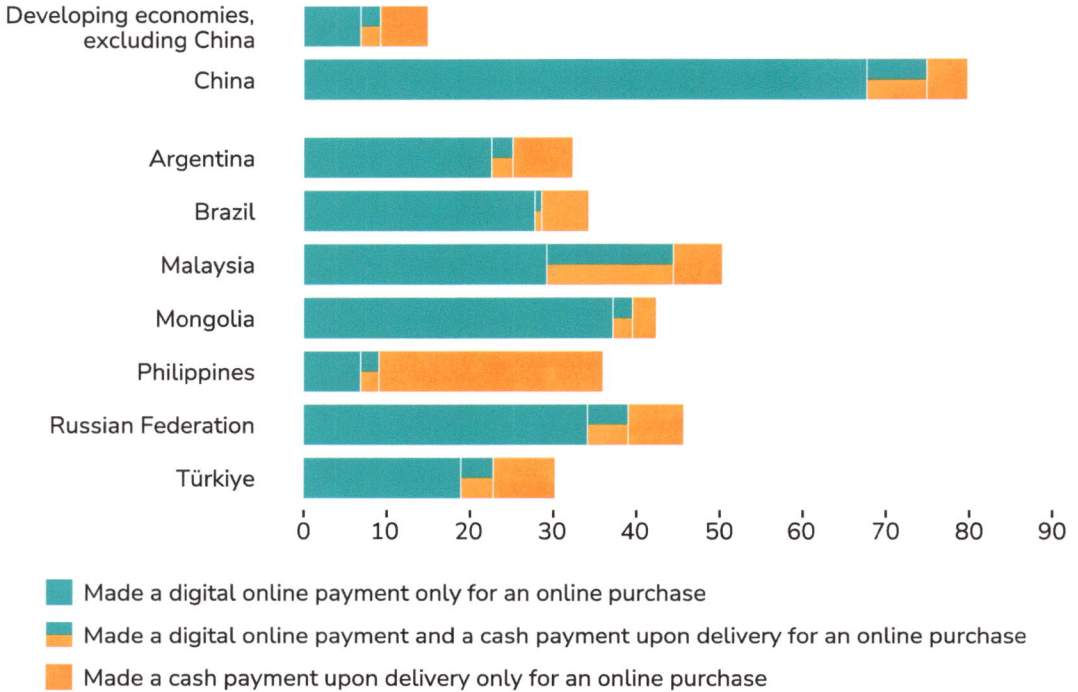

Made a digital online payment only for an online purchase

Made a digital online payment and a cash payment upon delivery for an online purchase

Made a cash payment upon delivery only for an online purchase

Source: Global Findex Database 2021.

Despite the general trend toward online payments, cash on delivery remains a common way to pay for online purchases in some economies. In the Philippines, 36 percent of adults bought something online, and three in four online shoppers paid only in cash for their purchase. The share of online shoppers that paid both online and in cash was low across nearly all of the surveyed economies, but in a handful of economies in the East Asia and Pacific region, including Malaysia, and in Europe and Central Asia, the proportion was greater than 10 percent.

Modes of making digital payments

Using a debit or credit card or a mobile phone or the internet to make digital payments

A digital payment can be made directly from an account without withdrawing cash in primarily two ways: using credit or debit cards or using a mobile phone or the internet.[22] In high-income economies, 90 percent of adults (93 percent of account owners) used one of these modes to make a payment, while in developing economies 45 percent of adults (64 percent of account owners) did so (figure 2.1.20). In both high-income and developing economies, adults who made digital payments were most likely to have used both methods—

---

22. Making a digital payment using a mobile phone or the internet can take different forms. Some make a payment directly from their mobile money account, while others use a smartphone app from their financial institution or one from a third-party payment provider linked to their account. Some also make digital payments directly on the website of their financial institution or a third-party payment service provider.

FIGURE 2.1.20

Adults who made digital payments directly from an account most commonly used both a debit or credit card and a mobile phone or the internet

Adults with an account (%), 2021

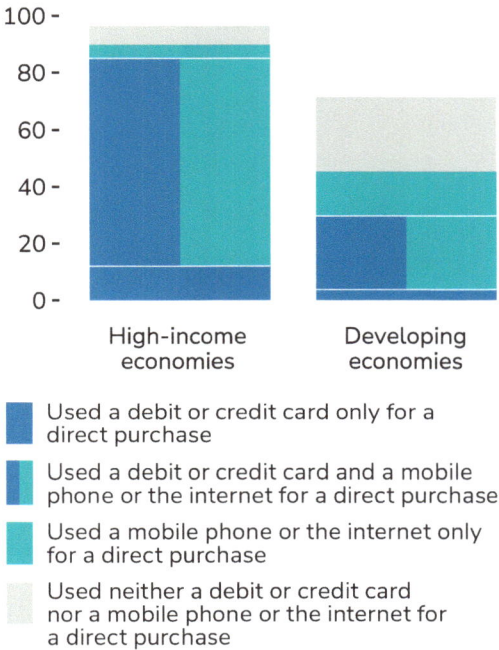

Used a debit or credit card only for a direct purchase

Used a debit or credit card and a mobile phone or the internet for a direct purchase

Used a mobile phone or the internet only for a direct purchase

Used neither a debit or credit card nor a mobile phone or the internet for a direct purchase

Source: Global Findex Database 2021.

a card payment and a mobile phone or the internet. This could include adults who made a card payment using a mobile phone or the internet. The second most common approach in high-income economies was use of only a debit or credit card (12 percent of adults, or 12 percent of account owners), whereas in developing countries the second most common approach was to only use a mobile phone or the internet (16 percent of all adults, or 22 percent of account owners).

The mode of making a digital payment varies considerably across developing economies, reflecting differences in payment infrastructure (figure 2.1.21). In Sub-Saharan African economies such as Côte d'Ivoire and Kenya, where mobile money accounts are common, use of a mobile phone or the internet

to make a payment was widespread among account owners (82 and 88 percent, respectively), and only using a mobile phone or the internet was by far the most common mode of making a payment (reported by three out of four account owners). The use of debit or credit cards was virtually nonexistent as the sole mode of making a payment in these economies. In China, the use of a mobile phone or the internet to make a digital payment was similarly universal. However, most account owners (60 percent) used both a debit or credit card and a mobile phone or the internet to make a digital payment. In many other developing economies, usage was distributed more evenly across the three groups: account owners who used a debit or credit card only; those who used a mobile phone or the internet only; or those who used both a debit or credit card and a mobile phone or the internet.

In some developing economies, the share of adults making a digital payment was low, and there is much room for growth in the use of payment cards or mobile phones or the internet to make payments directly from an account. In Egypt and India, for example, about 70 percent of account owners have not used payment cards nor a mobile phone or the internet to make a digital payment.

Using a mobile phone or the internet for sending money and paying bills

In addition to the questions reported previously in this chapter on domestic remittances and utility bill payments, the Global Findex 2021 survey included two questions that asked more broadly about using a mobile phone or the internet to send money to family and friends and for any type of bill payment.

Sending money to family and friends (distinct from domestic remittances)

Globally, 35 percent of adults used a mobile phone or the internet to send money to relatives or friends— 43 percent of adults in high-income economies and 33 percent in developing economies, or about 45 percent of account owners, on average, in both income groups (figure 2.1.22). Sending money to relatives or friends is broader than domestic remittances, which is typically understood as sending money to relatives or friends back in communities of

FIGURE 2.1.21

In developing economies, most adults used a mobile phone or the internet to make digital payments

Adults with an account (%), 2021

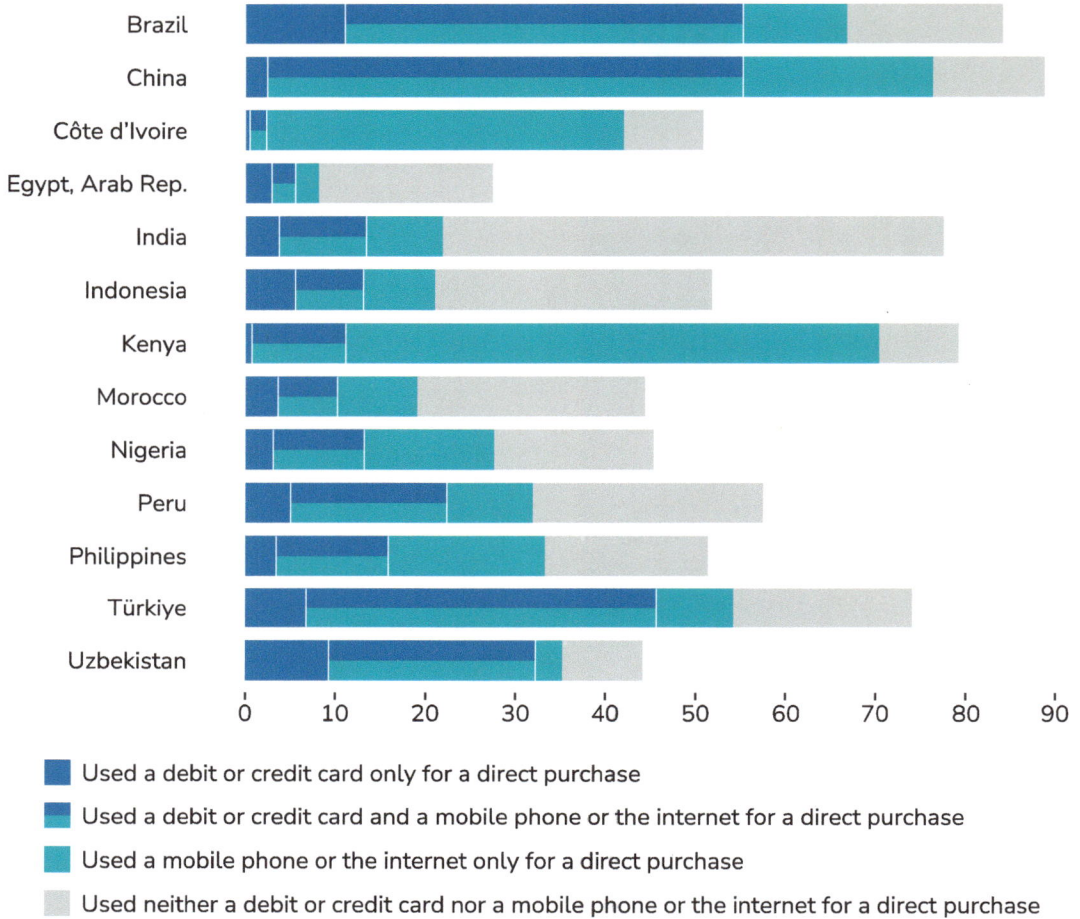

Legend:
- ■ Used a debit or credit card only for a direct purchase
- ■ Used a debit or credit card and a mobile phone or the internet for a direct purchase
- ■ Used a mobile phone or the internet only for a direct purchase
- ■ Used neither a debit or credit card nor a mobile phone or the internet for a direct purchase

Source: Global Findex Database 2021.

origin—in other words, in another city or area within a country. In developing economies, where the Global Findex 2021 survey also asked about domestic remittances, 21 percent of adults used a mobile phone or the internet to send money to relatives or friends but did not send a domestic remittance payment using an account.

Bill payment

Globally, 34 percent of adults used a mobile phone or the internet to make bill payments—56 percent of adults in high-income economies and 29 percent in developing economies (figure 2.1.23). However, these averages mask large variations. Although 10 percent or fewer of surveyed adults in economies in South Asia and the Middle East and North Africa (with the exception of the Islamic Republic of Iran) made such payments, in China and Russia more than half of adults do so. Even in high-income economies, the variation between countries was large: the share of adults using a mobile phone or the internet to make a bill payment ranged from 85 percent or more of adults in Estonia, Finland, and Norway to just over 30 percent in Italy and Japan.

FIGURE 2.1.22

Many adults used a phone or the internet to send money to family or friends

Adults with an account (%), 2021

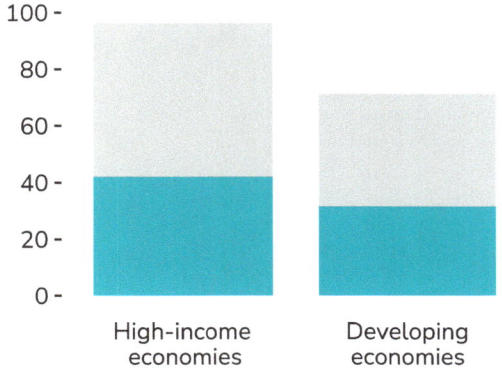

Used a mobile phone or the internet to send money to a relative or friend

Did not use a mobile phone or the internet to send money to a relative or friend

Source: Global Findex Database 2021.

Note: Sending money to relatives or friends is a broader definition than domestic remittances.

FIGURE 2.1.23

Many adults used a phone or the internet to make bill payments

Adults with an account (%), 2021

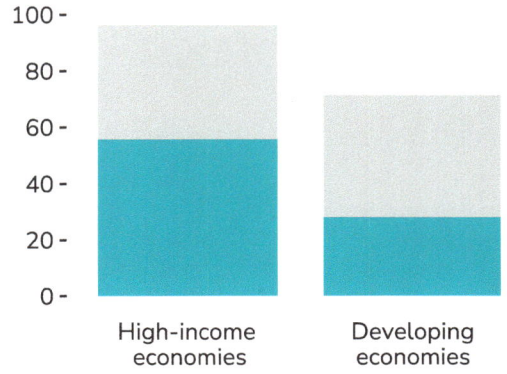

Used a mobile phone or the internet to make bill payments

Did not use a mobile phone or the internet to make bill payments

Source: Global Findex Database 2021.

2.2 Savings

2.2 SAVINGS

People save for several reasons: for large future expenses, for investments in education or a business, for their needs in old age, or for emergencies. Globally, 49 percent of adults responding to the Global Findex 2021 survey saved or set aside money in the past 12 months. In high-income economies, 76 percent of adults reported having saved, while 42 percent of adults saved in developing economies. The Global Findex 2021 survey data further highlight how and why people save. New data also reveal that a larger share of adults reported using their account to store money for cash management purposes than to save money.

Most savers used an account

People go about saving money in different ways. Globally, 31 percent of adults—or about two-thirds of people who saved any money—reported having saved formally at a financial institution or using a mobile money account.[23] Among all adults, the share who reported saving formally averaged 58 percent in high-income economies and 25 percent in developing economies (see figure 2.2.1 and map 2.2.1). Among those who saved in any form, three out of four in high-income economies and more than half in developing economies saved formally. This marks the first time that formal savings is the most common mode of saving in developing economies.

FIGURE 2.2.1

In both high-income and developing economies, more than half of adults who saved chose to do so formally

Adults saving any money in the past year (%), 2021

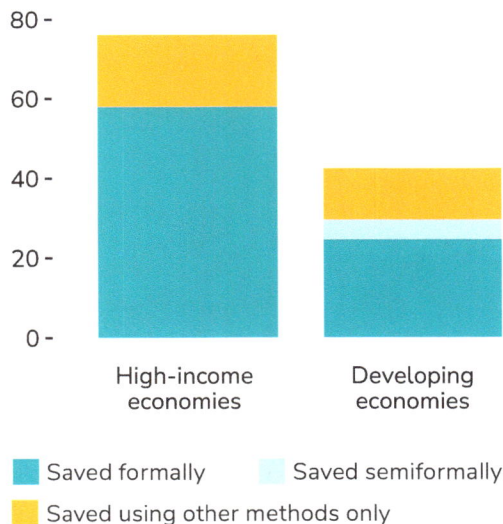

Saved formally Saved semiformally
Saved using other methods only

Source: Global Findex Database 2021.

Note: People may save in multiple ways, but categories are constructed to be mutually exclusive. "Saved formally" includes all adults who saved any money formally. "Saved semiformally" includes all adults who saved any money semiformally but not formally. Data on semiformal saving are not collected in most high-income economies.

A common alternative to saving formally in developing countries is to save semiformally by using a savings club or relying on a person outside the family. In 2021, 9 percent of adults reported saving in this manner, including 4 percent of adults who saved semiformally but not formally. One common type of savings club is a rotating savings and credit association (ROSCA). These associations generally operate by pooling weekly deposits and disbursing the entire amount to a different member each week. Saving semiformally is especially common in Sub-Saharan Africa, where 25 percent of adults reported having saved that way, including 16 percent who saved semiformally but not formally. In Sierra Leone, the share of those saving semiformally but not formally is as high as 26 percent of adults, or more than half of savers.

The options for saving go beyond doing so formally or semiformally. In both high-income and developing economies, about 14 percent of adults, on average, reported having saved only in some other way. This may include saving cash at home ("under the mattress") or saving in the form of assets such as livestock, jewelry, or real estate. It may also include using investment products offered by equity and other traded markets or by purchasing government securities. In 26 developing economies, more than half of those who saved did so only using some other way. In the Philippines, for example, 30 percent of

---

23. The Global Findex 2021 survey asks about saving money using a mobile money account only of adults with a mobile money account in economies where mobile money accounts exist.

MAP 2.2.1

Worldwide, the share of adults who save varies widely

Adults saving at a financial institution or using a mobile money account in the past year (%), 2021

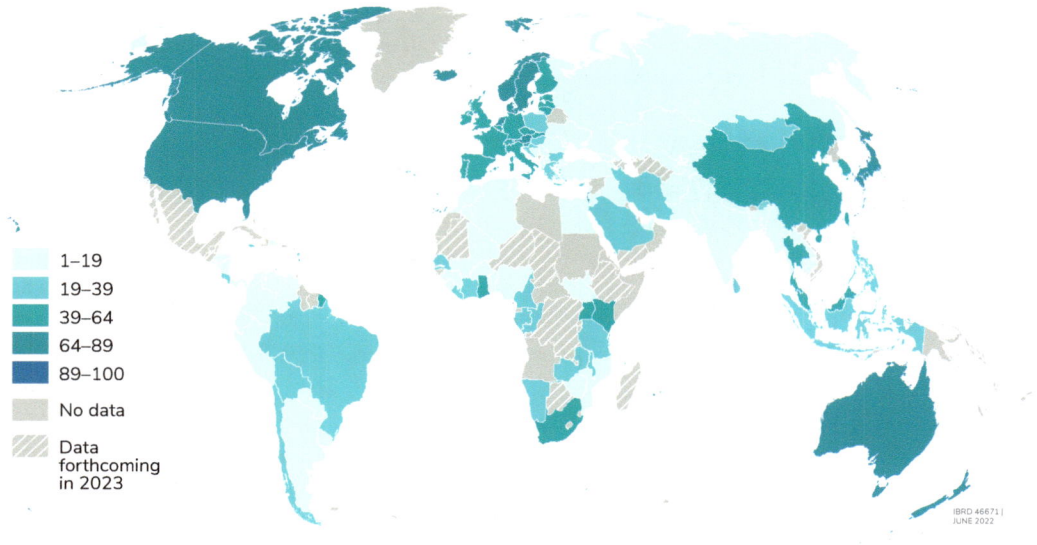

Legend:
- 1–19
- 19–39
- 39–64
- 64–89
- 89–100
- No data
- Data forthcoming in 2023

IBRD 46671 | JUNE 2022

Source: Global Findex Database 2021.

adults (55 percent of savers) saved in only some other way, making it one of the economies with the highest share of adults doing so.[24]

The share of adults saving formally grew around the world

The share of adults saving formally has increased over the past decade in both high-income and developing economies by 14 percentage points and 7 percentage points, respectively (figure 2.2.2). Because account ownership is a prerequisite for formal savings, it is no surprise that high-income economies, where account ownership is much higher, on average, than in developing economies, also have a higher average share of adults reporting that they saved formally.[25] Because those who have an account also tend to be wealthier and likelier to participate in the labor force, they may also have a greater capacity to save.

Mobile money accounts are becoming a popular way of saving formally in Sub-Saharan Africa

As mobile money account ownership has expanded in recent years, so has the use of these accounts—in some economies—to save money. The Global Findex 2021 survey asked for the first time about saving formally using a mobile money account. The share of adults who reported doing so is small (5 percent) in developing economies overall. However, in Sub-Saharan Africa, the region in which mobile money account ownership is most widespread, 15 percent of adults, on average—or 39 percent of mobile money account owners—reported

---

24. Only in Armenia (30 percent), Lao PDR (32 percent), and Moldova (38 percent) were the same or a higher share of adults saving only in some other way.
25. Globally, 0.6 percent of unbanked adults reported having saved formally.

FIGURE 2.2.2

Formal savings increased over the past decade in both high-income and developing economies

Adults saving at a financial institution or using a mobile money account in the past year (%), 2011–21

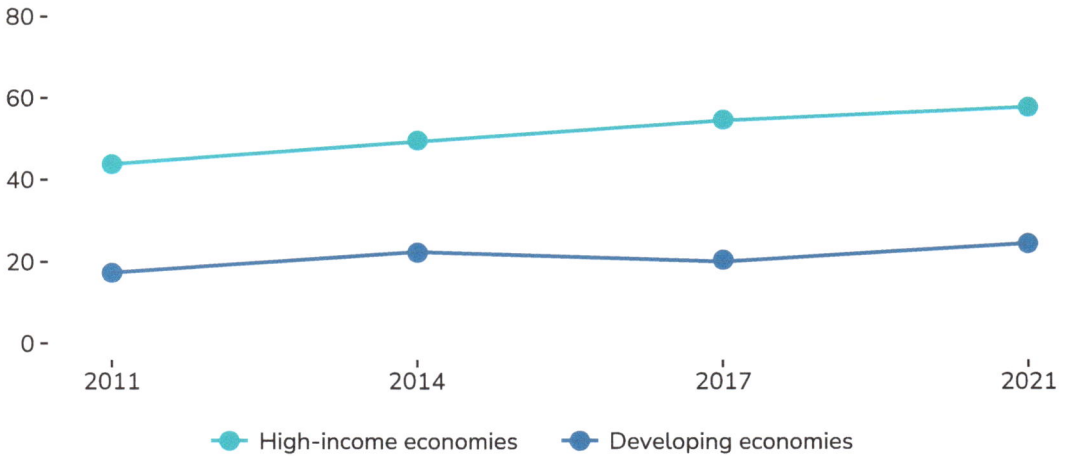

Source: Global Findex Database 2021.
Note: Data for 2021 include saving using a mobile money account.

having saved using their mobile money account. Indeed, in Sub-Saharan Africa, the average share of adults saving using a mobile money account is equal to the share of adults saving at a financial institution, including about one-third (5 percent of adults) who used both a mobile money account and a financial institution account for that purpose (figure 2.2.3). Saving using a mobile money account is especially widespread in Ghana and Kenya, where 37 percent of adults reported doing so, as well as in Senegal and Uganda, where about 30 percent did so. Meanwhile, in Gabon and Zambia between 22 and 26 percent did so, rounding out the list of economies with a mobile money savings share of at least 20 percent.

The share of adults who saved any money in Sub-Saharan Africa in 2021 was essentially unchanged from 2017 (figure 2.2.3). But saving using a mobile money account significantly expanded the share of adults who saved formally. On average, 26 percent of adults—or about half of savers—saved formally in 2021 in Sub-Saharan Africa, up from 15 percent in 2017. This increase in formal saving stemmed almost entirely from adults who reported having saved using a mobile money account but not at a financial institution.

Indeed, in some economies in the region the share of adults saving formally nearly or more than doubled thanks to the inclusion of saving using a mobile money account (figure 2.2.4). In Kenya, for example, the share of adults who saved any money in the past year was about 70 percent in both 2017 and 2021. But the share who saved formally increased to 45 percent in 2021, up from 27 percent in 2017. Notably, the share of adults saving at a financial institution fell by 5 percentage points over that period. At the same time, the share of adults who saved semiformally stayed about the same—about 32 percent in both 2017 and 2021. But close to two-thirds of these adults also saved using a mobile money account. As a result, these respondents show up in the "saved formally using a mobile money account" category based on how the mutually exclusive categories are constructed in figure 2.2.4. The fact that adults saved using a mobile money account in addition to saving semiformally or using other methods illustrates the convenience and security of mobile money accounts as a tool for saving.

FIGURE 2.2.3

In Sub-Saharan Africa, equal shares of adults saved at a financial institution and saved using a mobile money account

Adults saving any money in the past year (%), 2017–21

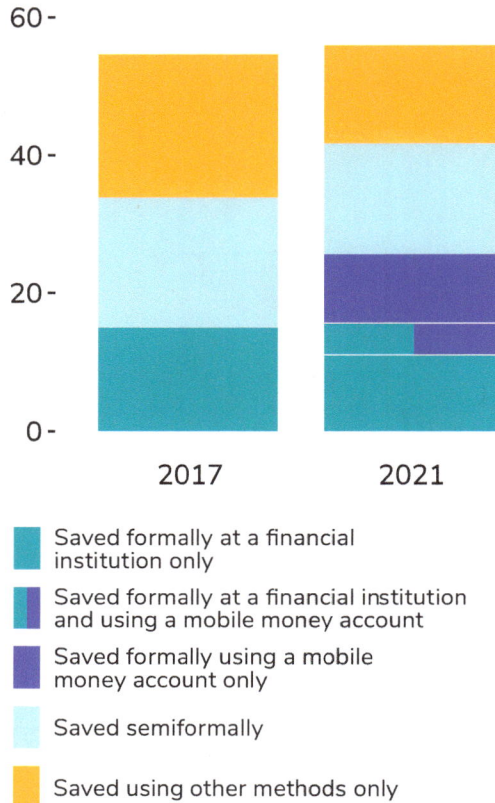

Saved formally at a financial institution only

Saved formally at a financial institution and using a mobile money account

Saved formally using a mobile money account only

Saved semiformally

Saved using other methods only

Source: Global Findex Database 2021.

Note: People may save in multiple ways, but categories are constructed to be mutually exclusive. "Saved formally" includes all adults who saved any money formally. "Saved semiformally" includes all adults who saved any money semiformally but not formally. Data on semiformal saving are not collected in most high-income economies. The Global Findex survey collected data on saving using a mobile money account for the first time in 2021.

Saving for old age was more common in high-income economies

The Global Findex 2021 survey asked whether people had saved money for their old age. Globally, 26 percent of adults were saving for old age—53 percent in high-income economies and 19 percent in developing economies. Among those saving for old age, about two-thirds in developing economies and more than three-quarters in high-income economies reported having saved money formally. The Global Findex 2021 survey asked adults in Russia a few additional questions on pension and retirement planning to better understand how adults prepare for and fund their retirement.[26] Respondents were questioned about their main sources of income once they are retired and receive a so-called old-age pension—a statutory compulsory pension insurance scheme—and about any retirement planning they might have done.[27] Those not yet receiving an old-age pension were asked about their expectations and planning for retirement. One question specifically

26. The data for the additional module on pension and retirement planning in Russia will be published separately.
27. OECD (2019).

FIGURE 2.2.4

Mobile money accounts are an important mode of formal saving in Sub-Saharan Africa

Adults saving any money in the past year (%), 2017–21

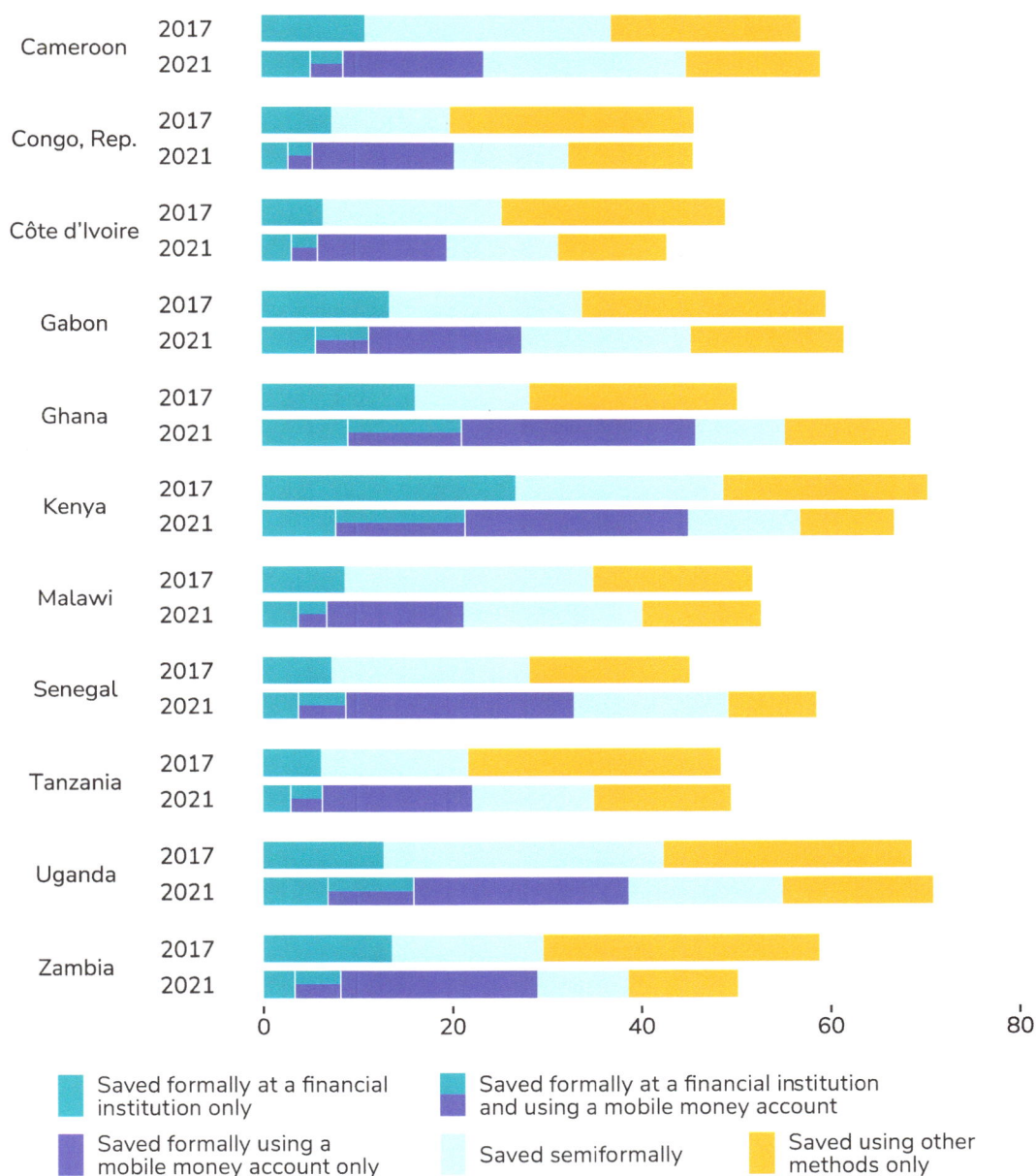

Saved formally at a financial institution only

Saved formally at a financial institution and using a mobile money account

Saved formally using a mobile money account only

Saved semiformally

Saved using other methods only

Source: Global Findex Database 2021.

Note: People may save in multiple ways, but categories are constructed to be mutually exclusive. "Saved formally" includes all adults who saved any money formally. "Saved semiformally" includes all adults who saved any money semiformally but not formally. Data on semiformal saving are not collected in most high-income economies. The Global Findex survey collected data on saving using a mobile money account for the first time in 2021.

FIGURE 2.2.5

In the Russian Federation, of the few adults who were planning for retirement, only one in three reported saving for old age

Adults not yet receiving an old-age pension (%), 2021

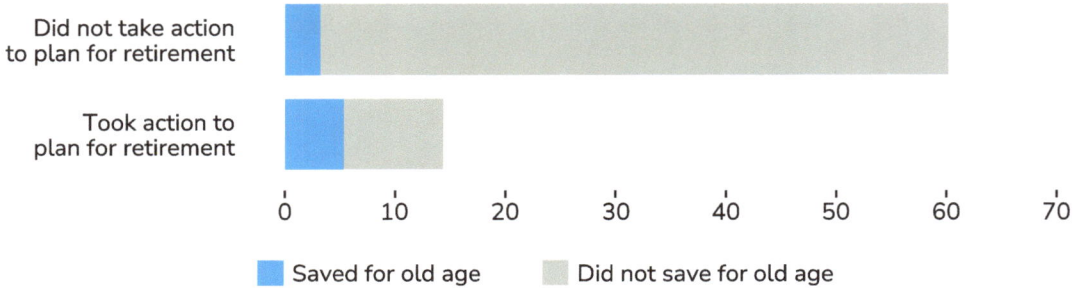

Source: Global Findex Database 2021.

posed was whether those who do not yet receive a pension—74 percent of adults—have taken any action to plan for retirement such as saving money or making investments. Most responded that they had not taken any action. Of those who had not yet received an old-age pension but reported having taken action to plan for retirement (such as by saving money or making investments), one-third reported having saved for old age. Among those who reported they had not taken action, only one in 20 had saved for that purpose (figure 2.2.5).

More adults used their account for cash management than for saving

Saving is a broad concept that can mean different things to different people. Many people think of savings as money put aside for longer-term goals or larger expenses that go beyond their day-to-day basic needs. But people also set aside money in the short term to pay for day-to-day basics, including bills due at the end of the month. Most do not think of setting aside money for day-to-day basics as savings; they think of doing so simply as cash management.

To better understand cash management behavior, the Global Findex 2021 survey asked adults for the first time whether they typically keep—"store"—any money in their accounts for shorter-term purposes. Globally, 48 percent of adults, or 63 percent of account owners, did so. Among adults in high-income economies, that share is 84 percent, or 88 percent of account owners, and in developing economies, the share is 39 percent, or 55 percent of account owners (figure 2.2.6). The share of account

FIGURE 2.2.6

Globally, more than half of account owners used their account to store money

Adults with an account (%), 2021

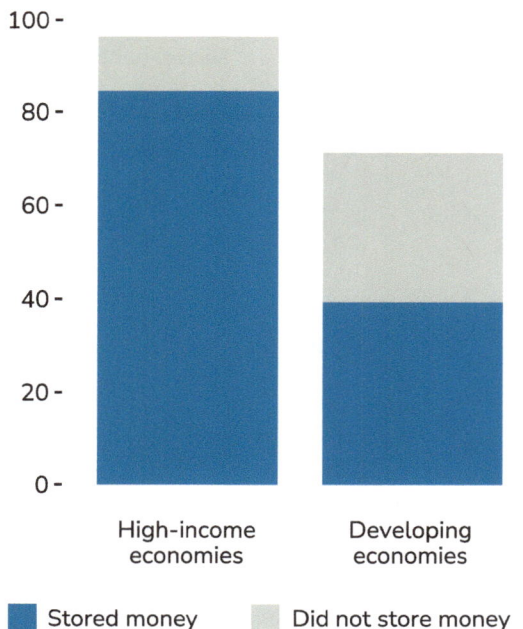

Source: Global Findex Database 2021.

FIGURE 2.2.7

More adults used their account to store money for cash management than to save

Adults with an account (%), 2021

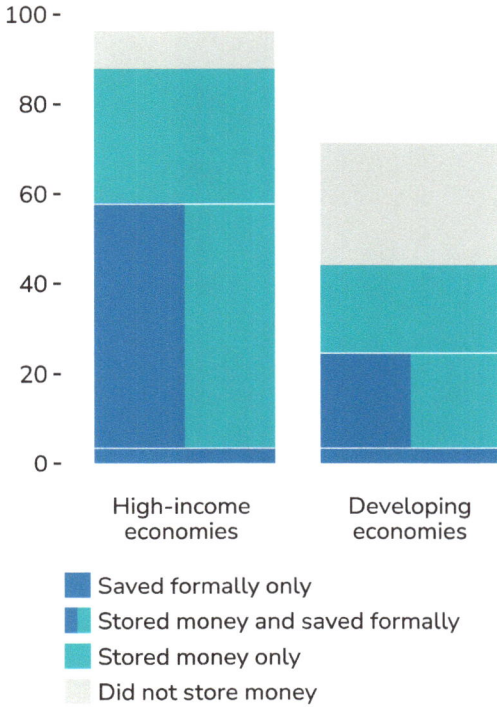

Saved formally only
Stored money and saved formally
Stored money only
Did not store money

Source: Global Findex Database 2021.

owners in developing economies using their account to store money is as high as 75 percent in Kenya and 80 percent in Ghana—two economies in which mobile money accounts are common and make it convenient to store money. The share of account owners who store money is similarly high in Malaysia and Mauritius, where most adults have an account at a financial institution.

Not surprisingly, a larger share of adults reported using their account to store money than to save money. Globally, 48 percent of adults stored money and 31 percent saved money using an account, including 26 percent who did both. Among adults in high-income economies, 84 percent stored money and 58 percent saved using an account, including 55 percent who did both (figure 2.2.7). Of adults in developing economies, 39 percent stored money and 25 percent saved money using an account, including 20 percent who did both.

2.3 Borrowing

2.3 BORROWING

In 2021, 53 percent of adults worldwide reported having borrowed any money in the past 12 months, including by using a credit card. The share of adults with new credit, formal or nonformal, averaged 65 percent in high-income economies and 50 percent in developing economies.

Formal borrowing is increasing as providers embrace additional methods

In high-income economies, formal borrowing—whether through a loan from a financial institution, using a credit card, or through a mobile money account—was by far the most common source of credit (figure 2.3.1 and map 2.3.1).[28] In developing economies, by contrast, 46 percent of borrowers did so formally. About an equal share of borrowers in developing economies cited family and friends as their only source of credit. In developing economies, 2 percent of adults borrowed semiformally from a savings club, such as rotation savings and credit associations, but did not borrow formally. Other sources of borrowing were reported by 5 percent of adults globally.[29]

FIGURE 2.3.1

Formal borrowing was the most common source of credit in both high-income and developing economies

Adults borrowing any money in the past year (%), 2021

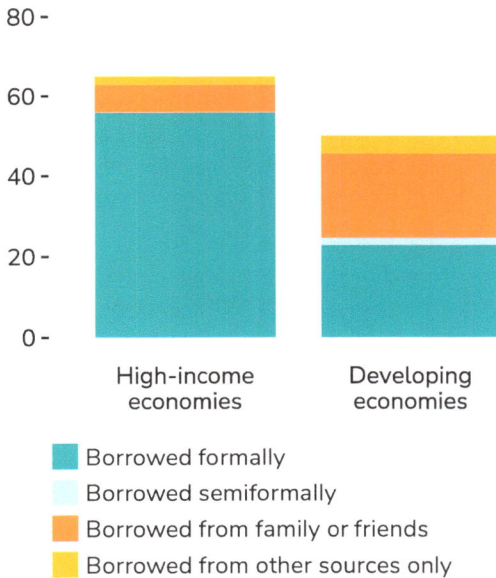

- Borrowed formally
- Borrowed semiformally
- Borrowed from family or friends
- Borrowed from other sources only

Source: Global Findex Database 2021.

Note: People may borrow from multiple sources, but the categories in the figure are constructed to be mutually exclusive. "Borrowed formally" includes all adults who borrowed any money from a financial institution or through the use of a credit card or mobile money account. "Borrowed semiformally" includes all adults who borrowed any money semiformally (from a savings club) but not formally. "Borrowed from family or friends" excludes adults who borrowed formally or semiformally.

The share of adults who borrowed formally grew in developing economies

The share of adults borrowing formally is, on average, low in developing economies, but it has increased over the last decade from about 16 percent of adults in 2014 and 2017 to 23 percent in 2021 (figure 2.3.2). In high-income economies, the share remained stable at about 56 percent.

FIGURE 2.3.2

In developing economies, formal borrowing increased over the past decade

Adults borrowing any money from a financial institution or through the use of a credit card or mobile money account in the past year (%), 2014–21

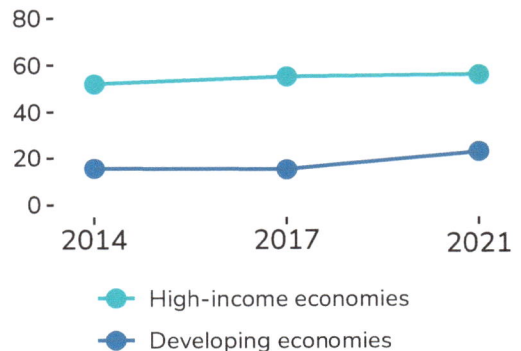

- High-income economies
- Developing economies

Source: Global Findex Database 2021.

Note: Data for 2021 include borrowing using a mobile money account.

---

28. The Global Findex survey asked about borrowing using a mobile money account only in economies where mobile money accounts exist and only of adults who reported having a mobile money account.
29. Other sources of borrowing can include private informal lenders.

MAP 2.3.1

The share of adults borrowing formally remains low in developing countries

Adults borrowing any money from a financial institution or through the use of a credit card or mobile money account in the past year (%), 2021

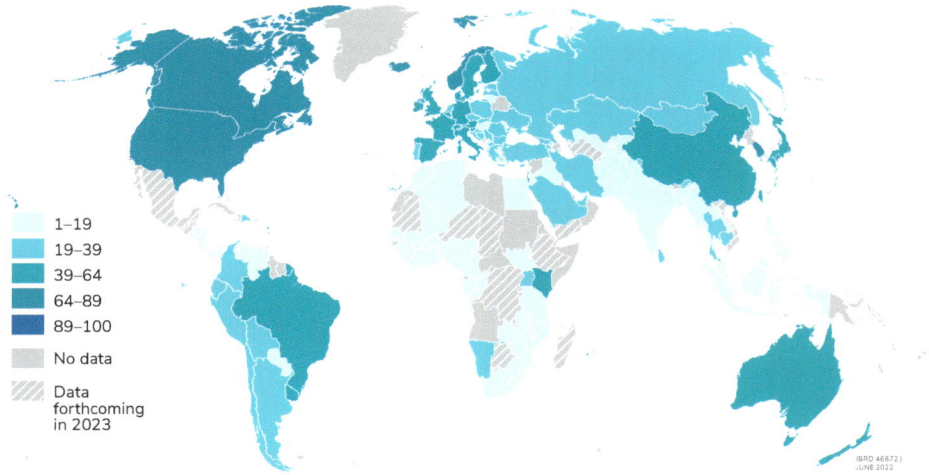

Legend:
- 1–19
- 19–39
- 39–64
- 64–89
- 89–100
- No data
- Data forthcoming in 2023

IBRD 46672 |
JUNE 2022

Source: Global Findex Database 2021.

Formal borrowing using credit cards dominated in high-income economies and is growing in developing economies

In high-income economies, the dominant way to borrow was by credit card, which is both a payment instrument and a source of credit. Credit cards provide short-term credit whenever they are used, even when credit card holders pay their balance in full each statement cycle and thus pay no interest on that balance. The introduction of credit cards in an economy might therefore have affected the demand for and use of short-term credit.

In high-income economies, 51 percent of adults used a credit card in the past 12 months. Among those who reported borrowing formally, about one-third borrowed from a formal financial institution or mobile money provider, whereas two-thirds borrowed using a credit card but not from a financial institution or mobile money provider (figure 2.3.3).

In developing economies, despite continuing growth in credit card use, on average only 14 percent of adults reported having used one. Exceptions were China, as well as Russia, Türkiye, and Ukraine in Europe and Central Asia, and Argentina and Brazil in Latin America and the Caribbean. In these economies, the share of adults borrowing by using a credit card, but not through a loan from a financial institution or mobile money provider, ranged from close to 40 percent in the three economies in Europe and Central Asia, about 50 percent in China, and about 60 percent in the two economies in Latin America and the Caribbean.

Most users paid off their credit card balance each month

To better understand practices around paying off credit card balances, the Global Findex 2021 survey asked for the first time whether adults who used a credit card paid off all their balances in full by the due date. In high-income economies, on average, 85 percent of adults who used a credit card paid off their balances in full (figure 2.3.4). In the six developing economies in which the share of credit card users exceeds 20 percent, payment patterns varied. In China, 90 percent of credit card users paid off their balances in full, while in Argentina and Brazil, 72 percent did so. In Russia, Türkiye, and Ukraine, about 60 percent did so.

In both high-income and developing economies, some adults own a credit card, but they have not used it in the past 12 months.

FIGURE 2.3.3

Credit card use dominated formal borrowing in high-income economies and in some developing economies

Adults borrowing formally in the past year (%), 2021

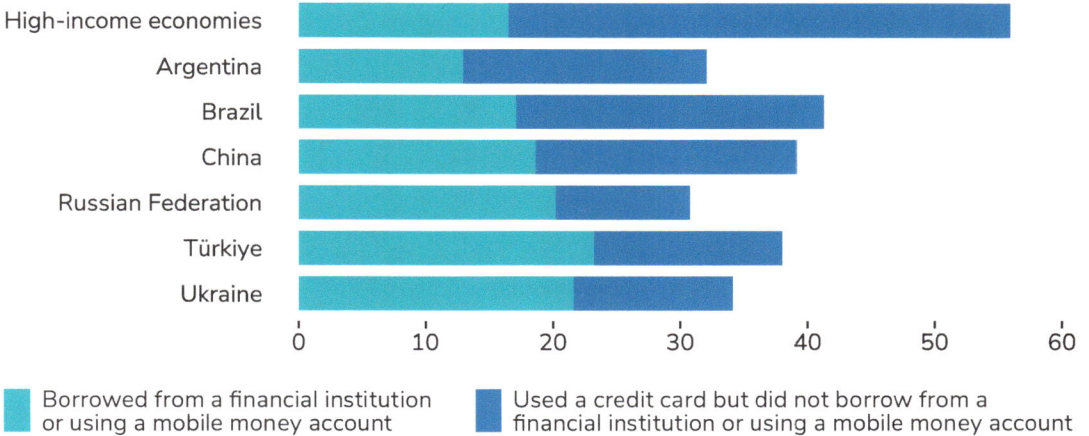

Legend:
- ■ Borrowed from a financial institution or using a mobile money account
- ■ Used a credit card but did not borrow from a financial institution or using a mobile money account

Source: Global Findex Database 2021.

FIGURE 2.3.4

Most credit card users reported paying off their balance in full in high-income economies and in some developing economies with high credit card use

Adults with a credit card (%), 2021

Legend:
- ■ Used a credit card in the past year and paid off balance in full
- ■ Used a credit card in the past year but did not pay off balance in full
- □ Owns a credit card but did not use it in the past year

Source: Global Findex Database 2021.

Mobile money accounts are playing a growing role in formal borrowing in some economies in Sub-Saharan Africa

As mobile money account ownership has expanded in recent years, so, too, have account features in some economies that allow account owners to borrow. The Global Findex 2021 survey asked for the first time about formal borrowing through the use of a mobile money account. This credit could be directly from a mobile money service provider or provided in partnership with a bank. Not surprisingly, the share of adults who reported having borrowed any money using their mobile money account was small (3 percent). Even in Sub-Saharan Africa, where mobile money account ownership is most widespread, just 7 percent of adults reported having borrowed using their mobile money account.

Economies with some of the highest mobile money account ownership rates nonetheless stand out with much higher-than-average borrowing patterns. In Kenya, the pioneer in mobile money in the region and the economy with the most mature mobile money market, 30 percent of adults reported having borrowed money using their mobile money account. In Uganda, that share was 16 percent. In both Kenya and Uganda, about one-third of borrowers using a mobile money account also borrowed from a financial institution or by using a credit card. Rounding out the list of economies where at least 10 percent of adults borrowed any money using a mobile money account are Ghana and Tanzania, each with a share of about 10 percent. In these two economies, the overwhelming majority (more than 80 percent) of those who borrowed using a mobile money account did not also borrow from a financial institution or through a credit card (figure 2.3.5).

FIGURE 2.3.5

Borrowing using a mobile money account is becoming more common in some economies in Sub-Saharan Africa

Adults borrowing any money in the past year (%), 2021

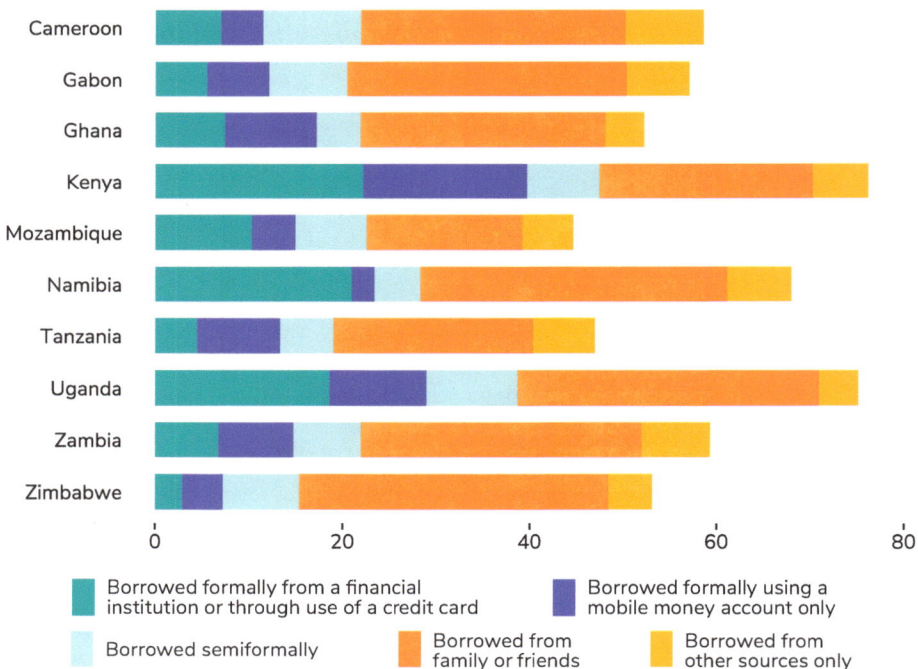

Source: Global Findex Database 2021.

Note: People may borrow from multiple sources, but the categories in the figure are constructed to be mutually exclusive. "Borrowed formally" includes all adults who borrowed any money from a financial institution or through the use of a credit card or mobile money account. "Borrowed semiformally" includes all adults who borrowed any money semiformally (from a savings club) but not formally. "Borrowed from family or friends" excludes adults who borrowed formally or semiformally.

In some developing economies, family and friends are the most common source of credit

As noted earlier, almost half of borrowers in developing economies borrowed formally, and about an equal share of borrowers cited family and friends as their only source of credit. But in some developing economies, family and friends are by far the most common source of credit. Afghanistan has the highest share of adults who borrowed only from family and friends in both absolute and relative terms: 59 percent of adults or 87 percent of borrowers (figure 2.3.6). Other economies where borrowing only from family and friends dominated include Morocco, where 77 percent of borrowers did so, and Egypt, Jordan, and Pakistan, where about two-thirds did so.

In addition, in some economies the share of adults borrowing semiformally only from a savings club, such as a rotating savings and credit association (ROSCA), was much higher than the average of 2 percent in developing economies. Usually, ROSCAs are structured around monthly contributions, which are paid out monthly to members on a rotating basis. Another type of savings club, an accumulating savings and credit association (ASCA), requires all members to make monthly contributions and allows some members to borrow from the group, which is repaid to the group with interest. Some economies with large shares of adults saving semiformally (see section 2.2) also have much higher rates of semiformal borrowing. For example, in seven Sub-Saharan Africa economies—Cameroon, Liberia, Malawi, Sierra Leone, South Africa, Togo, and Uganda—10–14 percent of adults only borrowed semiformally. In Liberia, Malawi, and Sierra Leone, this share translates to about a quarter of borrowers who only borrowed semiformally, the largest share in the world.

FIGURE 2.3.6

Family and friends were the dominant source of credit in some developing economies

Adults borrowing any money in the past year (%), 2021

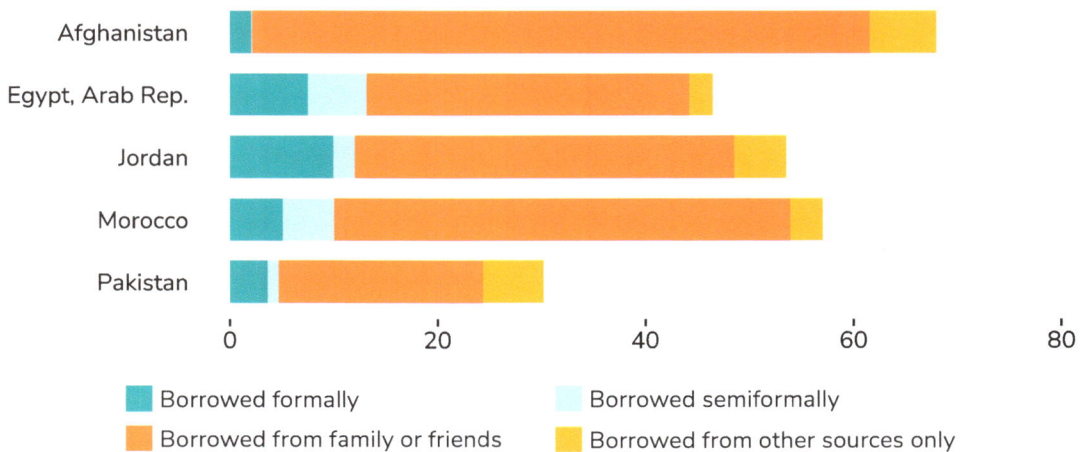

Source: Global Findex Database 2021.

Note: People may borrow from multiple sources, but categories are constructed to be mutually exclusive. "Borrowed formally" includes all adults who borrowed any money from a financial institution or through the use of a credit card or mobile money account. "Borrowed semiformally" includes all adults who borrowed any money semiformally (from a savings club) but not formally. "Borrowed from family or friends" excludes adults who borrowed formally or semiformally.

Some adults borrow for health or medical purposes

The Global Findex 2021 survey asked whether people borrowed money in the past 12 months for health or medical purposes. In developing economies, 17 percent of adults reported having borrowed money for this reason, up from about 11 percent of adults who reported having done so in 2017 and 2014. This increase may stem from fielding the Global Findex 2021 survey during the pandemic, although the survey did not ask whether such borrowing was due to COVID-19. By contrast, in high-income economies the share of adults who reported having borrowed money for health or medical purposes remained steady at about 6 percent.

2.4 The financial ecosystem

2.4 THE FINANCIAL ECOSYSTEM

Owning an account is an important step toward financial inclusion. To fully benefit from an account, however, people must be able to use it safely and conveniently. The first three sections in this chapter looked at the use of accounts for payments, savings, and borrowing. This section looks at how these services interact as part of a broader financial ecosystem.

Do people commonly use all three types of financial services, or just one or two? Among those who receive a payment into an account, what type of payments do they receive? What types of payments do they make? And do they also use their accounts to formally save, store, or borrow money? Finally, how do mobile money account owners in Sub-Saharan Africa use their accounts? Responses to the Global Findex 2021 survey help to answer these questions.

Globally, payments are the most-used financial service

In developing economies, 57 percent of adults, on average, used their account for payments, followed by 24 percent who formally saved and 22 percent who formally borrowed (figure 2.4.1, panel a).[30] Of the possible combinations of payments, borrowing, and savings, the use of payments alone was most common: 24 percent of adults used their account only for payments. About 10 percent of adults used their account for all three financial services. About the same share of adults (10 percent) used their account for payments and savings or for payments and credit. Virtually no one used their account only for savings or only for credit.

When the definition of saving is expanded to include both those who saved formally and those who used their account to store money (see section 2.2), the share of those who did so increases to 43 percent (figure 2.4.1, panel b). Considering all the possible combinations of financial services, combining payments with saving formally or storing money was the most common—22 percent of adults did so—followed by 16 percent who used their account for all three financial services and 15 percent who used it only for payments.

As in developing economies, adults in high-income economies used their accounts most commonly for payments: 95 percent did so, followed by 58 percent who formally saved and 56 percent who formally borrowed (figure 2.4.1, panel c).[31] However, the most common combination of financial services in high-income economies was use of all three services: 39 percent of adults used payments, savings, and borrowing. About 20 percent of adults used their account only for payments, and somewhat equal shares of adults (about 20 percent) used their account for payments and savings or for payments and borrowing.

When the definition of saving in high-income economies includes both those who saved formally and those who used the account to store money, the share of those who did so increased to 88 percent, and there was a near-perfect overlap with those who used their account for payments (figure 2.4.1, panel d). The share of adults who used their account for all three financial services expanded to 53 percent.

30. The numbers here refer to adults with an account who saved formally or borrowed formally. In developing economies, 1 percent of unbanked adults reported having saved formally and 1 percent having borrowed formally. As a result, the numbers here are lower than the numbers for all adults reported in the sections on savings and borrowing.
31. The numbers here refer to adults with an account who have saved formally or borrowed formally. In high-income economies, fewer than 0.2 percent of unbanked adults saved formally and 0.2 percent borrowed formally. As a result, the numbers here are lower than the numbers for all adults reported in the sections on savings and borrowing.

FIGURE 2.4.1

Globally, payments are the most-used financial service, and use of other financial services in combination differs across developing and high-income economies

a. In developing economies, the biggest share of adults only used payments

Adults using an account for financial services in developing economies (%), 2021

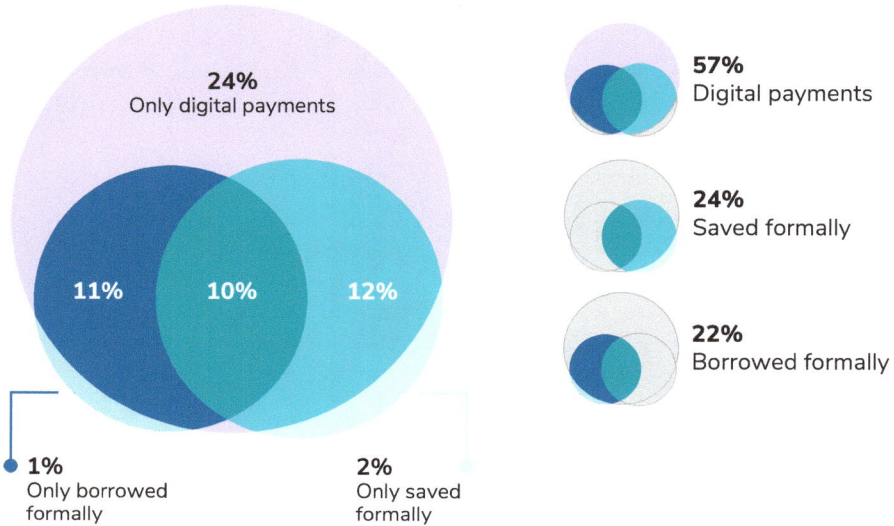

24%
Only digital payments

11%   **10%**   **12%**

1%
Only borrowed
formally

2%
Only saved
formally

57%
Digital payments

24%
Saved formally

22%
Borrowed formally

b. In developing economies, when storing money is considered part of saving, the biggest share of adults combines payments with saving or storing money

Adults using an account for financial services in developing economies (%), 2021

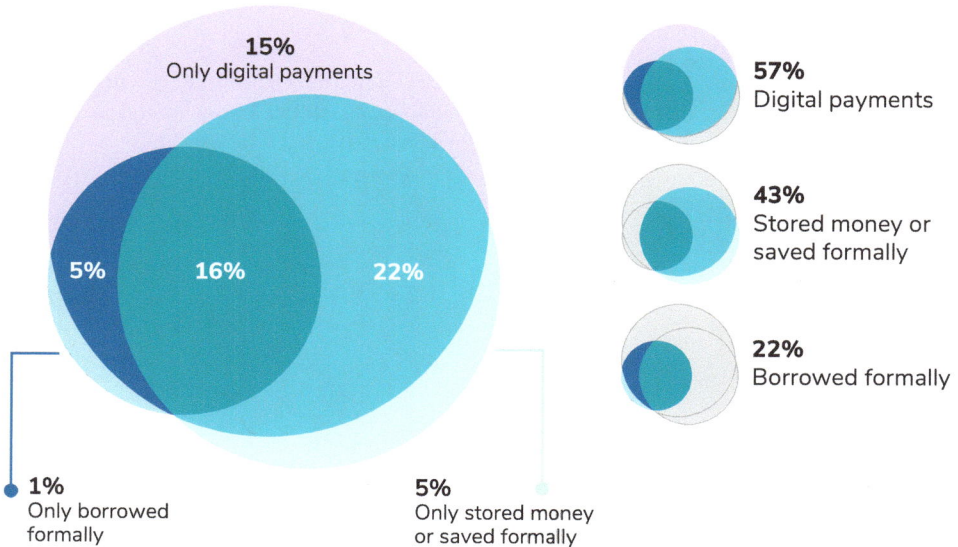

15%
Only digital payments

5%   **16%**   **22%**

1%
Only borrowed
formally

5%
Only stored money
or saved formally

57%
Digital payments

43%
Stored money or
saved formally

22%
Borrowed formally

(figure continues on next page)

FIGURE 2.4.1 *(continued from previous page)*

Globally, payments are the most-used financial service, and use of other financial services in combination differs across developing and high-income economies

c. Many more adults in high-income economies than in developing economies use all three financial services

Adults using an account for financial services in high-income economies (%), 2021

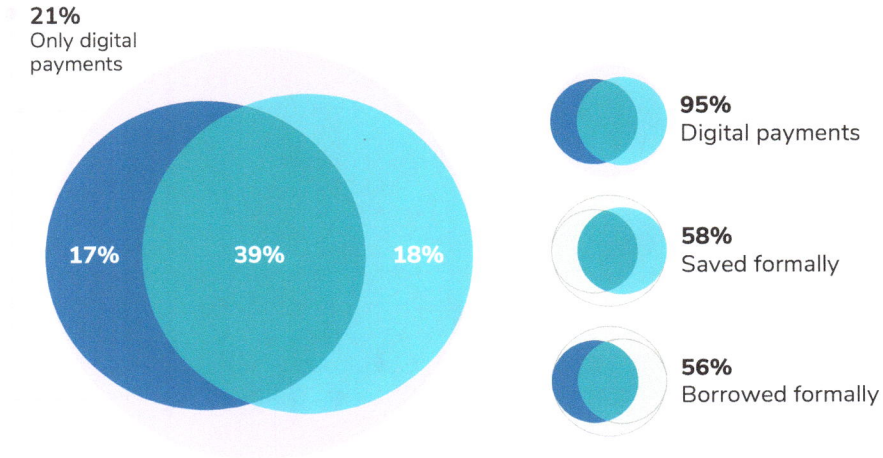

21%
Only digital payments

17%   39%   18%

95%
Digital payments

58%
Saved formally

56%
Borrowed formally

d. In high-income economies, the share of adults who either store or save money overlaps almost entirely with those who use accounts to make or receive payments

Adults using an account for financial services in high-income economies (%), 2021

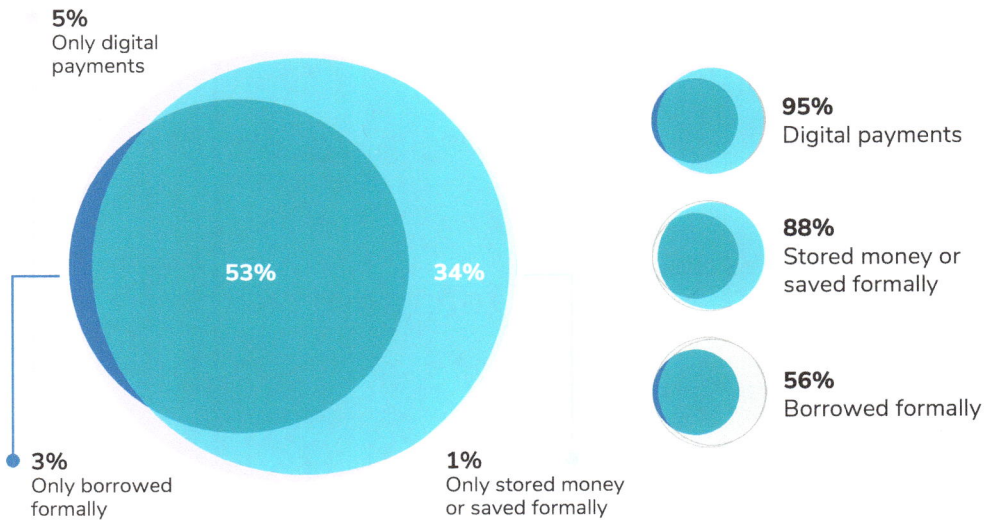

5%
Only digital payments

53%   34%

3%
Only borrowed formally

1%
Only stored money or saved formally

95%
Digital payments

88%
Stored money or saved formally

56%
Borrowed formally

Source: Global Findex Database 2021.

In developing economies, receiving a payment into an account was a gateway to using other financial services

In developing economies, 36 percent of adults received a payment into an account. Types of incoming payments include a private or public sector wage payment, a government transfer or pension payment, a domestic remittance payment, or a payment for the sale of agricultural products (figure 2.4.2). Of those who received a payment into an account, most (83 percent) also reported that they made a digital payment.[32] Payment recipients make one or more of the following digital payments: digital merchant payments (made by 65 percent of those who received a payment into an account), bill payments using a mobile phone or the internet (53 percent), a utility payment (33 percent), or a domestic remittances payment from an account (32 percent). Because many adults who received a payment into an account made more than one type of digital payment, the percentages add up to more than 83 percent.

Almost two-thirds of those who received a payment into their account also used the account to store money. About 40 percent of payment recipients reported saving money formally and about 40 percent borrowed money formally.

It is not surprising that adults who received a payment into an account were more likely than the general population to make a digital payment and to store, save, or borrow money. In developing economies, for example, the 83 percent of digital payment recipients making a digital payment was far higher than the 51 percent of all adults making a digital payment. Likewise, 63 percent stored money using an account, compared with 39 percent of all adults; 42 percent saved formally, compared with 25 percent of all adults; and 39 percent borrowed formally, compared with 23 percent of all adults.

Once money is received into an account, it is typically easiest for it to remain there until needed and then make a payment from the account. Similarly, once money is in an account, it is relatively easy to keep it there for savings. Receiving a payment into an account—especially if the payment can be used to document a regular income stream over time—can also make it easier to borrow money formally. As chapter 1 has shown, account owners are typically richer than adults without an account. There are important variations, however, between how recipients of different kinds of payments use their account.

Figure 2.4.2 shows the relationship between payment inflows and the use of financial services among payment recipients as developing economy averages. As discussed in previous sections, there are large variations in the use of accounts across economies.

The majority of adults receiving wage payments into an account also made digital payments and stored or saved money

Twenty percent of adults in developing economies received a wage payment—from the private sector or from the government—into an account (figure 2.4.3). Almost all (91 percent) of those recipients also made a digital payment from their account. This share includes the 79 percent who made a digital merchant payment, the 65 percent who made a bill payment using a mobile phone or the internet, and the about 35 percent each who made a utility payment or sent a domestic remittance payment. At the same time, about 70 percent of those who received a payment into their account also used their account to store money. Meanwhile, about half saved money formally and about half borrowed money formally.

When comparing adults who received a wage payment into an account with all payment recipients who received the money into an account, a larger share of them also made a digital payment—especially a digital merchant

---

32. See section 2.1 on digital payments for definitions of all the payments specified in the variable *making a digital payment*. The Global Findex 2021 survey collected no data on the sequence of financial transactions.

FIGURE 2.4.2

In developing economies, adults who receive a payment into an account are more likely than the general population to also make digital payments and to save, store, and borrow money

INFLOWS ▶▶   ▶▶ ▶▶ USAGES

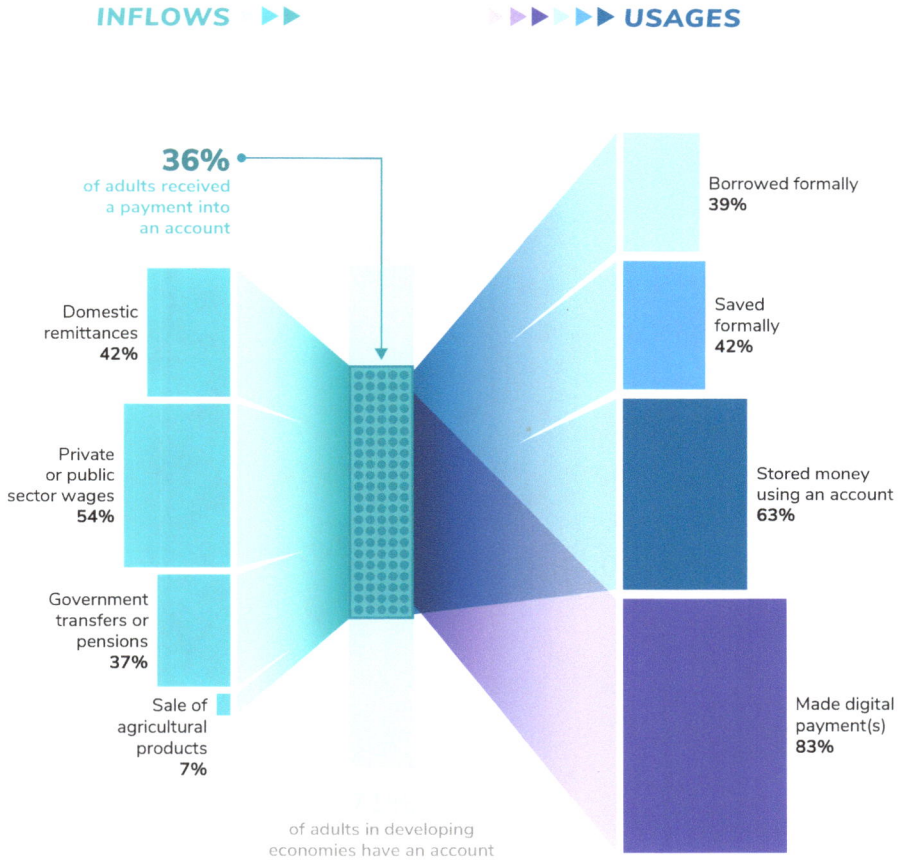

36%
of adults received
a payment into
an account

Domestic
remittances
42%

Private
or public
sector wages
54%

Government
transfers or
pensions
37%

Sale of
agricultural
products
7%

of adults in developing
economies have an account

Borrowed formally
39%

Saved
formally
42%

Stored money
using an account
63%

Made digital
payment(s)
83%

Source: Global Findex Database 2021.

Note: Inflows and usages are shown as percentages of the 36 percent of adults receiving a payment into an account.

payment and a bill payment using a mobile phone or the internet. Wage recipients were also more likely than overall payment recipients to use their account to store, save, and borrow money. Because those receiving a wage payment tend to receive such payments on a regular basis and tend to be relatively wealthier than adults receiving one of the other three types of payments, it is not surprising that they were more likely to also use these other services.

Many adults receiving a government transfer or pension payment into an account also made payments, but a smaller share stored, saved, or borrowed money

In developing economies, 13 percent of adults received a government transfer or pension payment into an account (figure 2.4.4). Of these payment recipients, 70 percent also made a digital payment from their account, including 50 percent who made a digital merchant payment; 40 percent who made a bill payment

In developing economies, adults receiving wage payments into an account also made digital payments and stored or saved money

INFLOWS ▶▶▶   ▶▶▶▶▶ USAGES

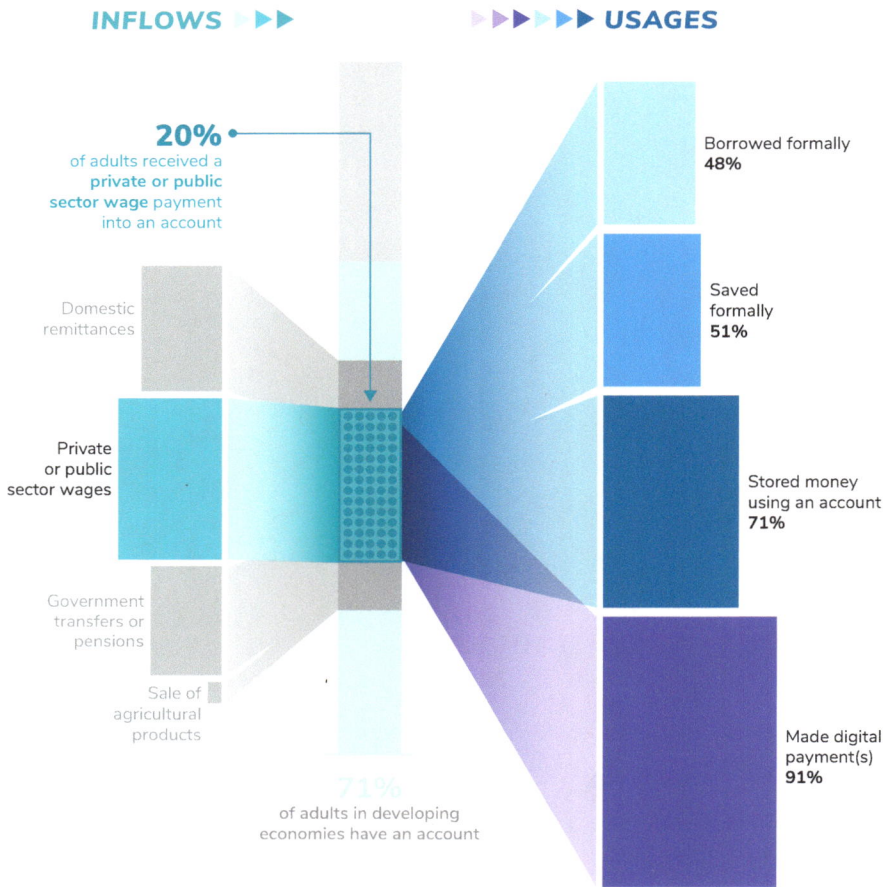

20%
of adults received a
**private or public
sector wage** payment
into an account

Domestic
remittances

Private
or public
sector wages

Government
transfers or
pensions

Sale of
agricultural
products

71%
of adults in developing
economies have an account

Borrowed formally
48%

Saved
formally
51%

Stored money
using an account
71%

Made digital
payment(s)
91%

Source: Global Findex Database 2021.
Note: Usages are shown as percentages of the 20 percent of adults receiving a private or public sector wage payment into an account.

using a mobile phone or the internet; 32 percent who made a utility payment from an account; and 22 percent who sent a domestic remittance payment from an account. At the same time, about half of those who received a government transfer or pension payment into their account also used their account to store money. About one-third of government transfer or pension recipients saved money formally, and one-third borrowed money formally.

Compared with recipients of wage payments, adults receiving a government transfer or pension payment were less likely to have made a digital payment, to have used their account to store money, or to save or borrow. Because government transfer and pension payments are typically much smaller in value and their recipients are likely relatively poorer, it is not surprising that a smaller share used their account for any of the financial services described. As for transfer payments, recipients may also receive such payments less frequently and potentially just as a one-off payment.

FIGURE 2.4.4

In developing economies, most adults receiving a government pension or transfer payment into an account also made digital payments

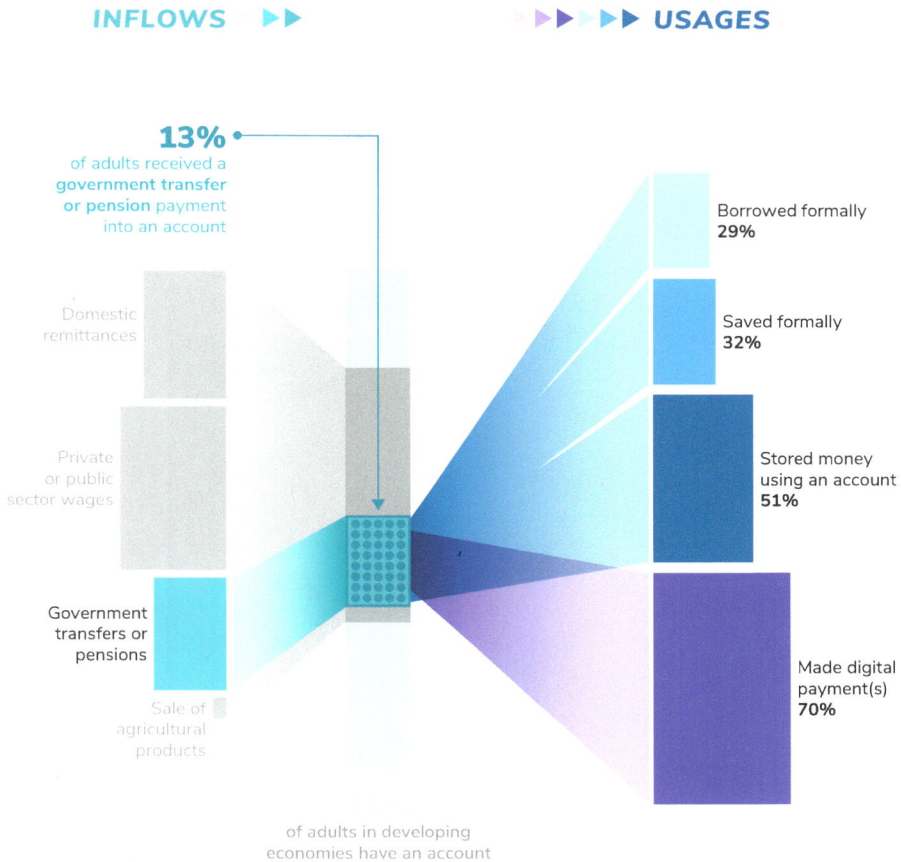

INFLOWS ▶▶   ▶▶ ▶▶ **USAGES**

13%
of adults received a
**government transfer
or pension** payment
into an account

Domestic
remittances

Private
or public
sector wages

Government
transfers or
pensions

Sale of
agricultural
products

Borrowed formally
29%

Saved formally
32%

Stored money
using an account
51%

Made digital
payment(s)
70%

of adults in developing
economies have an account

Source: Global Findex Database 2021.

Note: Usages are shown as percentages of the 13 percent of adults receiving a government transfer or pension payment into an account.

In Sub-Saharan Africa, recipients of domestic remittance payments into an account often sent domestic remittances as well

As discussed in section 2.1 on digital payments, domestic remittance payments are especially important in Sub-Saharan Africa, where 24 percent of adults, on average, received such a payment into an account (figure 2.4.5). Of those recipients, virtually all (94 percent) also made a digital payment. This share includes the 62 percent who sent a domestic remittance payment—likely passing on some of the funds they received to relatives or friends. Adults may be both recipients and senders of remittances at different points in time, if, for example, their income is seasonal or fluctuates widely within a year for other reasons, especially more than the income of relatives or friends. One-third of account owners who received their domestic remittances into an account also made a digital merchant payment, a utility payment from an account, or a bill payment using a mobile phone or the internet. About 70 percent of those who received a domestic remittance payment into their account also

FIGURE 2.4.5

In Sub-Saharan Africa, nearly all adults receiving domestic remittance payments into an account made digital payments

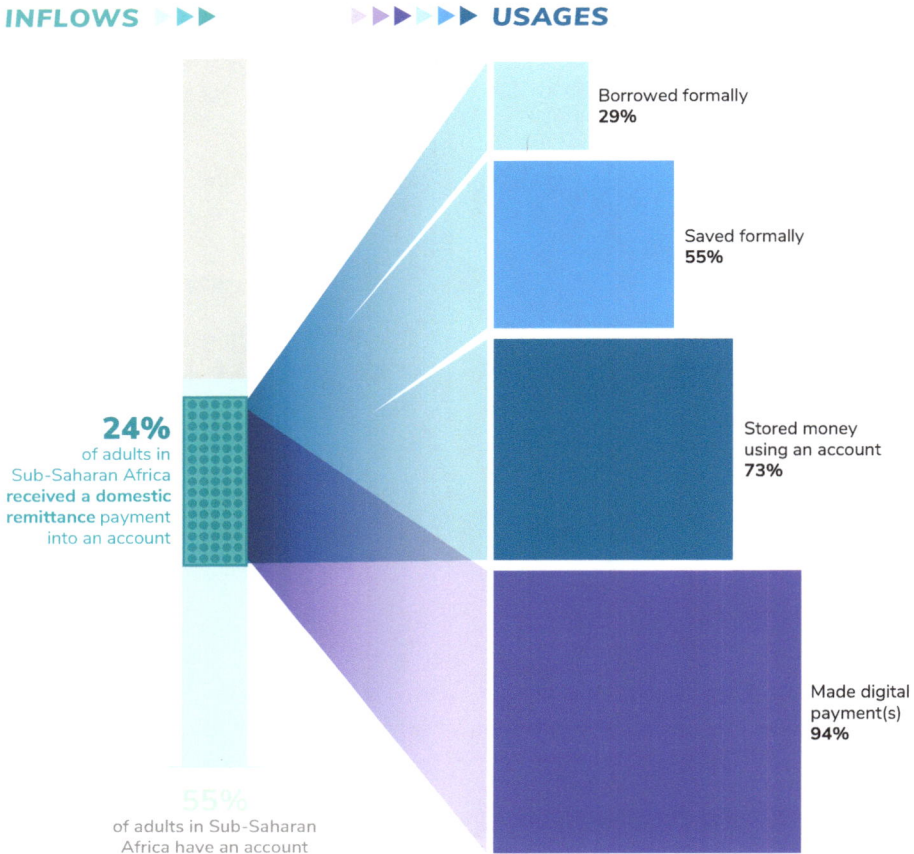

INFLOWS ▶▶▶   ▶▶▶▶▶ USAGES

24%
of adults in
Sub-Saharan Africa
**received a domestic
remittance** payment
into an account

55%
of adults in Sub-Saharan
Africa have an account

Borrowed formally
29%

Saved formally
55%

Stored money
using an account
73%

Made digital
payment(s)
94%

Source: Global Findex Database 2021.

Note: Usages are shown as percentages of the 24 percent of adults receiving a domestic remittance payment into an account.

used their account to store money or for cash management. Just over half saved formally, while about one-third borrowed formally.

A relatively small share of domestic remittance recipients in Sub-Saharan Africa made a digital merchant payment—around one-third—compared with the share of wage recipients in developing economies who went on to make digital merchant payments (79 percent) and even the share of wage recipients in Sub-Saharan Africa (52 percent). One explanation may be that recipients of domestic remittance payments live in more rural areas where the opportunities to make digital merchant payments are more limited.

Adults in Kenya used mobile money accounts to receive payments for the sale of agricultural products

Most adults in developing economies who were paid for agricultural products received their payment in cash. But, as discussed in section 2.1 on digital payments, Kenya—along with Mali and Uganda—stands out in terms of the share of adults receiving agricultural payments into an account. In Kenya, 19 percent of adults—63 percent of all those who received agricultural payments—received such a payment into an account, including 16 percent of adults who did so into a mobile money account. The comparatively high share of adults receiving agricultural payments into mobile money accounts in Kenya is an aspirational example for other Sub-Saharan African economies, where the share of adults receiving agricultural payments was more than twice the developing economy average and mobile money account ownership is high.

Among the 16 percent of adults in Kenya who received a payment into a mobile money account for the sale of agricultural products, 95 percent made a digital payment (figure 2.4.6). This share included 62 percent who made a digital merchant payment, 57 percent who used a mobile phone or the internet to make a bill payment, 54 percent who sent a domestic remittance payment from an account, and 40 percent who paid a utility bill directly from an account. About 70 percent of those who received an agricultural payment into their mobile money account used the account to store money. Half saved money using their mobile money account, and a little over 40 percent borrowed money using their mobile money account.

FIGURE 2.4.6

In Kenya, adults receiving payments for the sale of agricultural products into a mobile money account made digital payments and stored, saved, or borrowed money

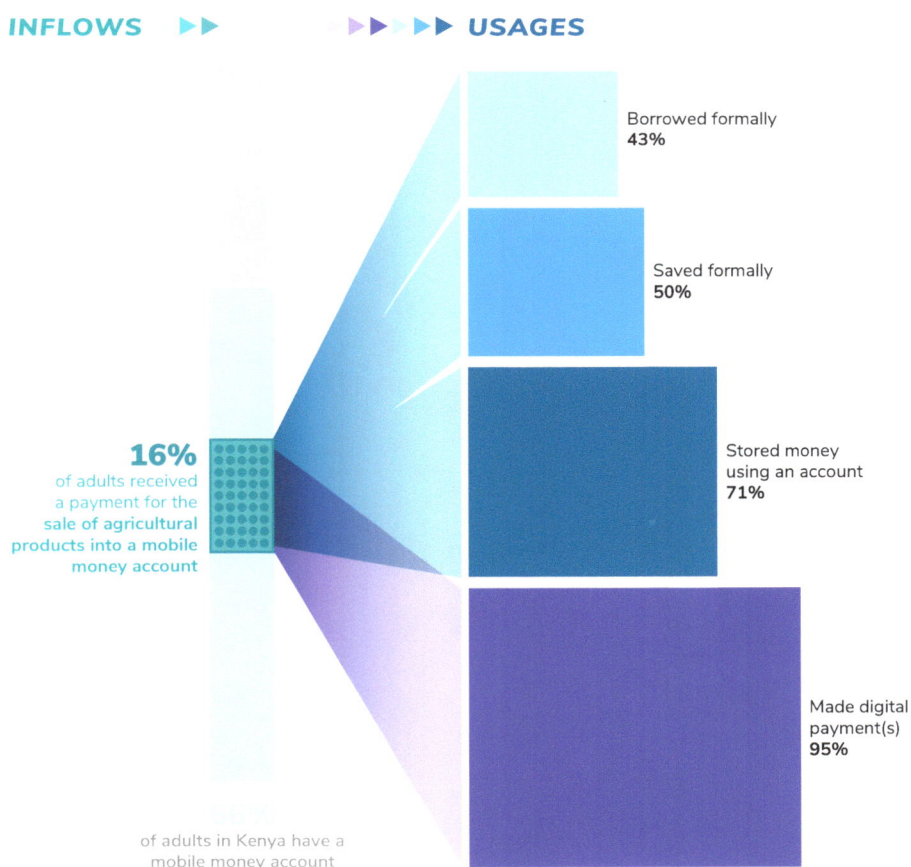

INFLOWS ►► ►►►► USAGES

16% of adults received a payment for the sale of agricultural products into a mobile money account

of adults in Kenya have a mobile money account

Borrowed formally
43%

Saved formally
50%

Stored money using an account
71%

Made digital payment(s)
95%

Source: Global Findex Database 2021.

Note: Usages are shown as percentages of the 16 percent of adults receiving a payment for the sale of agricultural products into a mobile money account.

Mobile money accounts in Sub-Saharan Africa are used for more than person-to-person payments

In Sub-Saharan Africa, 33 percent of adults have a mobile money account (figure 2.4.7). Of those who have such an account, two in three (68 percent) received a payment into their mobile money account. This share included about half of mobile money account owners who received a domestic remittance payment, 22 percent who received a wage payment, 13 percent who received a payment for the sale of agricultural products, and 8 percent who received a government transfer or pension payment. Virtually all mobile money account owners (98 percent) made a digital payment. This share included almost half who made a domestic remittance payment from an account, 37 percent who used a mobile phone or the internet to make a bill payment, about 30 percent who made a digital merchant payment, and about 30 percent who paid a utility bill directly from an account. Just over half of adults with a mobile money account used it to store money. About 40 percent reported having saved money using their mobile money account, and 20 percent borrowed money using their mobile money account.

FIGURE 2.4.7

In Sub-Saharan Africa, adults with a mobile money account used it for a range of purposes beyond person-to-person payments

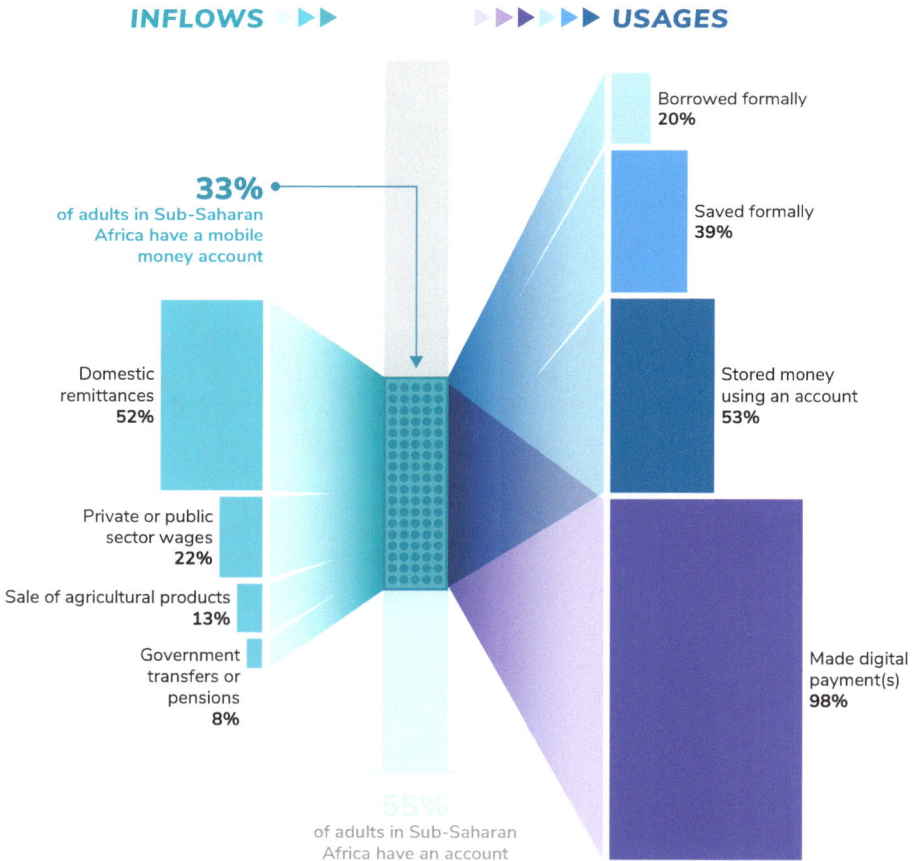

INFLOWS ▶▶   ▶▶▶▶▶ USAGES

33%
of adults in Sub-Saharan Africa have a mobile money account

Domestic remittances
52%

Private or public sector wages
22%

Sale of agricultural products
13%

Government transfers or pensions
8%

Borrowed formally
20%

Saved formally
39%

Stored money using an account
53%

Made digital payment(s)
98%

55%
of adults in Sub-Saharan Africa have an account

Source: Global Findex Database 2021.
Note: Inflows and usages are shown as percentages of the 33 percent of adults with a mobile money account.

The fact that a large share of mobile money account owners in Sub-Saharan Africa used their account for domestic remittance payments should come as no surprise. When the mobile money operator M-PESA launched its business in Kenya in 2007, it specifically targeted the domestic remittance market, promoting its services with the slogan "Send money home." As mobile money accounts spread across Sub-Saharan Africa, their use for domestic remittance payments also expanded, as well as their use for other types of payments. In 2021, about three in four (74 percent, or 25 percent of all adults) mobile account owners used their mobile money account to make or receive at least one payment that was not person-to-person. By contrast, just 18 percent (6 percent of adults) used their mobile money account only to send or receive person-to-person payments, and 7 percent (2 percent of adults) used their mobile money account only to make or receive an unspecified type of payment.[33]

---

33. *Person-to-person payment* is defined as sending or receiving a domestic remittance payment or sending money to a relative or friend using a mobile phone or the internet.

2.5 Opportunities for expanding the use of accounts

2.5 OPPORTUNITIES FOR EXPANDING THE USE OF ACCOUNTS

As described throughout this chapter, many account owners used their account to make or receive payments, to save or store money, or to borrow money. Yet 13 percent of account owners in developing economies did not use their account at all in the previous year. This section explores the data on account owners with "inactive" accounts and the reasons account owners with an inactive account in India gave for not using the account (India has the highest share of people who have accounts but do not use them). This section also explores opportunities for increasing the use of accounts among account owners, both those with inactive accounts and those who still make some financial transactions only in cash.

The share of account owners with an inactive account has fallen since 2017

In developing economies, 9 percent of adults overall—13 percent of account owners—have what could be considered an inactive account—that is, an account with no deposits or withdrawals and no incoming or outgoing digital payments in the past year (figure 2.5.1). The share of account owners in developing economies with an inactive account fell from 17 percent in 2017 to reach about the level (12 percent) it was in 2014.[34] In high-income economies, virtually all account owners have an active account.

The share of account owners with an inactive account varies across developing economies, but it is especially high in India at 35 percent, the highest in the world. That share is about seven times larger than the 5 percent average for all developing economies, excluding India (figure 2.5.2). One reason for India's high share of account inactivity may be that many of these accounts were opened as part of the Indian government's Jan Dhan Yojana scheme to increase account ownership. Launched in August 2014, the program had by April 2022 brought an

FIGURE 2.5.1

In developing economies, 13 percent of account owners had an inactive account in the past year

Adults with an account (%), 2014–21

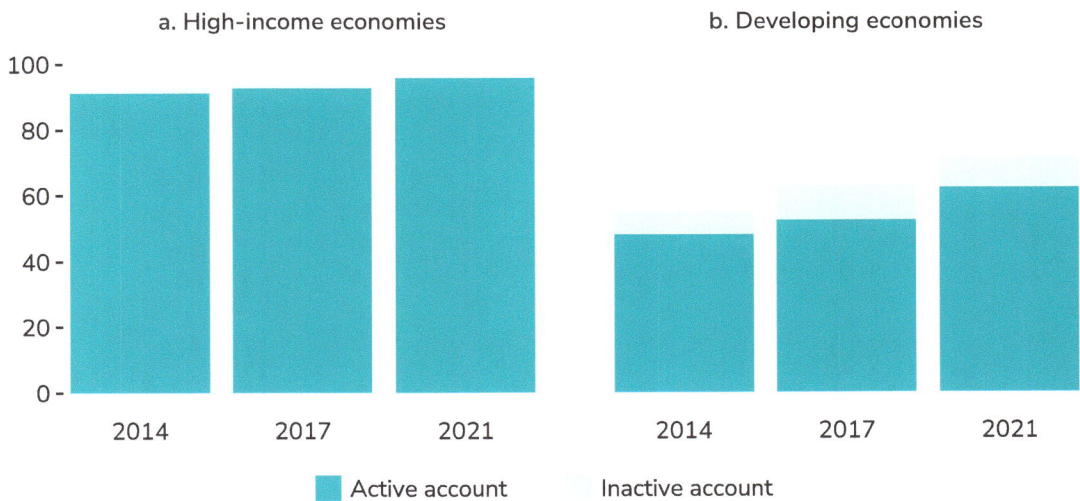

Source: Global Findex Database 2021.

---

34. The definition of an inactive account has been updated since Global Findex data on inactive accounts were first reported in 2017. The updated definition includes not having received or made a digital payment in the past year. It has been applied to all years in the database. The old definition was based only on the criterion of no deposit or withdrawal in the past year.

FIGURE 2.5.2

In India, about one-third of account owners had an inactive account in the past year

Adults with an account (%), 2021

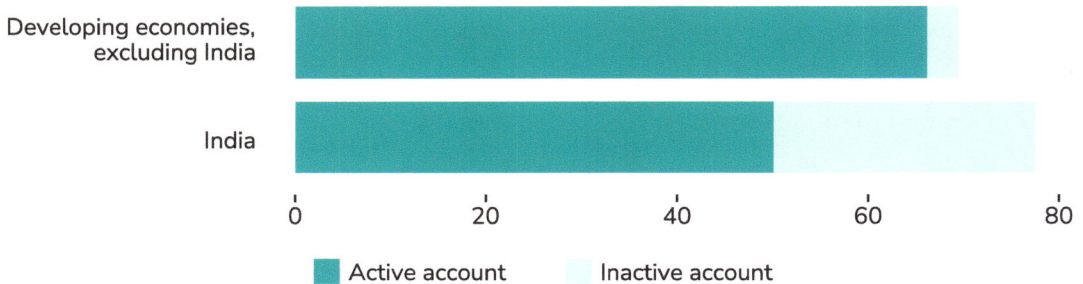

Source: Global Findex Database 2021.

additional 450 million Indians into the formal banking system.[35] Most of the new accounts had already been opened when the Global Findex 2017 survey was conducted. The share of adults with an inactive account in India remained about the same between 2017 and 2021.

In developing economies, women account owners are, on average, 5 percentage points more likely than men account owners to have an inactive account. However, India is driving this gap with a 12 percentage point difference between women account owners who had an inactive account (42 percent) and men account owners who did so (30 percent). The data on account inactivity in developing economies, excluding India, reveal that women and men have, on average, equal rates of inactivity.

Adults in India did not use their accounts for three main reasons: distance from a financial institution, lack of trust, and having no need

To shed light on why a large share of adults in India has inactive accounts, the Global Findex 2021 survey asked those with an inactive account why they did not use it. The three most common reasons were that financial institutions were too far away; lack of trust in financial institutions; and no need for an account. Each of these reasons was cited by about half of adults with an inactive account. As for other reasons, nearly 40 percent said they did not have enough money to use an account, and about 30 percent cited not feeling comfortable using an account by themselves (figure 2.5.3).

Notably, more men with an inactive account (34 percent) than women with an inactive account (26 percent) said they did not feel comfortable using an account by themselves. There was no income or educational attainment gap for inactive account holders who gave this reason.

Digitalizing payments, if offered in a context of reliable products and infrastructure, may increase the use of accounts by banked adults

Many account owners receive cash payments from a range of sources. For example, about 90 million account owners worldwide received a government payment in the form of a wage, pension, or transfer payment in cash, and 225 million account owners received a private sector wage in cash. In developing economies, 160 million account owners received cash payments for the sale of agricultural products. Although recipients

---

35. Ministry of Finance, India (2022).

FIGURE 2.5.3

In India, distance to financial institutions, lack of trust, and lack of need were the most commonly cited reasons for account inactivity

Adults with an inactive account reporting barrier as a reason for not using account (%), 2021

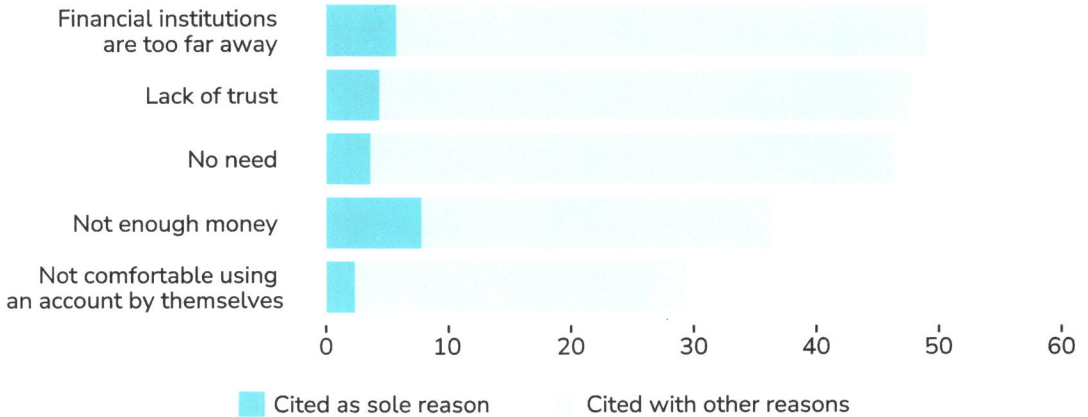

Source: Global Findex Database 2021.

often did not control how these payments were made, the sheer volume suggests opportunities to digitalize those transactions.

Payments made in cash by account owners likewise suggest opportunities to expand the use of accounts. For example, worldwide, 620 million adult account owners made utility bill payments in cash, and more than 1.6 billion account owners in developing economies used only cash for merchant payments.

Digitalizing cash payments is not simply a matter of incentivizing account owners to use an account, however. Financial infrastructure—enabled by actors such as governments, telecommunications providers, payment processors, and financial service providers (including fintechs)—also is needed to create an environment in which safe, affordable, and convenient products and functionality are widely available.

Progress is already under way, catalyzed by the wider availability of digital products and services offered by mobile money account providers, financial institutions, and third-party payment service providers, and executed through mobile phones, apps, and the internet. But mobile phones and the internet can only facilitate the use of accounts in locations with reliable electricity, data connectivity, and mobile networks. People will be less inclined to use digital payments if they view them as undependable because of network outages or other technical problems. This is just one way in which the broader business environment is an enabler of financial access.

Telecommunications access is a key enabler. Globally, 70 percent of adults have access to the internet via a mobile phone or a computer, according to the Gallup World Poll (map 2.5.1). In high-income economies, that share is 91 percent, and in developing economies it is 67 percent. In South Asia and Sub-Saharan Africa, less than half of adults have internet access. Most adults in these two regions do have a mobile phone, however—70 percent in South Asia and 81 percent in Sub-Saharan Africa—which may still enable them to use mobile money accounts, even on a text-based, non–internet-enabled phone.

MAP 2.5.1

Globally, 70 percent of adults have internet access

Adults with access to the internet (%), 2021

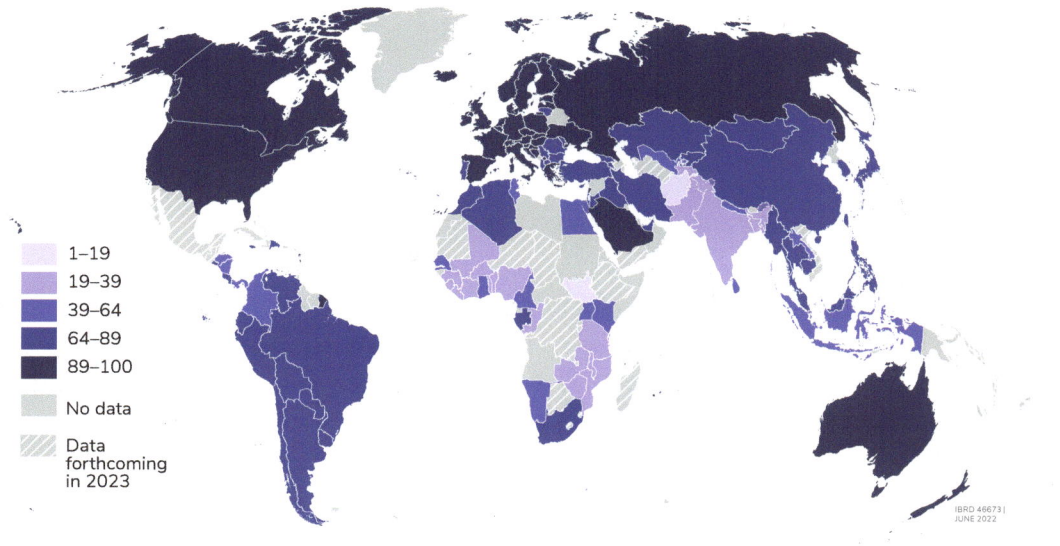

Legend:
- 1–19
- 19–39
- 39–64
- 64–89
- 89–100
- No data
- Data forthcoming in 2023

IBRD 46673 |
JUNE 2022

Source: Gallup World Poll.

Highlighting opportunities for account owners to make digital payments

There are many opportunities to further increase the use of accounts to make digital payments. Globally, 1 billion adults who have an account did not make a single digital payment in 2021 (map 2.5.2), which means that about a quarter of account owners globally did not make any digital payments. That share is much higher in some major developing economies. In India, about 70 percent of account owners did not make a single digital payment—one of the world's highest shares (figure 2.5.4). India's large population and the fact that 78 percent of adults have an account makes India home to about half—540 million—of the world's 1 billion adults who have an account but made no digital payment. Egypt has a similarly high percentage of account owners who did not make a digital payment, but on a smaller population base and with only about a third of India's account ownership rate.

By contrast, only 4 percent of adults in China with an account did not use it to make digital payments—one of the smallest shares among developing economies. In fact, use of accounts to make digital payments was nearly universal among China's 89 percent of adults with an account. In Kenya, as in many other Sub-Saharan African economies, making digital payments is also nearly universal among account owners because of the widespread use of mobile money accounts. About 17 percent of adults with an account in Brazil, South Africa, and Türkiye did not make a digital payment.

MAP 2.5.2

Globally, 1 billion adults who have an account made no digital payments—including 540 million in India

Adults with an account making no digital payment in the past year, 2021

1 million
50 million
100 million

IBRD 46674 |
JUNE 2022

Source: Global Findex Database 2021.
Note: Data are not displayed for economies for which no data are available.

FIGURE 2.5.4

Globally, about a quarter of account owners made no digital payments

Adults with an account (%), 2021

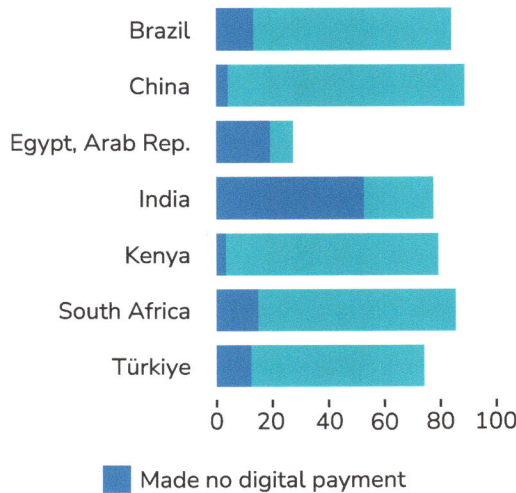

■ Made no digital payment

Source: Global Findex Database 2021.

Utility bill payments present an opportunity to increase the use of accounts by account owners

One of the best ways to increase account use is to more fully digitalize payments for water, electricity, and other utility bills. Globally, 620 million adults with an account paid their utility bills in cash in 2021 (map 2.5.3). This share translates into about 14 percent of account owners worldwide having paid utility bills in cash in 2021, with higher rates in certain major developing economies. For example, about 20 percent of account owners in Brazil and India paid utility bills in cash, 35 percent in Nigeria, and 55 percent in Indonesia. In Egypt, 72 percent of account owners paid utility bills in cash (figure 2.5.5). In some economies, people have the option of paying utility bills digitally, but choose not to because of high fees, lack of proof of payment, or other concerns. If more utilities offered convenient, reliable, and low- or no-cost options for digital utility payments, they could improve efficiency and usage.

FIGURE 2.5.5

Millions of account owners paid utility bills in cash

Adults with an account (%), 2021

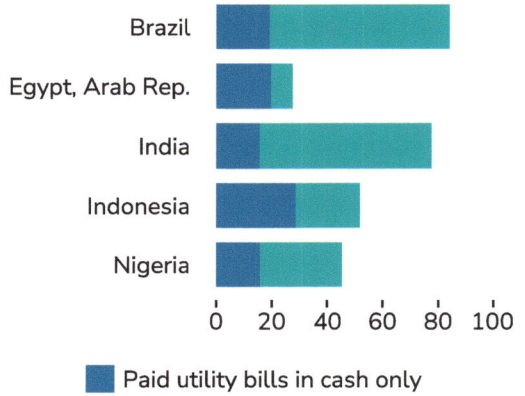

■ Paid utility bills in cash only

Source: Global Findex Database 2021.

MAP 2.5.3

Globally, about 620 million adults who have an account still paid utility bills in cash

Adults with an account paying utility bills in the past year in cash only, 2021

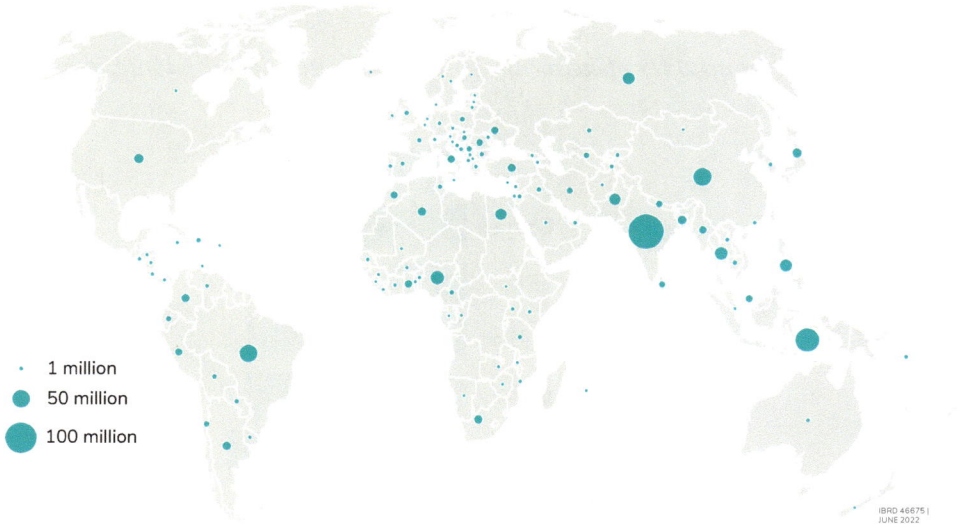

- 1 million
- 50 million
- 100 million

IBRD 46675 |
JUNE 2022

Source: Global Findex Database 2021.
Note: Data are not displayed for economies for which no data are available.

Banked adults who make merchant payments only in cash present another opportunity for increasing the use of digital payments

Another large opportunity to increase account use is to more fully digitalize merchant payments. In developing economies, 1.6 billion adults with an account made merchant payments only in cash (map 2.5.4). Although the Global Findex 2021 survey did not directly ask whether adults made at least one merchant payment, it is reasonable to assume that all adults had done so, meaning that, on average, almost half of adults with an account made merchant payments only in cash. This average is heavily skewed by the fact that just 8 percent of account owners in China only used cash to make merchant payments. Examining the data for developing economies without China reveals that two-thirds of adults with an account made merchant payments only in cash. In India, that share was 85 percent—or 670 million adults. In Bangladesh and Tanzania, more than 90 percent of adults with an account made merchant payments only in cash, and that share was 75 percent in Indonesia, 54 percent in Kenya, and about 40 percent in Brazil, South Africa, and Türkiye (figure 2.5.6).

Ideally, people with an account—and, in particular, those who receive a payment into their account—would keep their funds in the account and use them to make purchases or payments directly from the account. The Global Findex 2021 survey payments data show that many account owners did just that. However, in many developing economies digital payments are not yet widely accepted for everyday purchases at local retail stores and markets. Merchants may not find it attractive to accept digital payments if fees are high or if the enabling physical infrastructure—such as electricity and data network connectivity—is unreliable. A regulatory environment that makes it cumbersome to formalize a business, or one that taxes digital payments, may also discourage merchants from accepting digital payments.[36] Thus the challenge of transitioning more adults to digital payments is not just a matter of motivating demand, but also a matter of enabling supply, so that account owners have the option to pay digitally.

MAP 2.5.4

In developing economies, 1.6 billion adults with an account made no digital merchant payment—including 670 million in India

Adults with an account making no digital merchant payment in the past year, 2021

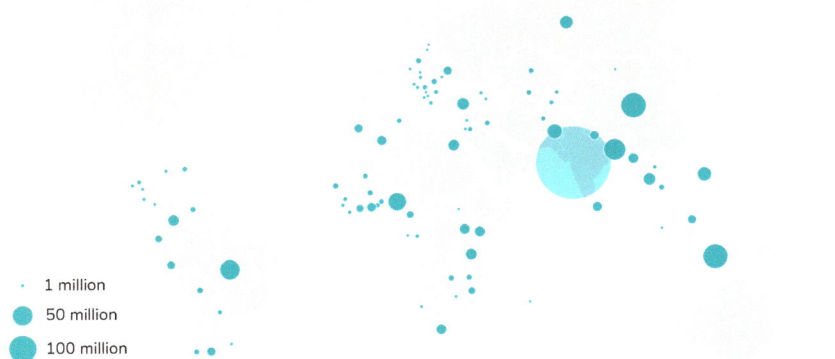

- 1 million
- 50 million
- 100 million

(IBRD 46676)
(JUNE 2022)

Source: Global Findex Database 2021.

Note: Data on digital merchant payments were not collected in most high-income economies. Data are not displayed for economies for which no data are available.

---

36. See Klapper, Miller, and Hess (2019) for a discussion of how digital financial services—including those accessed through mobile phones and the internet—can encourage businesses to formalize their operations.

FIGURE 2.5.6

In developing economies, about half of account owners made no digital merchant payment

Adults with an account (%), 2021

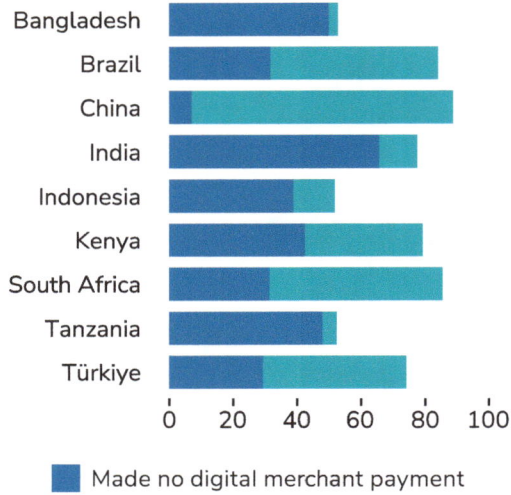

Made no digital merchant payment

Source: Global Findex Database 2021.

2.6 Opportunities for increasing account ownership for the unbanked through digitalizing payments

2.6 OPPORTUNITIES FOR INCREASING ACCOUNT OWNERSHIP FOR THE UNBANKED THROUGH DIGITALIZING PAYMENTS

This chapter opened with evidence on the ways in which using financial services—in particular, payments—gives recipients better privacy, security, and control over their money, while also increasing savings and financial resilience. For example, digital payments of wages can encourage workers to save using their account, and digital payments for agricultural products can make it easier for farmers to access additional financial products such as input financing and crop insurance. Digitalizing wage or government payments also helps recipients by reducing the time and cost of receiving such payments, and it can help payers by ensuring the money goes to the intended recipients and by reducing leakage. However, these benefits can accrue only to those who have an account and use it. This section explores opportunities to further increase account ownership based on the Global Findex 2021 survey findings on the use of financial services.

Digitalizing cash transactions offers a pathway to increasing account ownership

Just as there are opportunities to help people who have an account make more use of it, there are also opportunities to increase account ownership by digitalizing cash transactions for the unbanked.

Millions of unbanked adults around the world still receive regular payments in cash from employers or from the government. Digitalizing such payments is a proven way to increase account ownership. In developing economies, 39 percent of adults—or 57 percent of those with a financial institution account—opened their first account at a financial institution specifically to receive a wage payment or to receive money from the government (figure 2.6.1).[37]

The share is higher in some economies. In India, Malaysia, South Africa, and República Bolivariana de Venezuela, 70 percent of account owners opened their first account at a financial institution to receive a wage or government payment. The same is true for about two-thirds of account owners in Mongolia, as well as in a few economies in Europe and Central Asia, including Bosnia and Herzegovina, Kazakhstan, and Serbia.

FIGURE 2.6.1

Millions of adults opened their first account at a financial institution to receive a wage or government payment

Adults with an account at a financial institution (%), 2021

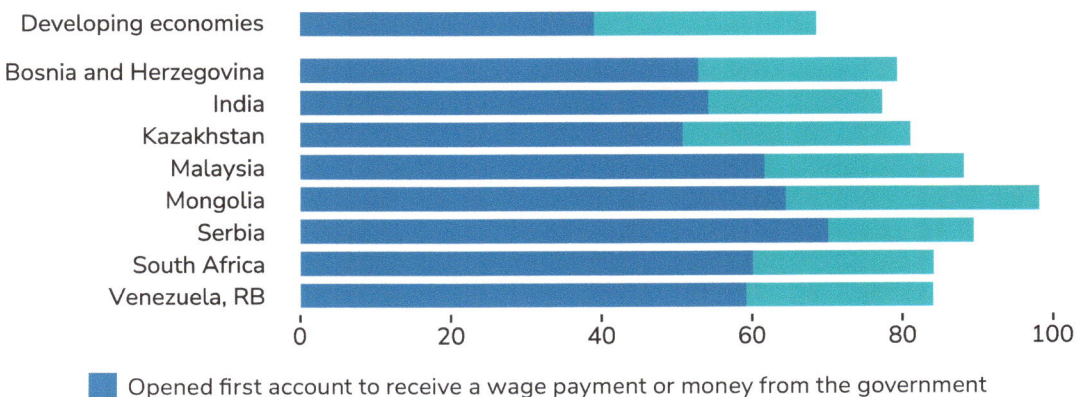

Opened first account to receive a wage payment or money from the government

Source: Global Findex Database 2021.

37. This question was asked in different ways in the Global Findex 2021 survey and the Global Findex 2017 survey.

Digitalizing government payments

The Global Findex 2021 survey data reveal that digitalizing government payments has already resulted in higher account ownership. Among adults in developing economies with an account at a financial institution, roughly 865 million opened their first account to receive money from the government, including 423 million women.

Governments send several types of payments to people. They pay wages to public sector employees, distribute public sector pensions, and provide those receiving social benefits with transfers. Globally, about 5 percent of unbanked adults—85 million people—received such payments in cash (map 2.6.1). They included about 45 million women, as well as 40 million adults with incomes in the poorest 40 percent of households in their economy. Among the unbanked adults receiving government payments in cash, many have a mobile phone, suggesting both potential and means for increasing account ownership by moving these payments into accounts.

Although the overwhelming majority of public sector wages are paid into an account (less than 1 percent of unbanked adults around the world received a government wage payment in cash), important opportunities remain in some economies to increase account ownership by paying government transfers and pensions into accounts. In Cambodia and the Philippines, about 20 percent of unbanked adults—or about 10 percent of all adults—received government transfer payments in cash (figure 2.6.2). More than 80 percent of the unbanked receiving such payments in these economies have a mobile phone. In Albania and Uzbekistan, 16 percent of unbanked adults—or nearly 10 percent of all adults—received pension payments in cash. In Moldova and Romania, the share of unbanked adults receiving a pension payment is even higher, 24 percent and 33 percent, respectively, translating into a similar share of nearly 10 percent of all adults in these economies who could be brought into the formal financial system if these payments were paid into accounts. Among the adults receiving a government pension payment in cash in these four Europe and Central Asia economies, at least half have a mobile phone.

MAP 2.6.1

Globally, about 85 million unbanked adults received government payments in cash

Adults without an account receiving government payments in the past year in cash only, 2021

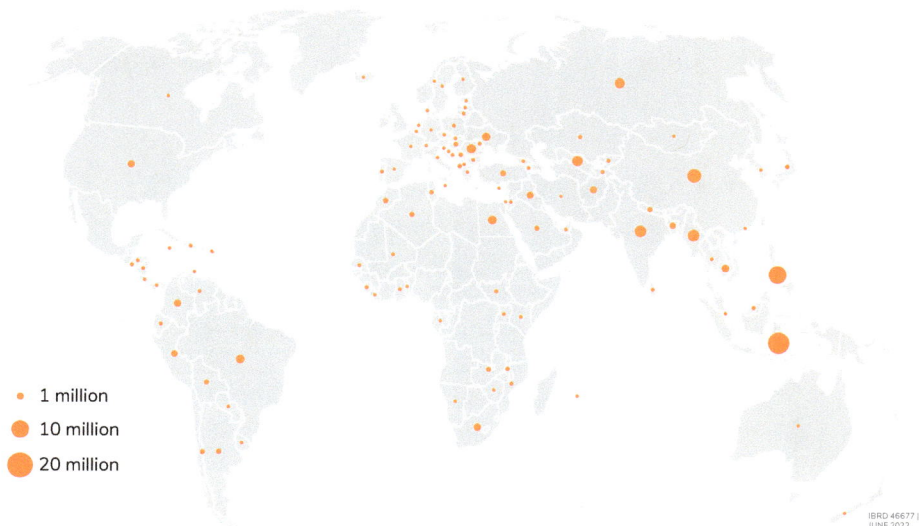

- 1 million
- 10 million
- 20 million

IBRD 46677 | JUNE 2022

Source: Global Findex Database 2021.

Note: Public sector wage questions were not posed in China in 2021. Data are not displayed for economies where the share of adults without an account was 5 percent or less or the share receiving government payments was 10 percent or less or for economies for which no data are available.

FIGURE 2.6.2

Digitalizing government payments could reduce the number of unbanked adults

Adults without an account (%), 2021

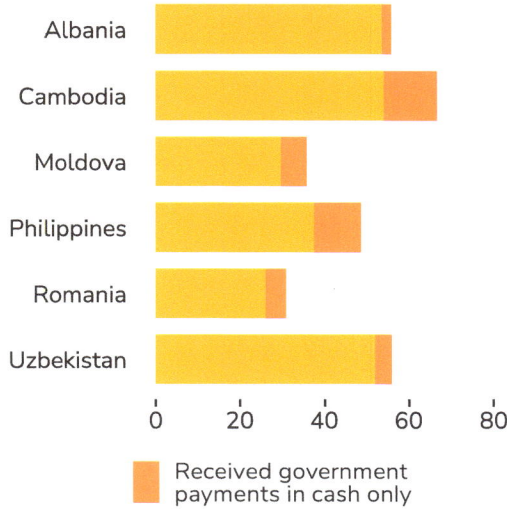

Received government payments in cash only

Source: Global Findex Database 2021.

Digitalizing private sector wage payments

Global Findex 2021 survey data reveal that businesses, like government, could also boost account ownership by paying their unbanked employees through accounts rather than in cash. Globally, 12 percent of unbanked adults—about 165 million people—received private sector wage payments in cash, including about 50 million women and about 70 million adults with incomes in the poorest 40 percent of households in their economy (map 2.6.2). Many of these wage earners already have a mobile phone.

Digitalizing private sector wage payments could reduce the share of unbanked adults by up to 36 percent in Myanmar and by up to about 20 percent in Cambodia, Egypt, Indonesia, and Pakistan, among other economies. In Pakistan, such digitalization would result in a 13 percentage point increase in account ownership and would bring around 20 million unbanked adults into the formal financial system. In Indonesia, digitalizing private

MAP 2.6.2

Globally, about 165 million unbanked adults received private sector wages in cash

Adults without an account receiving private sector wages in the past year in cash only, 2021

1 million
10 million
20 million

IBRD 46678 |
JUNE 2022

Source: Global Findex Database 2021.

Note: Data are not displayed for economies where the share of adults without an account was 5 percent or less or the share receiving private sector wages was 10 percent or less or for economies for which no data are available.

sector wage payments would similarly reduce the number of unbanked by up to 17 million adults and increase the account ownership rate by 9 percentage points (figure 2.6.3). Mobile phones could help facilitate electronic wage payments because more than 80 percent of adults who received private sector wages in cash in Cambodia, Egypt, and Pakistan, and about two-thirds in Indonesia, have a mobile phone.[38]

Digitalizing payments for agricultural products

Another opportunity to increase account ownership is by digitalizing payments for the sale of agricultural products. About 11 percent of unbanked adults in developing economies—145 million people— received agricultural payments in cash, according to the Global Findex 2021 survey findings, among them about 65 million women and 70 million adults with incomes in the poorest 40 percent of households in their economy (map 2.6.3). Nearly half of these

FIGURE 2.6.3

Digitalizing private sector wages could reduce the number of unbanked adults

Adults without an account (%), 2021

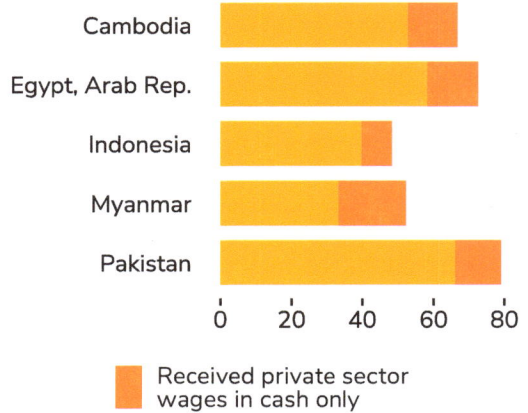

Received private sector wages in cash only

Source: Global Findex Database 2021.

MAP 2.6.3

In developing economies, about 145 million unbanked adults received agricultural payments in cash

Adults without an account receiving payments for agricultural products in the past year in cash only, 2021

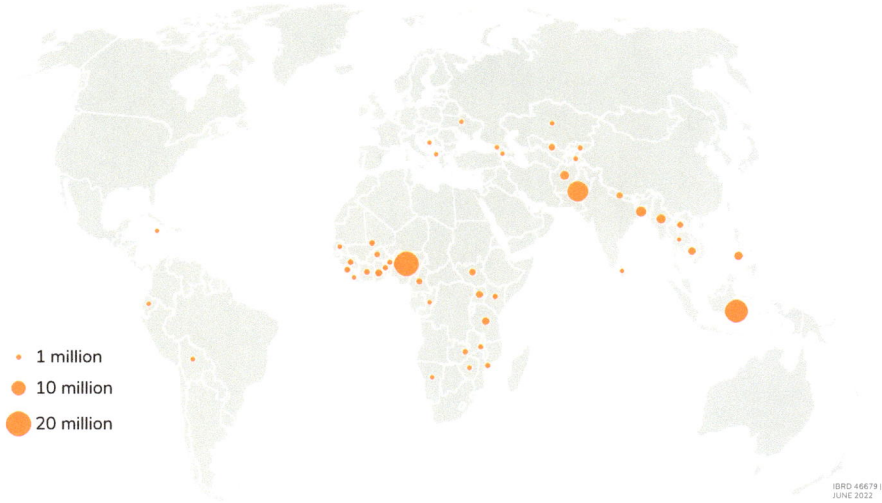

- · 1 million
- ● 10 million
- ⬤ 20 million

IBRD 46679 | JUNE 2022

Source: Global Findex Database 2021.
Note: Data on payments for agricultural products were not collected in most high-income economies. Data are not displayed for economies where the share of adults without an account was 5 percent or less or the share receiving payments for agricultural products was 10 percent or less or for economies for which no data are available.

---

38. Data in Myanmar were collected by phone survey and, by design, virtually all adults surveyed had a mobile phone.

FIGURE 2.6.4

Digitalizing agricultural payments could reduce the number of unbanked adults

Adults without an account (%), 2021

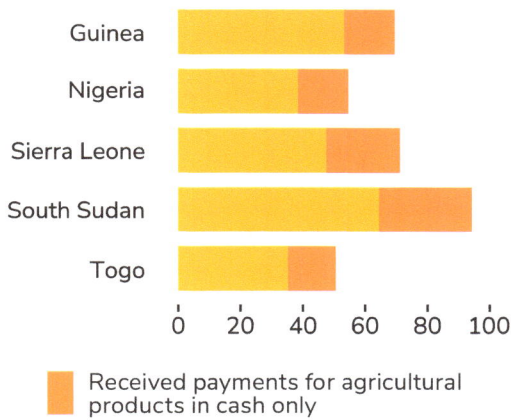

Received payments for agricultural products in cash only

Source: Global Findex Database 2021.

FIGURE 2.6.5

In developing economies, about 85 million unbanked adults saved semiformally

Adults without an account (%), 2021

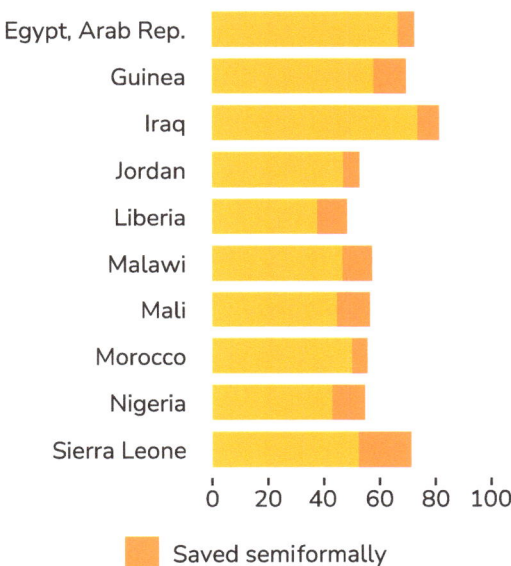

Saved semiformally

Source: Global Findex Database 2021.

145 million adults are in Sub-Saharan Africa. Digitalizing agricultural payments could increase the share of banked adults in this region by, on average, up to 10 percentage points, including by up to 30 percentage points in South Sudan, 24 percentage points in Sierra Leone, and up to 16 percentage points in Guinea, Nigeria, and Togo (figure 2.6.4).

Making agricultural payments through mobile phones could be especially helpful for unbanked farmers living in remote rural areas, many of whom have access to a phone. Fifty-five percent of unbanked adults in Sub-Saharan Africa who received agricultural payments in cash have a mobile phone.

Moving semiformal savings to accounts

Unbanked adults use a variety of methods to save, including semiformal methods such as entrusting money to a person outside the family or participating in a savings club. Rotating savings and credit associations are particularly important in Sub-Saharan Africa. Many people who choose this method may be drawn to the social aspect of savings clubs. But using an account might be an attractive alternative if financial institutions offered free or low-cost, interest-bearing savings products requiring little or no minimum balance.

Moving semiformal savings into accounts is an important opportunity to increase financial inclusion in some economies. The Global Findex 2021 survey finds that in developing economies about 85 million people—6 percent of unbanked adults—saved semiformally. In Sub-Saharan Africa alone, about 50 million unbanked adults saved semiformally, including about 35 million women. Moving semiformal savings into accounts could reduce the share of adults without an account by up to 19 percentage points in Sierra Leone and about 12 percentage points in Guinea, Liberia, Malawi, Mali, and Nigeria (figure 2.6.5). Outside of Sub-Saharan Africa, moving semiformal savings into accounts could reduce the share of adults without an account by up to 6–8 percent in Egypt, Iraq, Jordan, and Morocco.

Creating an enabling environment to leverage payments for increased financial inclusion

Shifting payments from cash into accounts can serve as an entry point to the formal financial system. The challenge for businesses and governments, however, is to ensure that digital payments are safer, more affordable, and more transparent than cash-based alternatives. Moreover, because the benefits of account ownership can accrue only to those who use an account to manage their finances, it will be important to design financial products to ensure that first-time users are able to use their account for more than simply cashing out the payment they receive into it.

Mobile phones and the internet can drive financial inclusion only if they are underpinned by reliable physical infrastructure—such as reliable electricity and mobile networks—and financial infrastructure—such as an adequate payments system with interoperability between providers, including both financial institutions and mobile money providers, and infrastructure and mechanisms to identify and verify users' identification. Financial infrastructure also includes a physical network to deliver payments to all corners of an economy and the regulations that protect consumers, help them develop the financial literacy skills they need to effectively use accounts, and create incentives for financial providers to deliver high-quality services.

Installing a physical network of branches or automated teller machines (ATMs) in every place that currently has none is not always a cost-effective way to reach an unbanked population. A common alternative is to form partnerships with post offices or retail shops to offer basic financial services using an "agent banking" model. The benefit is that these agents give account holders a way to deposit and withdraw cash safely, reliably, and conveniently at cash-in and cash-out points. Even if the ultimate goal is to promote digital payments, cash is still likely to be part of the financial ecosystem for a long time to come, especially where digital payments are not yet widely accepted for everyday purchases. A reliable cash-out experience is key to the success of digital payments.[39] Here, the "agent" could be a bank agent, a mobile money agent, or an ATM.[40]

It is important as well for governments to ensure that appropriate regulations and consumer protection safeguards are in place so that all users, and especially first-time account owners, benefit from digital financial services. Regardless of how people access and use their accounts, financial services need to be accessible for disadvantaged groups, including those who may have low literacy and numeracy skills. It is also important to determine the level of access that targeted users have to the devices they need to use digital financial services.

Finally, efforts to expand financial access through usage must take into account product design and operations to ensure their success. Although government payments have successfully increased the number of people worldwide who have accounts, past efforts have suffered from solvable shortcomings. A common complaint among those receiving government transfers as digital payments is, for example, that the payment products are difficult to use. Recipients have reported long lines at bank agents and have said that they struggle to get help when they have a question or a problem with their payments. Financial service providers now have a great opportunity to create value by designing and delivering positive customer experiences grounded in customer needs.[41]

---

39. Kendall and Voorhies (2014).
40. See Klapper and Singer (2017).
41. See CGAP (2016).

References

Aker, Jenny, Rachid Boumnijel, Amanada McClelland, and Niall Tierney. 2016. "Payment Mechanisms and Antipoverty Programs: Evidence from a Mobile Money Cash Transfer Experiment in Niger." *Economic Development and Cultural Change* 65 (1): 1–37.

Blumenstock, Joshua, Michael Callen, and Tarek Ghani. 2018. "Why Do Defaults Affect Behavior? Experimental Evidence from Afghanistan." *American Economic Review* 108 (10): 2868–901.

Breza, Emily, Martin Kanz, and Leora Klapper. 2020. "Learning to Navigate a New Financial Technology: Evidence from Payroll Accounts." Policy Research Working Paper 9495, World Bank, Washington, DC.

Breza, Emily, and Cynthia Kinnan. 2021. "Measuring the Equilibrium Impacts of Credit: Evidence from the Indian Microfinance Crisis." *Quarterly Journal of Economics* 136 (3): 1447–97.

CGAP (Consultative Group to Assist the Poor). 2016. "Customer Experience Toolkit." CGAP, Washington, DC. https://www.cgap.org/research/publication/customer-experience-toolkit#:~:text=The%20CGAP%20 Customer%20Experience%20Toolkit,advocate%20for%20it%20with%20leadership.

Dusza, Brian. 2016. "Liberian Teacher ePayments: Stepping Stones to Inclusion." *CGAP Blog*, December 1, 2016. https://www.cgap.org/blog/liberian-teacher-epayments-stepping-stones-inclusion.

Field, E., R. Pande, N. Rigo, S. Schaner, and C. Troyer Moore. 2021. "On Her Own Account: How Strengthening Women's Financial Control Impacts Labor Supply and Gender Norms." *American Economic Review* 11 (7): 2342–75.

Gelb, Alana, Anit Mukherjee, Kyle Navis, Mahmuda Akter, and Jannatul Naima. 2019. "Primary Education Stipends in Bangladesh: Do Mothers Prefer Digital Payments over Cash?" CGD Note, Center for Global Development, Washington, DC.

Gentilini, Ugo, Mohamed Almenfi, Hrishikesh T. M. M. Iyengar, Yuko Okamura, John Austin Downes, Pamela Dale, Michael Weber, et al. 2022. "Social Protection and Jobs Responses to COVID-19: A Real-Time Review of Country Measures" (English). Working paper, World Bank, Washington, DC. http://documents.worldbank .org/curated/en/110221643895832724/Social-Protection-and-Jobs-Responses-to-COVID-19-A-Real -Time-Review-of-Country-Measures.

Kendall, Jake, and Rodger Voorhies. 2014. "The Mobile-Finance Revolution: How Cell Phones Can Spur Development." *Foreign Affairs* 93 (2): 9–13.

Klapper, Leora, Margaret Miller, and Jake Hess. 2019. "Leveraging Digital Financial Solutions to Promote Formal Business Participation." World Bank, Washington, DC.

Klapper, Leora, and Dorothe Singer. 2017. "The Opportunities and Challenges of Digitizing Government-to -Person Payments." *World Bank Research Observer* 32 (2): 211–26.

Kvaran, Páll, and Gram Peters. 2017. "Making Mobile Money More Attractive to Farmers." Blog, UN Capital Development Fund. https://www.uncdf.org/article/2536/making-mobile-money-more-attractive-to-farmers.

Lasse, Brune, Xavier Giné, Jessica Goldberg, and Dean Yang. 2016. "Facilitating Savings for Agriculture: Field Experimental Evidence from Malawi." *Economic Development and Cultural Change* 64 (2): 187–220.

Ministry of Finance, India. 2022. "Pradhan Mantri Jan Dhan Yojana." Progress Report, Department of Financial Services. https://pmjdy.gov.in/account.

Muralidharan, Karthik, Paul Niehaus, and Sandip Sukhtankar. 2016. "Building State Capacity: Evidence from Biometric Smartcards in India." *American Economic Review* 106 (10): 2895–929.

OECD (Organisation for Economic Co-operation and Development. 2019. "Pensions at a Glance 2019: Country Profiles—Russian Federation." https://www.oecd.org/els/public-pensions/PAG2019-country-profile-Russian -Federation.pdf.

Wright, Richard, Erdal Tekin, Volkan Topalli, Chandeler McClellan, Timothy Dickson, and Richard Rosenfeld. 2017. "Less Cash, Less Crime: Evidence from the Electronic Benefit Transfer Program." *Journal of Law and Economics* 60 (2): 361–83.

CHAPTER 3

Financial Well-Being

Introduction

As highlighted in the introductions to chapters 1 and 2, the growth in ownership and usage of accounts could have positive impacts in the form of lower poverty rates, higher consumption, and more spending on education, health, and income-generating opportunities. Development goals also include improvements in well-being, which is related to a person's financial resilience (the ability to deal with an unexpected financial event), level of stress generated by common financial issues, and level of confidence in using financial resources. Financial inclusion can support well-being by helping people feel secure in their financial future.

The Global Findex 2021 survey assessed financial resilience by asking respondents whether they could come up with extra money if they had a significant unexpected expense and where they would get the money.

Global Findex 2021 survey headline findings on financial well-being

Financial resilience

- Fifty-five percent of adults in developing economies could access emergency money within 30 days without much difficulty.

- Family and friends are the first-line source of emergency money for 30 percent of adults in developing economies, but nearly half of those say the money would be hard to get. Reliance on family and friends is as high as 50 percent in the Middle East and North Africa.

- Women and the poor are less likely than men and richer individuals to successfully raise emergency money, and they are more likely to rely on family and friends as their go-to source.

- Adults in developing economies who save formally and use savings as their first-line source of money in an emergency are most likely to get money when they need it.

Financial worrying

- Sixty-three percent of adults in developing economies are very worried about one or more common financial expenses; the share for high-income economies is 33 percent of adults.

- About 50 percent of adults in developing economies are very worried about covering health expenses in the event of a major illness or accident, and over 36 percent say health care costs are their biggest worry.

- In Sub-Saharan Africa, worry over school fees is much more common than in other regions—54 percent of adults in Sub-Saharan Africa say they worry about it, and about 30 percent say it is their biggest worry.

- In developing economies, 82 percent of adults are very worried (52 percent) or somewhat worried (30 percent) about the continued financial toll of the COVID-19 pandemic.

Opportunities to support financial well-being

- One-third of mobile money account holders in Sub-Saharan Africa cannot use their account without help from a family member or an agent.

- One in five adults in developing economies who receive a wage payment into a financial institution account paid unexpected fees on the transaction.

These findings collectively point to a key area of concern related to financial inclusion: poor and financially inexperienced users may not be able to benefit from account ownership if they do not understand how to use financial services in a way that optimizes benefits and avoids consumer protection risks such as high and hidden fees, overindebtedness, fraud, and discrimination.[1] For example, inexperienced account owners who must ask a family member or a banking agent for help using an account may be more vulnerable to financial abuse. Consumer safeguards are also important for building public trust in the financial system.

Clear and easy-to-understand product terms may be especially important for adults with limited financial experience and capability. A mystery shopper audit of 1,000 microfinance firms in Uganda found that information on account costs was inconsistent; inexperienced borrowers received less information than experienced borrowers; and printed materials with product specifications were missing or in violation of regulatory guidelines.[2] A similar multicountry mystery shopper study evaluating financial institutions in Ghana, Mexico, and Peru found that when actors posed as potential customers, they were rarely offered the cheapest product or given the correct cost.[3] The reason may be that bank and microfinance institution staff are often paid more when they sign up customers for more expensive products, which gives them an incentive to withhold information or mislead potential customers.

Developing and enforcing clearer guidelines about effective disclosure and pricing transparency could help build trust in the financial system and help account holders recognize the difference between legitimate fees that are part of the price of service and illicit fees or overly high interest rates. Lab experiments in Mexico and Peru found that presenting participants with simplified statements of key facts about credit and savings products was strongly correlated with choosing a financial product that best fit their needs. By contrast, financial literacy had a much weaker impact on good financial decisions.[4]

Traditional classroom-based financial education has yielded mixed results,[5] whereas evidence suggests that financial training structured as learning-by-doing during financial account onboarding may lead to regular use of accounts and help users become savvier financial customers.[6] The evidence also points to the importance of real-time information to increase trust and usage—for example, through functionality that allows users to check balances using a card, phone, or the internet.[7]

The first section of this chapter on financial well-being presents the findings from the Global Findex 2021 survey related to financial resilience in the face of an unexpected expense. Specifically, the section presents answers to survey questions about the ability to access emergency money and where it would come from. Section 3.2 then examines financial stress and its causes, and section 3.3 explores opportunities to more effectively leverage financial products and the enabling infrastructure to help improve resilience.

---

1. For a discussion of consumer financial protection, see Garz et al. (2020).
2. Atuhumuza et al. (2019).
3. Giné and Mazer (2022).
4. Giné, Martínez, and Mazer (2017).
5. Bruhn et al. (2016); Bruhn, Ibarra, and McKenzie (2014); Doi, McKenzie, and Zia (2014); Fernandes, Lynch, and Netemeyer (2014).
6. Breza, Kanz, and Klapper (2020); Lee et al. (2021).
7. Bachas et al. (2021).

3.1 Financial resilience

3.1 FINANCIAL RESILIENCE

Every year, adults around the world face a significant financial repercussion stemming from, for example, job loss, ill health, crop failure, new caring responsibilities, or an essential repair to a vehicle or home. Failure to cope with these events can cause short-term harm and have long-lasting consequences. The ability of adults to cope financially when faced with a sudden drop in income or an unavoidable expense is known as financial resilience.

There are many ways to build financial resilience, and people may adopt different approaches, depending on the cause of the financial event, the size of the impact, how long-lasting it is likely to be, and other factors. Common approaches include calling on family and friends to bridge a finance gap, working additional hours to boost income, drawing down savings, taking out a formal loan, or selling an asset.

Yet these strategies may not be easy to deploy when a person needs them. For example, adding work hours may not be possible if the person's employer or informal labor market is in a slow season. A systemic shock that causes widespread economic damage across a community, such as the COVID-19 pandemic or an extreme weather event, can affect the ability of close family and friends to help. Savings committed to a community group, such as a rotating savings and credit association (ROSCA), may be inaccessible in the time frame needed.

Personal circumstances also affect financial resilience. Individuals' income level, whether they have an account, and how they use it all increase the probability that they have savings or the ability to receive an outside payment. Other factors, such as where individuals live and the size and diversity of their social network, also play a role because larger and more diverse social networks increase the chance that friends are not exposed to the same risks at the same time. There are also personal factors that go beyond income or social networks that influence individual choices—for example, how willing an individual is to negotiate for help with family members or concern about social status.

Rather than identify specific factors of the broader context and their importance in accounting for how people manage their financial challenges, the Global Findex 2021 survey findings presented in this chapter report on how respondents around the world evaluate their ability to manage financial shocks that fall outside routine and expected living costs.

To gauge financial resilience, the Global Findex 2021 survey asked respondents three questions:

1. Imagine that you have an emergency, what would be the main source of money you would use to come up with an amount equal to 5 percent of gross national income (GNI) per capita in local currency within the next 30 days? This is equivalent to about US$3,300 in the United States or US$320 in India.

2. How difficult would it be for you to come up with this money in the next 30 days?

3. How difficult would it be for you to come up with this money in the next seven days?

People can often access emergency money, but it is not always easy, and it takes time

In developing economies, 87 percent of adults said they could access one of several sources of emergency money within 30 days, including savings, formal borrowing, money from family or friends, work, or the sale of assets (figure 3.1.1). However, nearly one in three adults said it would be very difficult to come up with those funds. As a result, a much smaller share, 55 percent, was confident they could access the money when needed. In high-income economies, 79 percent of adults said they could raise emergency money with no or only some difficulty in 30 days. When asked about the difficulty of getting the emergency money in a week rather than a month, more adults responded by saying that the money would be very difficult to come up with. In developing economies, 85 percent of adults said they could come up with the money in a week, but only 41 percent could do so without significant difficulty.

All of the economies in which at least three in four adults feel confident about their ability to cover the costs of an emergency are high-income ones, except China and Ukraine.[8] National income per capita does not always correlate with financial resilience at the level of the economy, however. In high-income Chile, for example, 57 percent of adults said they could come up with emergency money without major difficulty, or roughly the same share as in upper-middle-income Ecuador, which has less than half of Chile's GNI per capita. In Mongolia, a lower-middle-income economy, 68 percent of adults can reliably raise emergency money, while in South Africa, an upper-middle-income economy, only 40 percent can (figure 3.1.2).

FIGURE 3.1.1

In developing economies, 55 percent of adults could access emergency money in 30 days with little or no difficulty

Adults assessing how difficult it would be to access emergency money in 30 and 7 days (%), 2021

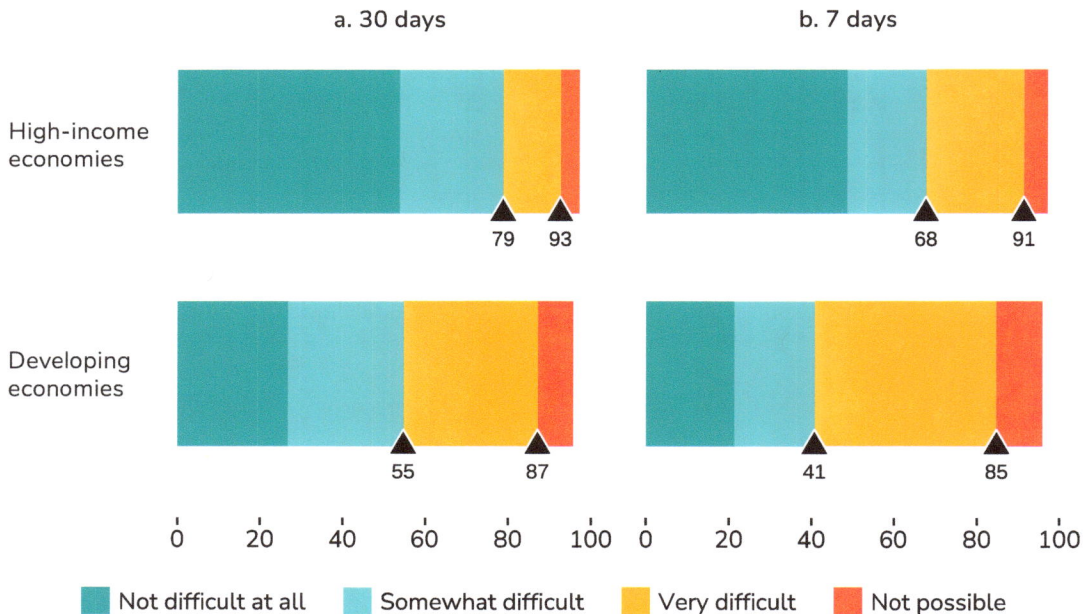

Source: Global Findex Database 2021.

Note: A small share of adults did not know or refused to disclose the level of difficulty they would face obtaining emergency money.

---

8. The data on China showed that a large share of adults in the country depended on savings to cover an emergency. By contrast, a dominant share of adults in Ukraine would have turned to family and friends.

FIGURE 3.1.2

Among economies, income group is not the sole driver of financial resilience

Adults who could come up with emergency money in 30 days with some or no difficulty (%), 2021

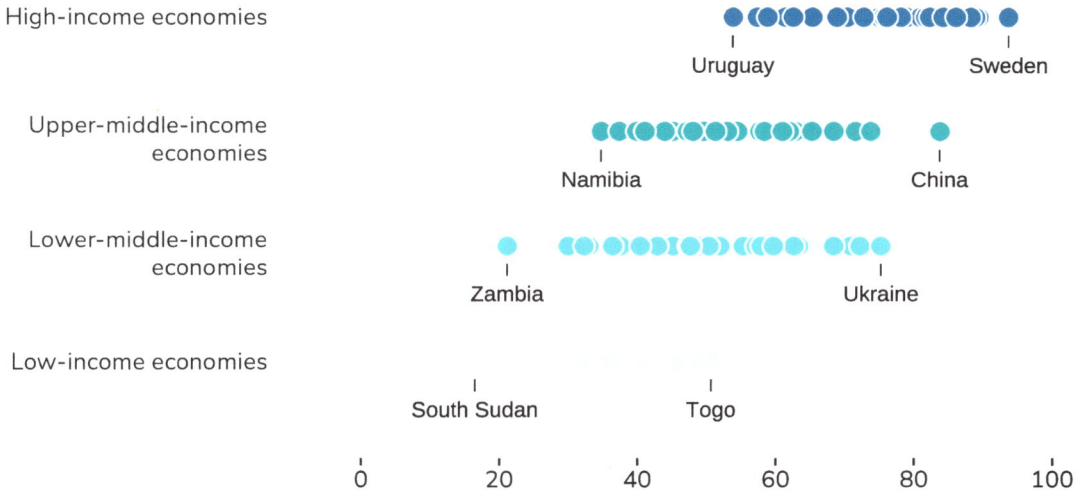

Source: Global Findex Database 2021.

These examples highlight the point made at the opening of this chapter that beyond differences between individuals (such as income, preferences, and behaviors), differences in financial resilience across economies are likely to be strongly influenced by country context (such as culture, policies, and financial development). This context could include differences in the financial infrastructure that shapes whether people have access to and use formal financial products (see chapter 2), government policies and social safety nets, and cultural factors that influence how optimistic people are and the types of emergencies people imagine when asked this question.

The source of emergency money varies among high-income and developing economies

Adults in different economies and income groups vary in how likely they are to turn to certain sources of emergency money. In high-income economies, savings is the preferred source of financing in an emergency: nearly 50 percent of adults say they would mainly use savings to come up with emergency money in 30 days (figure 3.1.3). In developing economies, by contrast, the two most common sources of funds are money from family or friends and earnings from work—nearly 60 percent of adults would rely on one of these as their main source of emergency money.

However, reliance on a certain source of emergency money is a separate issue from reliability. In developing economies, more than 50 percent of adults who say they would borrow or sell assets in an emergency also say that coming up with the money would be very difficult. Savings and earnings from work, on the other hand, are perceived as more reliable. On average, only 16 percent of adults who would use savings and 33 percent of adults who would work more also say it would be difficult to come up with the money.

FIGURE 3.1.3

In developing economies, work and social networks are the most common sources of emergency money, but they are not as reliable as savings

Adults identifying the source of, and assessing how difficult it would be to access, emergency money (%), 2021

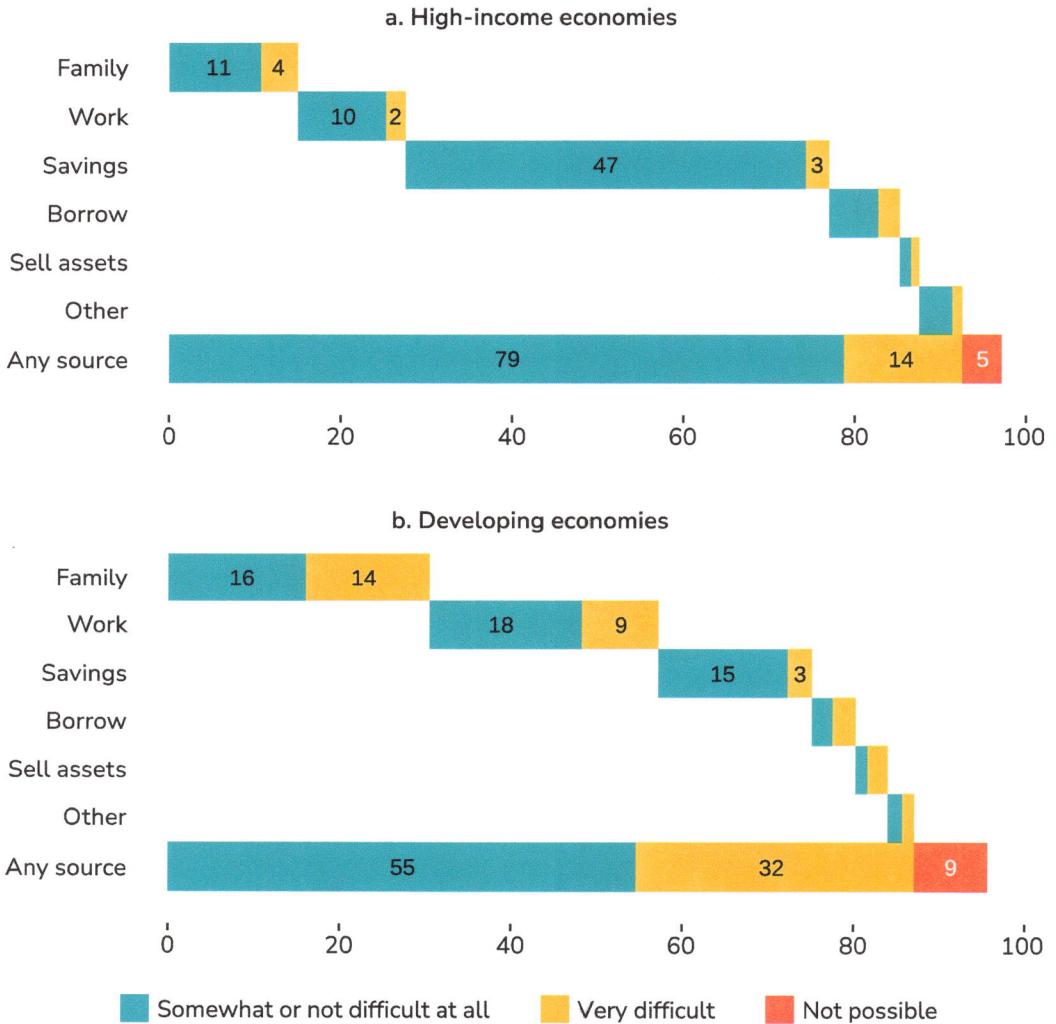

a. High-income economies

Family	11	4
Work	10	2
Savings	47	3
Borrow		
Sell assets		
Other		
Any source	79	14	5

b. Developing economies

Family	16	14
Work	18	9
Savings	15	3
Borrow		
Sell assets		
Other		
Any source	55	32	9

■ Somewhat or not difficult at all   ■ Very difficult   ■ Not possible

Source: Global Findex Database 2021.

Note: A small share of adults did not know or refused to disclose their main source of emergency money.

Family and friends are the most common source of emergency money in developing economies but are often unreliable

Digging deeper into the data from developing economies reveals that 30 percent of adults, on average, rely on their personal social network of family and friends for money in an emergency (figure 3.1.3). Four of the top five economies with the greatest dependence on family and friends for emergency financial assistance have had recent or ongoing episodes of violent conflict (Afghanistan, Iraq, Kosovo, and the West Bank and Gaza). More than half of adults depend on family in emergencies in the Middle East and North Africa (figure 3.1.4)—a region that also has relatively lower account ownership and usage of savings and borrowing (see chapters 1 and 2).

Even though social networks are the most common source of emergency money in developing economies, nearly half of adults who depend on their family and friends to navigate unexpected financial challenges say it would be very difficult to come up with the money. That number is higher, at 60 percent or more of the adults, in eight Sub-Saharan African economies (Kenya, Liberia, Mali, Namibia, Senegal, South Africa, South Sudan, and Zambia). In India, where a third of adults (33 percent) would mainly use family or friends to raise emergency money, about two-thirds of those adults say it would be very difficult to get the money.

The challenges associated with raising money from family may in part reflect the fact that the data were collected during the COVID-19 pandemic, when many members of the same family or community lost jobs or income simultaneously, making it difficult to help friends or relatives. The same dynamics may be in play during natural disasters or extreme weather events that affect an entire community—events that are becoming more frequent in the developing world.

Social networks are particularly important, and particularly unreliable, for adults living in the poorest 40 percent of households in an economy and for women (figure 3.1.5).

FIGURE 3.1.4

Adults in different regions prioritize different sources of emergency money—and see wide variations in resilience

Adults identifying the source of, and assessing how difficult it would be to access, emergency money (%), 2021

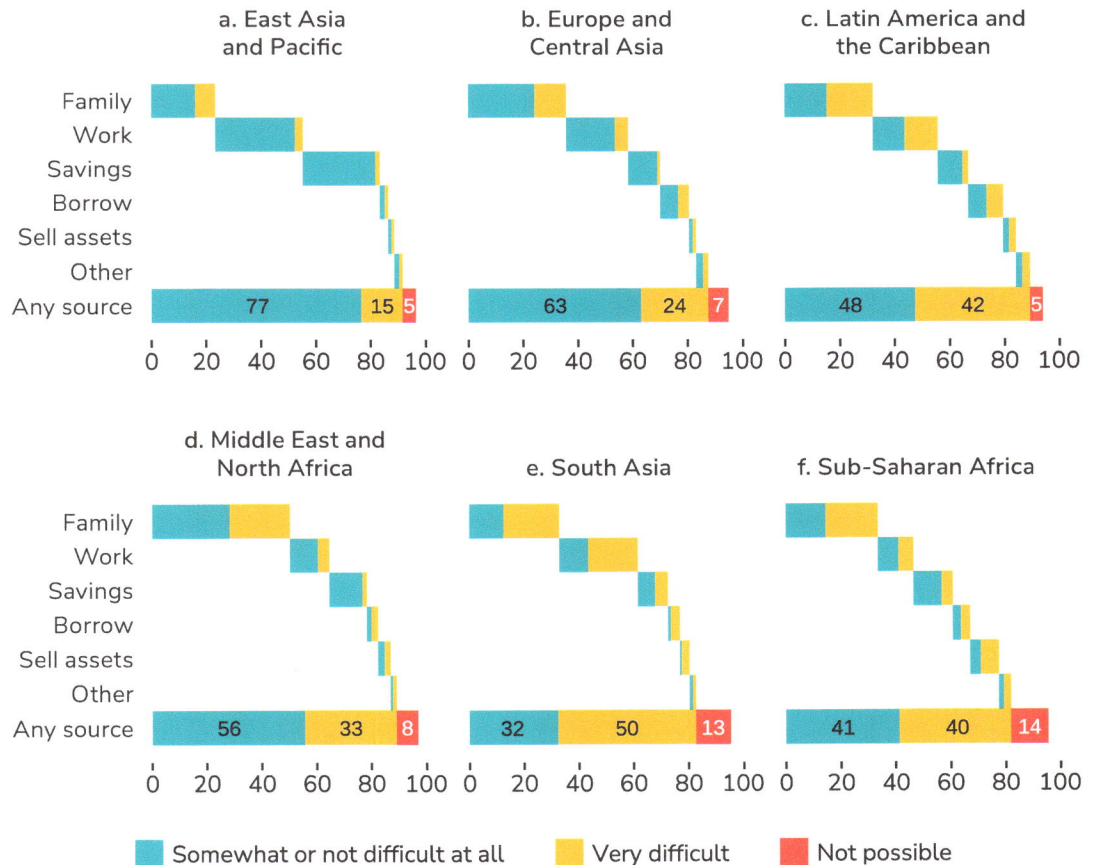

Source: Global Findex Database 2021.

Note: A small share of adults did not know or refused to disclose their main source of emergency money.

FIGURE 3.1.5

In developing economies, women and the poor are less resilient than men and those who are rich

Adults identifying the source of, and assessing how difficult it would be to access, emergency money (%), 2021

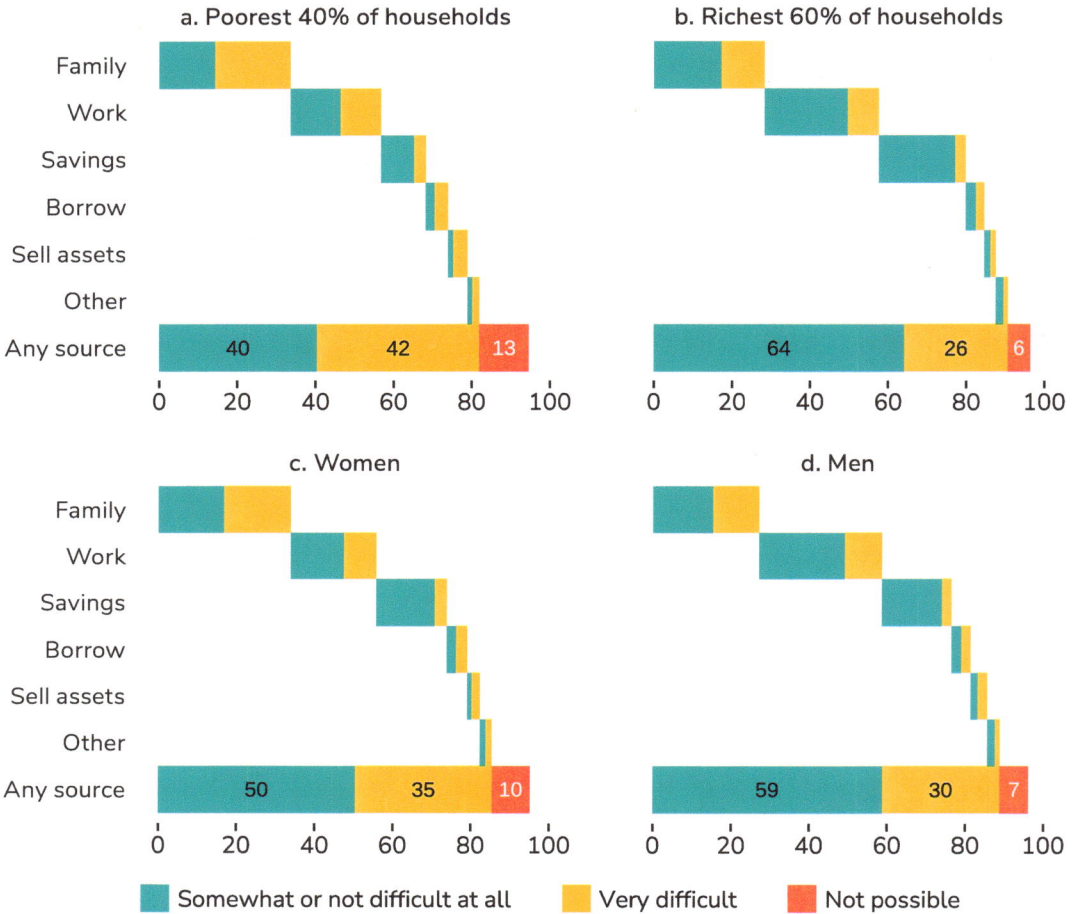

a. Poorest 40% of households

Family
Work
Savings
Borrow
Sell assets
Other
Any source | 40 | 42 | 13 |
0 20 40 60 80 100

b. Richest 60% of households

Family
Work
Savings
Borrow
Sell assets
Other
Any source | 64 | 26 | 6 |
0 20 40 60 80 100

c. Women

Family
Work
Savings
Borrow
Sell assets
Other
Any source | 50 | 35 | 10 |
0 20 40 60 80 100

d. Men

Family
Work
Savings
Borrow
Sell assets
Other
Any source | 59 | 30 | 7 |
0 20 40 60 80 100

■ Somewhat or not difficult at all   ■ Very difficult   ■ Not possible

Source: Global Findex Database 2021.

Note: A small share of adults did not know or refused to disclose their main source of emergency money.

In both high-income and developing economies, the poorest 40 percent of households are less able to cover the costs of an emergency than those in the richest 60 percent. Adults in lower-income households are less likely to use savings and more likely to rely on family support than adults in higher-income households, and they are more likely to find it very difficult to get the money.

Women are also more likely than men to say it would be very difficult to access emergency money. In developing economies, 50 percent of women said they could reliably come up with emergency money, compared with 59 percent of men. Gender differences in financial resilience are largest in Latin America and the Caribbean, where the resilience gender gap is 16 percentage points—that is, 39 percent of women say they can reliably access emergency money, compared with 56 percent of men.

One reason women may struggle to access emergency money is that their most popular source of funds in an emergency is family, which, as noted earlier, can be unreliable. In developing economies, women seem to have a harder time getting those funds from family as well: 50 percent of women who rely on family as their main source of emergency money say it would be very difficult, compared with 44 percent of men. These differences may also have to do with the composition of men's compared to women's social networks. Since men are more likely to work outside the home, they have greater opportunities to establish wider networks.

In developing economies, leveraging wages is more difficult for the self-employed than for the employed

Labor income is another common source of emergency money in developing economies. In some cases, adults facing an unexpected expense might work additional hours for a known employer or try to pick up additional, short-term work. In others, it could mean waiting for a paycheck or getting an advance from an employer.

In developing economies, 27 percent of adults, on average, would use labor earnings in an emergency. This share is higher in some East Asian economies and lower in the Middle East and North Africa and in Sub-Saharan Africa. For example, in China and Mongolia about 40 percent of adults would use labor income in an emergency. In Bangladesh, Brazil, and India, about 30 percent would do the same.

The difficulty encountered in raising money from work varies dramatically from one economy to the next. In Bangladesh, Brazil, and India, for example, over half of adults who would rely on work also said that it would be very difficult to raise the money in 30 days. Only 5 percent of adults in China who would use work said the same.[9]

In developing economies, adults who receive wage payments from an employer, when compared with adults who are self-employed, are significantly more likely either to use income from work in an emergency and to say raising money from work is not difficult. Regional or economy-level factors might also drive differences in the propensity to rely on work as a source of emergency money. These factors could include labor formality or informality or the amount of labor demand in relation to supply, both of which could influence how reliable wage work is compared with casual work and how easy it is to find additional work when needed.

In developing economies, formal savings is the most reliable source of emergency money, although less relied on

Among developing economies, the share of adults who primarily use savings as a source of emergency funds is between 1 percent in Afghanistan and 40 percent in Malaysia. Savings is the third most common source of emergency funds. On average, savings is perceived to be a more reliable source of emergency funds than other sources.

In developing economies, 18 percent of adults say they would rely on savings, and over 80 percent of adults who rely on savings say they could reliably get the money. In several developing economies, the share of adults who would rely on savings in an emergency is substantially higher. These economies include upper-middle-income economies such as China and Malaysia, where 33 percent and 40 percent of adults, respectively, say they would use savings to finance an emergency. Almost 90 percent of these adults also say they could reliably get the money. This finding is not surprising because about half of all adults in these two economies save formally. The reliability of formal savings in an emergency is also evident in Sub-Saharan Africa, where 14 percent of adults say they would rely on savings in an emergency. Seventy-two percent of these adults have an account, and 77 percent say it would not be difficult to get the money.[10]

---

9. In East Asia, wage and salaried workers make up 61.4 percent of total employment, compared with 25.1 percent of total employment in South Asia. In Europe and Central Asia, wage and salaried workers make up 82.4 percent of total employment, compared with 63.4 percent in Latin America and the Caribbean. These estimates correspond to data sourced from the International Labour Organization and compiled by the World Bank (https://datatopics.worldbank.org/jobs/topic/employment).

10. See section 2.2 in chapter 2 for data and analysis on how adults around the world use formal, semiformal, and other forms of savings.

Financial accounts could be used more consistently to boost resilience

Because richer individuals are more likely to own an account and have disposable income to save, determining the role of accounts in financial resilience is not straightforward. However, studies in developing economies that control for income and other factors find evidence linking account ownership to greater financial resilience, including increases in liquid savings or more effective risk sharing through social networks.

Among adults living in both the poorest 40 percent of households and the richest 60 percent, owning an account is associated with an increase in the likelihood of using savings as a primary source of emergency money and in the reliability of savings. These differences are amplified among richer individuals. For example, in low-income economies adults living in the poorest 40 percent of households with an account are more than twice as likely as adults without an account to say they would use savings in an emergency, whereas adults living in the richest 60 percent of households with an account are three times more likely to use savings than adults without one. Globally, people in developing economies who save formally and use savings as their first-line source of money in an emergency are most likely to get money when they need it.

Yet most adults in developing economies with accounts are not using them for emergency savings. In high-income economies, 96 percent of adults own an account, and 48 percent of account owners said they would use savings and not find it difficult to come up with the money to cope with an unexpected shock. But in developing economies, 71 percent of adults own an account, yet only 19 percent said they would use savings to cope with an emergency and that they would not find it very difficult to come up with emergency money. As discussed in chapter 2, digitalizing payments, expanding bank and mobile money agent networks, offering commitment savings accounts (which have features to discourage withdrawals), and leveraging technology (such as auto-deposit of savings) may help adults build stronger financial resilience.

3.2 Financial worrying

3.2 FINANCIAL WORRYING

The previous section on financial resilience focused on the ability to access financial resources to deal with an emergency expense or loss of income. Another dimension of financial well-being is the anxiety or worry that people feel about their financial lives. Not having sufficient protection from shocks, having trouble paying for basic family needs, or falling behind on personal financial goals influence how financially secure or stressed people feel. Of course, real-life circumstances have a huge impact on all of these factors. When people are barely meeting their living expenses with the income they have—and with no extra money for unexpected expenses—they are likely to worry more than people who have an income buffer. For that reason, it is logical to assume that poor people—and, in particular, poor people with limited or no savings and limited access to appropriate credit—are, on average, more likely to worry about money. That assumption is borne out in the findings from the Global Findex 2021 survey.

Beyond the objective reality of simply not having enough money, people also have subjective perceptions about their financial lives. These are complicated by personality traits, cultural norms, the economic context, social dynamics, available information about financial needs, and the social support programs available to people. The likely timing of an expense and how far away it is in the future are other major factors in worrying. For example, younger people may be more likely to worry about school fees and less likely to worry about old age. That does not mean that youth do not care about having enough money when they are older, but rather that they have more immediate concerns.

All of these factors influence how respondents answered the questions posed in the Global Findex 2021 survey intended to highlight the financial worries that prevail in a society. The answers can shed light on challenges that may not be clearly reflected in the data on account ownership and usage. Yet for all of the reasons just given, it is important when using the data in this section not only to have a concept of what worry means for an individual, but also to contextualize it in order to identify potential gaps that policies, financial access, product design, or user experience could address.

This section specifically examines responses to questions in the 2021 Global Findex survey asking respondents whether they were worried about their finances, how worried (somewhat worried or very worried) they were about four common issues that can lead to financial anxiety, and which issue they worry about the most. The specific issues are:

- Living expenses for old age
- Medical costs arising from a serious illness or accident
- Monthly bills and expenses
- School or education fees.

Adults in developing economies are more likely to worry about finances than adults in high-income economies

Adults in developing economies are considerably more worried about their financial lives than adults in high-income economies. In developing economies, about two-thirds of adults say they are very worried about any one of the four specified financial issues, whereas in high-income economies 21 percent or less say they are very worried about any one of these issues.

Nor do adults in developing economies worry about only one thing. Instead, 22 percent of adults are very worried about all four of the specified issues. In high-income economies, the share of adults very worried about all four financial concerns is only 4 percent (figure 3.2.1).

In developing economies, medical costs are the most common financial worry

In developing economies, the largest share of adults—52 percent—say they are very worried about not being able to pay medical bills in case of a serious illness or accident. Although paying medical bills is a common

Adults in developing economies were much more likely to be very worried about all four financial issues than were adults in high-income economies

Adults assessing their level of worry (%), 2021

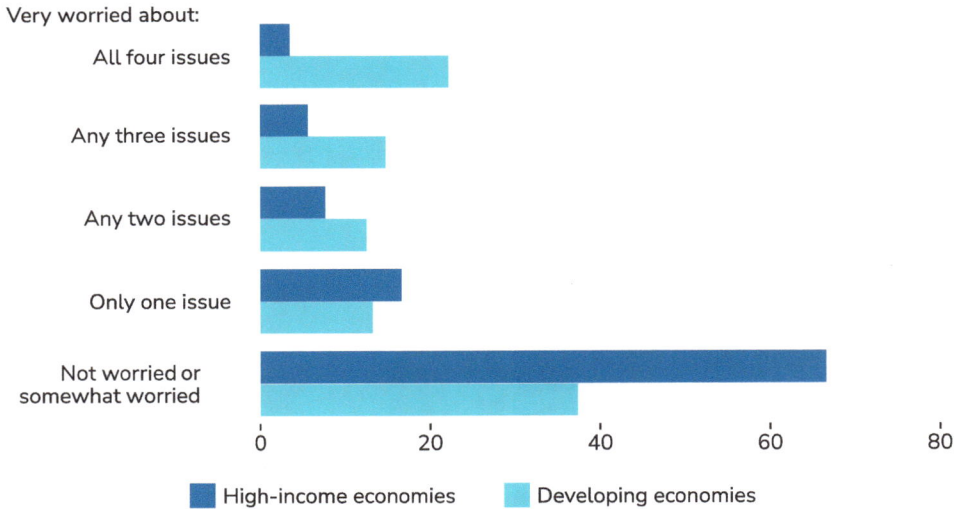

Source: Global Findex Database 2021.

Note: Survey respondents were asked to assess their level of worry about four common sources of financial stress: (1) money for old age; (2) paying for medical costs in the event of a serious illness or accident; (3) money to pay for monthly expenses or bills; (4) paying school or education fees.

financial concern, the Global Findex 2021 survey was fielded in 2021 during the COVID-19 pandemic, and, as a result, health and medical expenses may have been more on the mind of respondents. Responses may also reflect the quality and affordability of local health care providers.

Concerns around medical expenses are highest in Sub-Saharan Africa and South Asia, where about 64 percent of adults are very worried about them, and lowest in East Asia and the Pacific, where 38 percent of adults are very worried about them. In East Asia, there is considerable variation, however. For example, in China, Malaysia, and Thailand (all upper-middle-income economies), fewer than 40 percent of adults are very worried about medical expenses. In the lower-middle-income economies of Cambodia, Indonesia, and the Philippines, by contrast, nearly two in three adults (64 percent) are very worried about medical expenses. In low-income economies, over 70 percent of adults are very worried about medical expenses.

As for the common worries in high-income economies, one in five adults (20 percent) are very worried about paying for health care, and an equal share (21 percent) is very worried about finances in old age.

Respondents who worry about more than one financial issue were also asked which one they worry about the most. Including those who are only worried about a single issue (which is assumed to be their most significant worry), 36 percent of adults in developing economies say that medical costs is their biggest financial worry. Not having enough money for medical bills is the top financial concern in 64 of the 80 developing economies surveyed—again, not surprising because of the recent impact of the COVID-19 pandemic.

When broken down by region, worry about health costs remains the biggest worry for the largest share of adults in every developing region of the world (figure 3.2.2). Significant health events can force a person to stop working, creating both an income shock and an expense shock. It is therefore logical that worry about medical costs ranks so highly. This is, then, an opportunity for better financial protection related to health risks that require hospitalization or specialist care.

FIGURE 3.2.2

In developing economies in every world region, adults named medical expenses as their biggest financial worry

Adults identifying their biggest financial worry (%), 2021

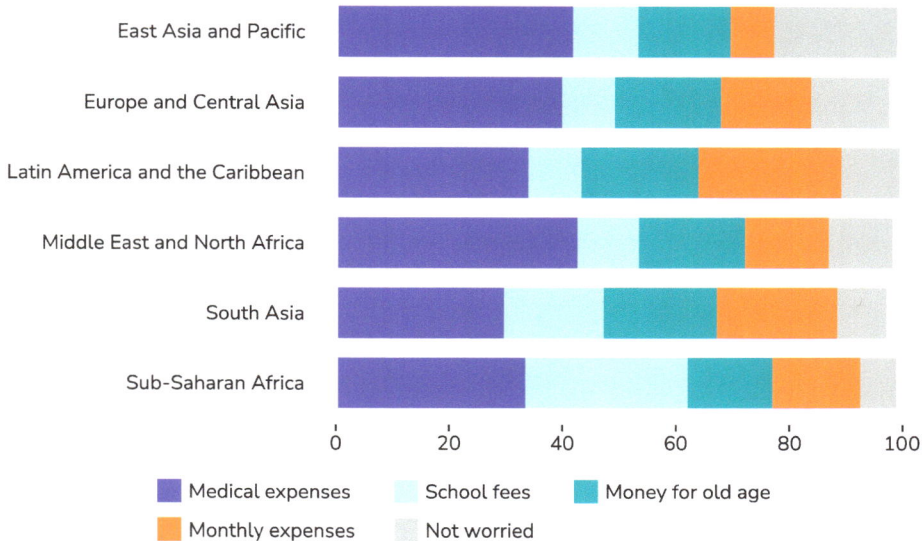

Source: Global Findex Database 2021.

Note: A small share of adults did not know or refused to disclose their main cause of worry.

Adults in Sub-Saharan Africa worry about school fees

Paying for education is a close second-biggest source of worry in Sub-Saharan Africa, where over half of adults (54 percent) are very worried about school financing, and 29 percent of adults name school fees as the issue of most concern. In part, this finding reflects demographics: 52 percent of the population in the region is below the age of 25, and so a large share of the adult population has school-age children.[11] The financial stress around education may also reflect the high out-of-pocket spending on school fees common in the region. Even families that use public schools are required to pay fees for uniforms and books in many Sub-Saharan African economies. Depending on whether the school in question requires a one-time payment for the entire school term or allows families to spread payments over months, the expense can put a significant dent in household finances. Meanwhile, fees can be higher for families that enroll their children in private schools. In Liberia, for example, 48 percent of primary school enrollment and 58 percent of secondary school enrollment are in private schools, and over 80 percent of adults are very worried about school financing.[12]

Some worry about paying for old age

Concerns around making ends meet in old age are most common in Sub-Saharan Africa and South Asia—over half of adults are very worried about old age in both regions. But frequently old age is not the biggest worry. Because adults typically have concerns about more than one area of financial life at the same time and because old age can seem further away than the medical bills or school fees due today, old age rarely ranks as the biggest financial worry. In Sub-Saharan Africa and South Asia, only 15 percent and 20 percent of adults, respectively, put old age at the top of their worry list.

---

11. United Nations (2019).
12. School enrollment data are from World Bank, World Development Indicators (SE.PRM.PRIV.ZS and SE.SEC.PRIV.ZS), https://databank.worldbank.org /source/world-development-indicators; United Nations (2019).

The region with the smallest share of adults who worry about old age is East Asia, where 28 percent of adults are very worried about old age. China pulls down this average because only one in five adults there are very worried about paying for old age. High savings rates in China may play a role in reducing concerns about retirement funding. In some of East Asia's lower-middle-income economies (such as Cambodia, Indonesia, the Lao People's Democratic Republic, and the Philippines), over half of adults are very worried about old age.

The financial impacts of COVID-19 are a significant source of worry

The COVID-19 pandemic has been both a major public health crisis and an economic crisis because of the financial impacts of public health measures such as lockdowns and restrictions on business operations. Financial worries related to the pandemic bridge the gap between concerns about medical bills and concerns about having sufficient income to meet day-to-day expenses.

When asked, over half of adults in the developing world feel very worried about the potential for continued financial hardship because of COVID-19 (figure 3.2.3). In South Asia and Sub-Saharan Africa, some two out of three adults (67 percent and 65 percent, respectively) say they are very worried about the personal financial toll of COVID-19. Women, the unemployed and self-employed, and adults in the poorest 40 percent of households are

FIGURE 3.2.3

In developing economies, women, the poor, and working-age adults were worried about the ongoing financial impacts of COVID-19

Adults assessing their worry about severe financial hardship due to COVID-19 (%), 2021

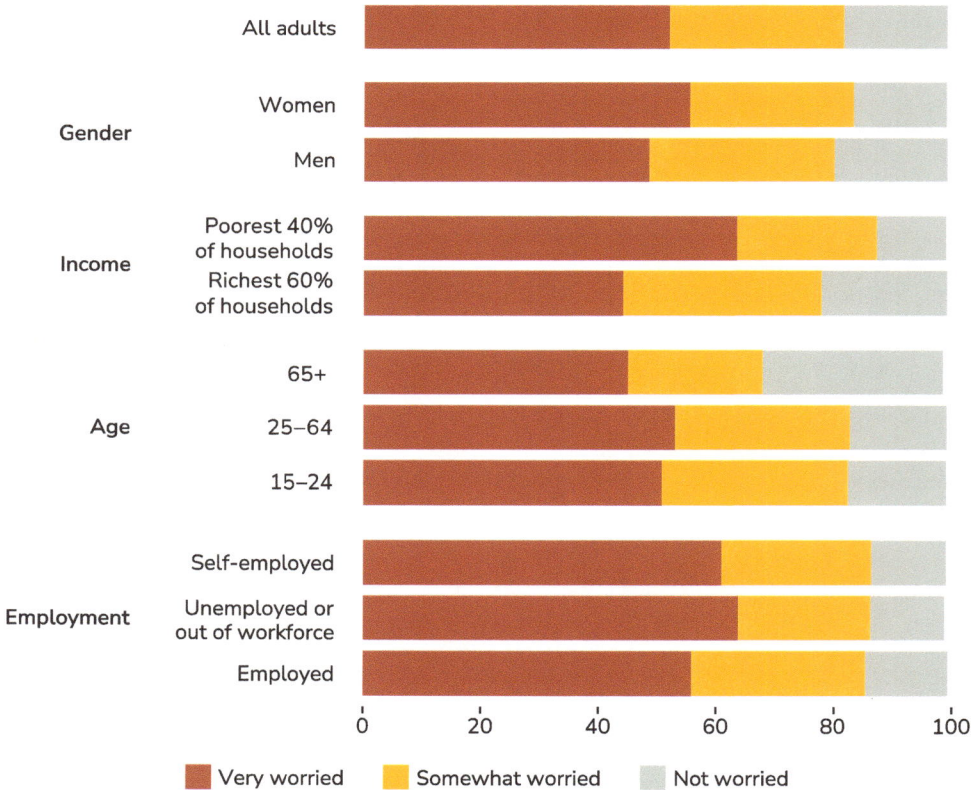

Source: Global Findex Database 2021.

Note: This question was only asked in developing economies. A small share of adults did not know or refused to disclose their level of worry.

more likely than men, wage employed workers, and adults in the richest 60 percent of households, respectively, to say they are very worried about facing continued financial hardship because of the pandemic.

Overall, these data provide one perspective on the toll the pandemic has taken on financial well-being, especially in low-income and lower-middle-income economies. The data confirm the regressive impact of the pandemic on more vulnerable populations. And this micro-level evidence on the experiences of individuals is consistent with the macro-level reality of a slower recovery in low-income economies.

Not surprisingly, poor adults worry more than higher-income adults about having enough money to pay monthly bills

The relationship between income and worry is also apparent for issues beyond COVID-19. Adults living in households in the poorest 40 percent of their economy's income distribution are about 20 percentage points more likely to be very worried about each of the four financial issues than adults in the richest 60 percent. In some economies, the differences are more extreme. In Brazil, for example, 72 percent of adults in the poorest 40 percent of households are very worried about not having enough money for monthly expenses, compared with the 35 percent of adults in the richest 60 percent of households. In Sri Lanka, 53 percent of the adults in the poorest 40 percent of households are very worried about not having enough money for old age, compared with only 19 percent of adults in the richest 60 percent of households.

In high-income economies, there are also differences in financial worrying between adults living in the poorest 40 percent of households and in the richest 60 percent of households. For example, in the United States, a third (33 percent) of adults in the poorest 40 percent of households are very worried about not being able to pay monthly bills, compared with 6 percent of adults in the richest 60 percent of households. In Greece, two-thirds (66 percent) of adults in the poorest 40 percent of households are very worried about not having enough money in old age, compared with 37 percent of adults in the richest 60 percent of households.

Globally, women and the poor are more likely than men and adults with higher incomes to worry about money

On average, women are moderately more worried about money issues than men. In developing economies, for example, 44 percent of women say they are very worried about not having enough money for routine monthly expenses or bills, compared with 39 percent of men. This difference of about 6 percentage points holds for other financial issues as well.

Both men and women tend to rank the same financial issues as the most pressing in both developing and high-income settings. However, men and women in a specific economy may rank their biggest financial concerns differently. For example, in India and Kenya women are over 10 percentage points more likely than men to say school fees are their biggest financial worry. Men in India and Kenya, on the other hand, are more likely to say that medical expenses worry them the most.

These findings are worth considering in light of recent research on intrahousehold bargaining between women and men, which has highlighted the different roles that household members play in generating and managing household finances.[13] These roles interact with social norms in a given economy and with the specific roles adopted in a given household, which may help put the gender-based differences in worrying in some context.

---

13. For a review of recent approaches to intrahousehold analysis, see Gomes, Haliassos, and Ramadorai (2020).

3.3 Opportunities to support financial well-being through the financial system

3.3 OPPORTUNITIES TO SUPPORT FINANCIAL WELL-BEING THROUGH THE FINANCIAL SYSTEM

The previous sections in this chapter highlighted two financial outcomes distinct from financial account ownership and usage that nevertheless matter for individuals and families: (1) their ability to come up with money to cover an extra or unexpected expense, and (2) their subjective concerns related to four common sources of potential financial stress. As those sections describe, unlike account ownership and account usage—which can be directly influenced by the financial sector by making products available, accessible, and helpful—financial well-being outcomes such as resilience and stress are influenced by many factors outside the financial system.

Meanwhile, within the financial system, financial service institutions and supportive regulators can play a role in driving financial well-being outcomes for consumers. The key question for financial service providers and policy makers is how can financial products and services, and the regulatory environment in which they operate, effectively help people achieve financial well-being? One answer is to create incentives for service providers to design and deliver products and services with demonstrated benefits to consumers. Another is to prevent and mitigate consumer risk and harm by identifying and weeding out bad actors and bad practices. Both are critical for improving resilience and reducing financial stress.

In developing economies, many adults need help using an account, which makes them vulnerable to bad information

The marketplace for retail financial services can be inherently complex to navigate. Furthermore, the speed with which technological advances and other innovations enter the market can create challenges for the regulators tasked with ensuring a stable, safe, and equitable financial system, and for the consumers to whom new products and services appeal. Mobile devices, agent networks, and software applications have transformed how people move and manage their money in every region of the world. Although millions of people have been able to take advantage of these offerings, the ability to use them requires access to a mobile device, enough income to afford mobile network access costs, and digital skills such as the ability to activate a digital wallet or account, navigate user interfaces, manage passwords, and use authentication services. For example, a recent study in Malawi found that digital loans taken out in response to a text message–driven mass marketing campaign were less likely to be repaid.[14] And in Mexico, the speed with which internet-based loans can be arranged is associated with lower loan repayment.[15]

Atop these challenges are risks for consumers, including lack of transparency about fees and other terms of service, aggressive marketing, poor dispute resolution, data or identity theft, mobile app fraud, and other threats.[16] Many of these risks are not new, but they can be amplified given the reach and convenience of digital technologies. Women, who often have less prior financial experience, may be more exposed to financial abuse. For example, a nationally representative survey in Côte d'Ivoire found that women are less likely to understand the financial products offered through their phones (22 percent of women, compared with 18 percent of men) and more likely to lose money to scams (16 percent of women, compared with 12 percent of men).[17]

Responses to Global Findex 2021 survey questions reveal the ways in which respondents may be ill-equipped to use financial account functionality or, in the case of credit, to pay back a loan. As for a consumer's capacity to use digital financial services, the survey asked respondents about their ability to use their account and found that in Sub-Saharan Africa, one in three (31 percent) mobile money account holders cannot use their account without help (figure 3.3.1). This finding is instructive for the way it quantifies the share of adults who could be vulnerable to certain forms of consumer risks. In some economies, this share is substantially higher.

---

14. Brailovskaya, Dupas, and Robinson (2021).
15. Burlando, Kuhn, and Prina (2021).
16. Chalwe-Mulenga and Duflos (2021).
17. CGAP (2022).

FIGURE 3.3.1

In Sub-Saharan Africa, about 30 percent of mobile money account owners, on average, need help to use their account

Adults with a mobile money account (%), 2021

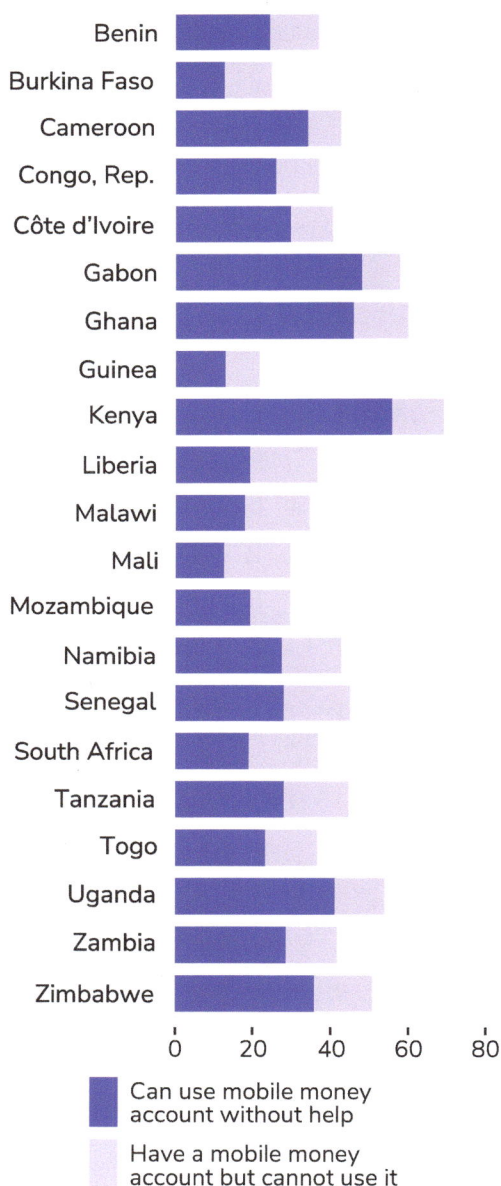

Legend:
- ■ Can use mobile money account without help
- ▨ Have a mobile money account but cannot use it

Source: Global Findex Database 2021.

For example, in Liberia, Malawi, and South Africa more than 50 percent of mobile money users need help using their account. Women are more likely than men to need assistance and therefore are at higher risk. For example, one study of government-to-person (G2P) mobile payments found that women were significantly more likely than men to send a representative to cash out government transfer payments.[18] Women are also more likely to report that their transfer was spent by another family member and to say they had to pay a fee or a tip to an agent to get their money when, officially, there should have been no charge. A proven way to improve financial skills is by encouraging use of accounts, such as by making payments directly into an account, as discussed in chapter 2. Research has shown the benefits of "learning by doing"—for example, factory workers in Bangladesh paid into an account also learned to use their account without assistance.[19]

As for consumer risks, the Global Findex 2021 survey asked adults in developing economies who reported receiving a wage payment into an account whether they paid higher fees than expected to receive it (figure 3.2.2).[20] Although the responses do not reveal whether a bank or an agent charged illicit fees, or whether recipients did not understand the established fee schedule for their account, they do indicate that one in five adults in developing economies who received a private or public sector wage payment into a financial institution account paid higher fees than expected. In several Europe and Central Asia economies such as Bulgaria, Moldova, North Macedonia, and Serbia, where wages are typically paid into financial institution accounts, more than one in four adults receiving a wage payment into a financial institution account paid unexpected fees.

Unexpected fees were also reported for wage payments put directly into a mobile money account (figure 3.3.3). For example, in Uganda over 40 percent of adults receiving wage payments reported unexpected fees, as did almost one in four wage payment recipients in Kenya. Several studies cited in the introduction to this chapter

---

18. Glynn-Broderick and Koechlein (2021).
19. Breza, Kanz, and Klapper (2020).
20. A caveat is that it is not known whether the payment was recently digitalized because research shows that digital payment recipients build financial capability over time. It may be that adults who recently received their first digital payments, such as a pandemic relief payment, were less familiar with related fees.

FIGURE 3.3.2

In developing economies, one in five wage recipients, on average, paid higher fees than expected to receive their wages directly into an account

Adults receiving a wage payment into a financial institution account (%), 2021

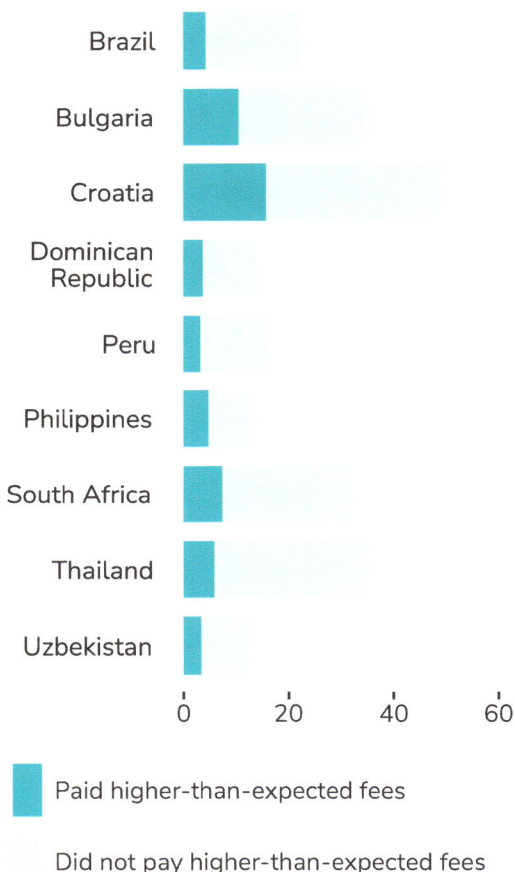

- Paid higher-than-expected fees
- Did not pay higher-than-expected fees

Source: Global Findex Database 2021.

FIGURE 3.3.3

In certain economies, the share of wage recipients paying unexpected fees to receive their money into an account was as high as 40 percent

Adults receiving a wage payment into a mobile money account (%), 2021

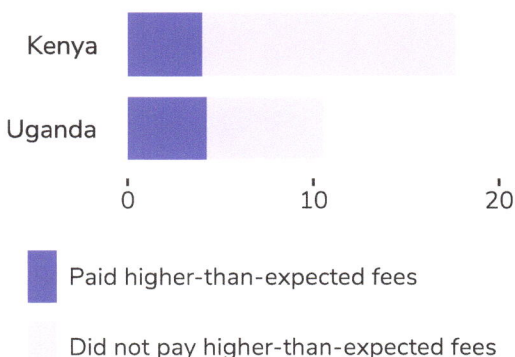

- Paid higher-than-expected fees
- Did not pay higher-than-expected fees

Source: Global Findex Database 2021.

charges, which allow people without a smartphone or data or internet connection to use mobile banking, were hidden and therefore completely unexpected by users.[21]

These examples highlight the large asymmetries of information that can be used to take advantage of consumers. Digital technology can also help bridge those asymmetries, however, and empower consumers with the information needed to build trust and greater confidence in the financial system.[22] Product functionality and design can help. Between 2017 and 2021, the share of adults with an account at a financial institution who used a mobile phone or the internet to check their balance went up from 18 percent to 33 percent in developing economies and from 56 percent to 70 percent in high-income economies (figure 3.3.4). Brazil, China, the Russian Federation, and South Africa saw substantial gains in the share of adults using mobile devices or the internet to check account balances. Other economies with high rates of account ownership, such as India and Indonesia, still have room to increase the share of account holders that use digital channels to look up account information (figure 3.3.5).

reveal inconsistencies in account disclosures and transparency related to transaction prices, either of which could explain these real-world experiences shared by respondents. In many cases highlighted in the literature, the true costs of digital transactions were inconsistent with the prices published in tariff guides or reported by an agent. Some fees, such as Unstructured Supplementary Service Data (USSD)

---

21. See, for example, Annan (2022); Annan and Giné (n.d.); Gwer et al. (2019).
22. For a discussion, see Feyen et al. (2021).

FIGURE 3.3.4

In developing economies, a third of adults used digital channels to check account balances

Adults with a financial institution account (%), 2017–21

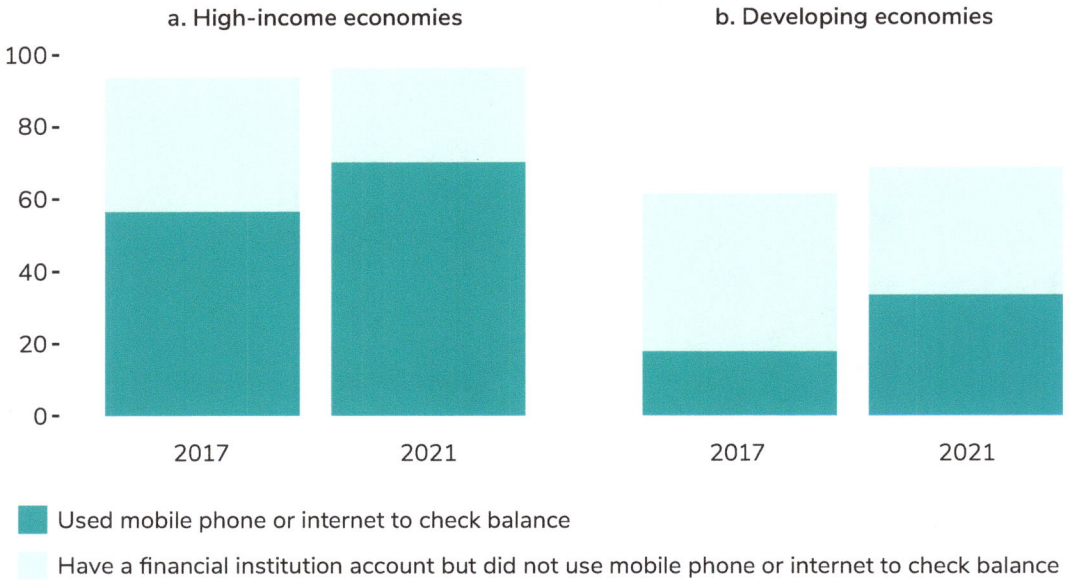

a. High-income economies

b. Developing economies

■ Used mobile phone or internet to check balance

▢ Have a financial institution account but did not use mobile phone or internet to check balance

Source: Global Findex Database 2021.

Sharing the responsibility for financial well-being among consumers, regulators, and financial institutions

There is growing recognition that financial well-being should not fall exclusively on the shoulders of consumers but should be a shared responsibility. As the financial industry and consumers shift to digital financial services, financial regulators and supervisory agencies should develop better supervisory monitoring systems to identify the types of financial risks in the market and measure their frequency and impact.[23] Frauds, scams, and pricing and marketing practices can evolve quickly using technology and as a result require more diligent monitoring by supervisors.

Meanwhile, it is also important to require financial providers to take steps to ensure that users of digital financial services fully understand providers' disclosures about product features and fees. Although disclosures are important for all financial products and much of the same information will apply, expanded disclosures for digital and fintech offerings may be necessary. For example, financial product terms and conditions may be harder to review using digital channels (such as a mobile phone) and thus require different approaches to the disclosure of basic features and key terms.[24] Although consumers understand that financial institutions must charge fees to cover operational costs, they often complain about the lack of transparency about when and how much they will be charged. Research in the United States has found that consumers became significantly more attentive to expense ratios and short-term performance after a 2012 reform mandating fee and performance

---

23. For additional information, see Consultative Group to Assist the Poor, "Market Monitoring for Financial Consumer Protection," https://www.cgap.org /topics/collections/market-monitoring/tools.

24. Boeddu and Chien (2018).

FIGURE 3.3.5

In some developing economies with high account ownership, many used digital channels to check account balances

Adults with a financial institution account (%), 2017–21

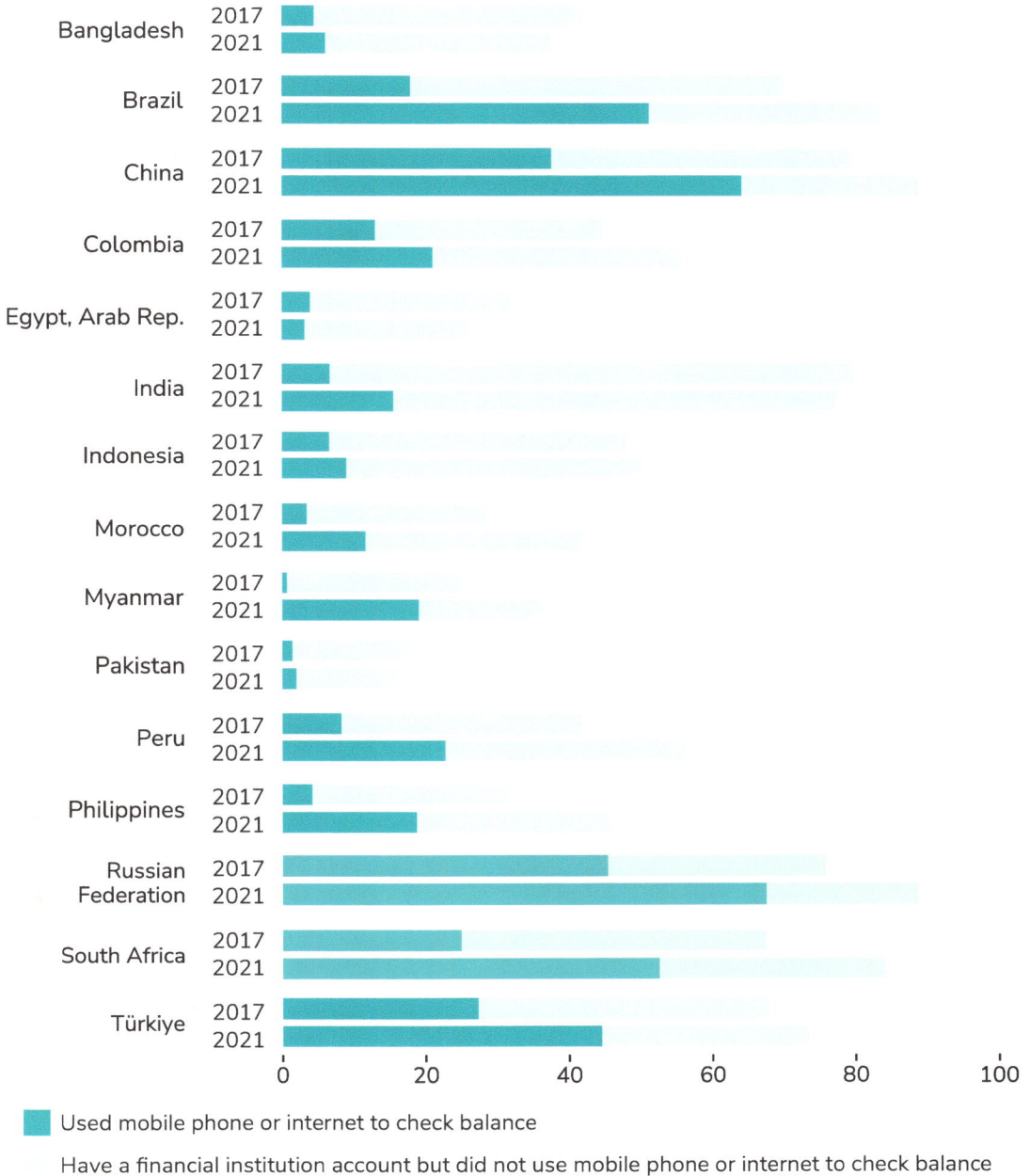

		Used mobile phone or internet to check balance	Have a financial institution account but did not use mobile phone or internet to check balance

Bangladesh — 2017, 2021

Brazil — 2017, 2021

China — 2017, 2021

Colombia — 2017, 2021

Egypt, Arab Rep. — 2017, 2021

India — 2017, 2021

Indonesia — 2017, 2021

Morocco — 2017, 2021

Myanmar — 2017, 2021

Pakistan — 2017, 2021

Peru — 2017, 2021

Philippines — 2017, 2021

Russian Federation — 2017, 2021

South Africa — 2017, 2021

Türkiye — 2017, 2021

(x-axis: 0, 20, 40, 60, 80, 100)

■ Used mobile phone or internet to check balance

Have a financial institution account but did not use mobile phone or internet to check balance

Source: Global Findex Database 2021.

disclosures for the investment options in individual retirement plans.[25] A possible remediation approach might be to establish clear guidelines for financial institutions about disclosures and transparency, as well as sound enforcement practices to ensure compliance.

Although the idea is to hold financial institutions accountable for harmful practices, preventing harm also includes informing consumers about the risks of predatory financial practices and what they look like. Because of the growing use of digital financial services by less educated adults and other vulnerable groups, it is important that financial service providers offer this information in plain language and in a format that users can easily understand.

Financial service providers can also invest in and draw on behavioral insights and design research. Examples include incorporating product design features that help people act on preestablished intentions, such as building savings for an emergency or for a specific goal. Behavioral insights can also help financial institutions communicate more effectively with customers, provide clear and complete information about costs, highlight salient details, and ensure that the benefits and risks of financial products and services are understood by customers.

25. Kronlund et al. (2021).

References

Annan, Francis. 2022. "Misconduct and Reputation under Imperfect Information." https://ssrn.com/abstract=3691376.

Annan, Francis, and Xavier Giné. No date. "Measuring the True Cost of Digital Transactions in Uganda." Research Brief, Innovations for Poverty Action, Washington, DC.

Atuhumuza, Elly, Xavier Giné, Rafe Mazer, and Joeri Smits. 2019. "Mystery Shopping Assessment of Credit Cost Disclosures in Uganda." Study Summary, Innovations for Poverty Action, New Haven, CT.

Bachas, Pierre, Paul Gertler, Sean Higgins, and Enrique Seira. 2021. "How Debit Cards Enable the Poor to Save More." *Journal of Finance* 76 (4): 1913–57.

Boeddu, Gian Luciano, and Jennifer Chien. 2018. *Financial Consumer Protection and Fintech: An Overview of New Manifestations of Consumer Risks and Emerging Regulatory Approaches*. Washington, DC: World Bank.

Brailovskaya, Valentina, Pascaline Dupas, and Jonathan Robinson. 2021. "Is Digital Credit Filling a Hole or Digging a Hole? Evidence from Malawi." Working Paper No. 1096, Stanford King Center on Global Development, Stanford, CA.

Breza, Emily, Martin Kanz, and Leora F. Klapper. 2020. "Learning to Navigate a New Financial Technology: Evidence from Payroll Accounts." Working paper, National Bureau of Economic Research, Cambridge, MA.

Bruhn, Miriam, Gabriel Lara Ibarra, and David McKenzie. 2014. "The Minimal Impact of a Large-Scale Financial Education Program in Mexico City." *Journal of Development Economics* 108 (May): 184–89. https://doi.org/10.1016/j.jdeveco.2014.02.009.

Bruhn, Miriam, Luciana de Souza Leao, Arianna Legovini, Rogelio Marchetti, and Bilal Zia. 2016. "The Impact of High School Financial Education: Evidence from a Large-Scale Evaluation in Brazil." *American Economic Journal: Applied Economics* 8 (4): 256–95.

Burlando, Alfredo, Michael A. Kuhn, and Silvia Prina. 2021. "Too Fast, Too Furious? Digital Credit Delivery Speed and Repayment Rates." UC Berkeley CEGA Working Papers, University of California Berkeley.

CGAP (Consultative Group to Assist the Poor). 2022. "CGAP and Côte d'Ivoire's Ministry of Economy and Finance Host Roundtable." Press release. https://www.cgap.org/news/cgap-and-cote-divoires-ministry-economy-and-finance-host-roundtable.

Chalwe-Mulenga, Majorie, and Eric Duflos. 2021. "The Evolving Nature and Scale of Consumer Risks in Digital Finance." CGAP (blog), October 19, 2021. Consultative Group to Assist the Poor, Washington, DC.

Doi, Yoko, David McKenzie, and Bilal Zia. 2014. "Who You Train Matters: Identifying Combined Effects of Financial Education on Migrant Households." *Journal of Development Economics* 109: 39–55.

Fernandes, Daniel, John G. Lynch, Jr., and Richard G. Netemeyer. 2014. "Financial Literacy, Financial Education, and Downstream Financial Behaviors." *Management Science* 60 (8): 1861–83.

Feyen, Erik, Jon Frost, Leonardo Gambacorta, Harish Natarajan, and Matthew Saal. 2021. "Fintech and the Digital Transformation of Financial Services: Implications for Market Structure and Public Policy." BIS Paper No. 117, Bank for International Settlements, Basel, Switzerland.

Garz, Seth, Xavier Giné, Dean Karlan, Rafe Mazer, Caitlin Sanford, and Jonathan Zinman. 2020. "Consumer Protection for Financial Inclusion in Low and Middle Income Countries: Bridging Regulator and Academic Perspectives." Working Paper 28262, National Bureau of Economic Research, Cambridge, MA.

Giné, Xavier, Cristina Martínez, and Rafe Mazer. 2017. "Information Disclosure and Demand Elasticity of Financial Products: Evidence from a Multi-Country Study." Policy Research Working Paper 8210, World Bank, Washington, DC.

Giné, Xavier, and Rafael Keenan Mazer. 2022. "Financial (Dis-)Information: Evidence from a Multi-Country Audit Study." *Journal of Public Economics* 208 (April).

Glynn-Broderick, Kate, and Liz Koechlein. 2021. "Are Mobile Payments Reaching Men and Women Equally? Latest Findings on How G2P Payments Are Working in Bangladesh." *Innovations for Poverty Action* (blog), July 7, 2021. https://www.poverty-action.org/blog/are-mobile-payments-reaching-men-and-women -equally-latest-findings-how-g2p-payments-are-working.

Gomes, Francisco, Michael Haliassos, and Tarun Ramadorai. 2020. "Household Finance." *Journal of Economic Literature* 59 (3): 919–1000.

Gwer, Francis, Paul Gubbins, Edoardo Totolo, and Jack Odero. 2019. *Cost of Banking, 2019*. Nairobi: FSD Kenya. https://www.fsdkenya.org/wp-content/uploads/2019/12/Cost-of-banking-2019.pdf.

Kronlund, Mathias, Veronika K. Pool, Clemens Sialm, and Irina Stefanescu. 2021. "Out of Sight No More? The Effect of Fee Disclosures on 401(k) Investment Allocations." *Journal of Financial Economics* 141 (2): 644–68.

Lee, Jean N., Jonathan Morduch, Saravana Ravindran, Abu S. Shonchoy, and Hassan Zaman. 2021. "Poverty and Migration in the Digital Age: Experimental Evidence on Mobile Banking in Bangladesh." *American Economic Journal: Applied Economics* 13 (1): 38–71.

United Nations. 2019. *World Population Prospects 2019, Volume II, Demographic Profiles* (ST/ESA/SER.A/427). https://population.un.org/wpp/Graphs/1_Demographic%20Profiles/Sub-Saharan%20Africa.pdf.

Survey Methodology

The indicators in the Global Findex 2021 database are drawn from survey data covering almost 128,000 people in 123 economies, representing 91 percent of the world's population (see table A.1 for a list of the economies included). The survey was carried out over the 2021 calendar year by Gallup, Inc., as part of its Gallup World Poll, which since 2005 has annually conducted surveys of approximately 1,000 people in each of more than 160 economies and in over 150 languages, using randomly selected, nationally representative samples. The target population is the entire civilian, noninstitutionalized population age 15 and up.

Interview procedure

In most developing economies, Global Findex data have traditionally been collected through face-to-face interviews. Surveys are conducted face-to-face in economies where telephone coverage represents less than 80 percent of the population or where in-person surveying is the customary methodology. However, because of ongoing COVID-19–related mobility restrictions, face-to-face interviewing was not possible in some of these economies in 2021. Phone-based surveys were therefore conducted in 67 economies that had been surveyed face-to-face in 2017 (see map A.1). These 67 economies were selected for inclusion based on population size,

A number of economies switched from face-to-face to phone-based surveys in 2021

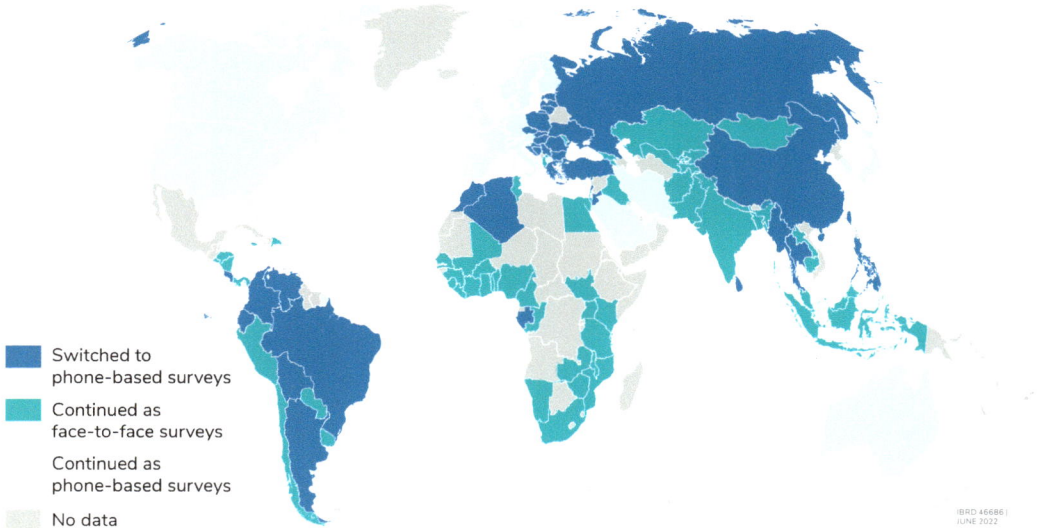

Switched to phone-based surveys

Continued as face-to-face surveys

Continued as phone-based surveys

No data

IBRD 46686
JUNE 2022

Sources: Global Findex Database 2021; Gallup World Poll.
Note: Iraq was surveyed using a phone-based survey in 2017 but switched to face-to-face in 2021.

phone penetration rate, COVID-19 infection rates, and the feasibility of executing phone-based methods where Gallup would otherwise conduct face-to-face data collection, while complying with all government-issued guidance throughout the interviewing process. Gallup takes both mobile phone and landline ownership into consideration. According to Gallup World Poll 2019 data, when face-to-face surveys were last carried out in these economies, at least 80 percent of adults in almost all of them reported mobile phone ownership.[1] All samples are probability-based and nationally representative of the resident adult population. Phone surveys were not a viable option in 17 economies that had been part of previous Global Findex surveys, however, because of low mobile phone ownership and surveying restrictions. Data for these economies will be collected in 2022 and released in 2023.[2]

In economies where face-to-face surveys are conducted, the first stage of sampling is the identification of primary sampling units. These units are stratified by population size, geography, or both, and clustering is achieved through one or more stages of sampling. Where population information is available, sample selection is based on probabilities proportional to population size; otherwise, simple random sampling is used.

Random route procedures are used to select sampled households. Unless an outright refusal occurs, interviewers make up to three attempts to survey the sampled household. To increase the probability of contact and completion, attempts are made at different times of the day and, where possible, on different days. If an interview cannot be obtained at the initial sampled household, a simple substitution method is used.

Respondents are randomly selected within the selected households. Each eligible household member is listed, and the hand-held survey device randomly selects the household member to be interviewed. For paper surveys, the Kish grid method is used to select the respondent.[3] In economies where cultural restrictions dictate gender matching, respondents are randomly selected from among all eligible adults of the interviewer's gender.

In traditionally phone-based economies, respondent selection follows the same procedure as in previous years, using random digit dialing or a nationally representative list of phone numbers. In most economies where mobile phone and landline penetration is high, a dual sampling frame is used.

The same respondent selection procedure is applied to the new phone-based economies. Dual frame (landline and mobile phone) random digital dialing is used where landline presence and use are 20 percent or higher based on historical Gallup estimates. Mobile phone random digital dialing is used in economies with limited to no landline presence (less than 20 percent).

For landline respondents in economies where mobile phone or landline penetration is 80 percent or higher, random selection of respondents is achieved by using either the latest birthday or household enumeration method. For mobile phone respondents in these economies or in economies where mobile phone or landline penetration is less than 80 percent, no further selection is performed. At least three attempts are made to reach a person in each household, spread over different days and times of day.

---

1. In 2019, mobile phone ownership was reported as 78 percent in Myanmar, 76 percent in Sri Lanka, and 69 percent in República Bolivariana de Venezuela.
2. Due to challenges in collecting representative samples by phone, these economies include Mexico and Vietnam, and the data will be collected face-to-face in 2022.
3. The Kish grid is a table of numbers used to select the interviewee. First, the interviewer lists the name, gender, and age of all permanent household members age 15 and up, whether or not they are present, in order by age. Second, the interviewer finds the column number of the Kish grid that corresponds to the last digit of the questionnaire and the row number for the number of eligible household members. The number in the cell where the column and row intersect is the person selected for the interview.

Data preparation

Data weighting is used to ensure a nationally representative sample for each economy. Final weights consist of the base sampling weight, which corrects for unequal probability of selection based on household size, and the poststratification weight, which corrects for sampling and nonresponse error. Poststratification weights use economy-level population statistics on gender and age and, where reliable data are available, education or socioeconomic status. Table A.1 shows the data collection period, number of interviews, approximate design effect, and margin of error for each economy as well as sampling details where relevant.

Additional information about the Global Findex data, including the complete database, can be found at http://www.worldbank.org/globalfindex.

Additional information about the methodology used in the Gallup World Poll can be found at http://www.gallup.com/178667/gallup-world-poll-work.aspx.

TABLE A.1

Details of survey methodology for economies included in the Global Findex 2021 survey and database

Economy	Region[a]	Income group	Data collection date	Number of interviews	Design effect[b]	Margin of error[c]	Mode of interview	Languages	Exclusions and other sampling details (samples are nationally representative unless otherwise noted)
Afghanistan	SAR	Low	Aug 8–Sep 27, 2021	1,002	1.6	3.9	Face-to-face (HH)[d]	Dari, Pashto	Gender-matched sampling was used during the final stage of selection.
Albania	ECA	Upper-middle	Jun 29–Aug 27, 2021	1,000	1.65	4	Face-to-face (HH)[d]	Albanian	People living in remote or difficult-to-access rural areas were excluded. The excluded area represents approximately 2 percent of the total population.
Algeria	MENA	Lower-middle	Oct 2–Nov 1, 2021	1,002	1.88	4.2	Mobile telephone	Arabic	
Argentina	LAC	Upper-middle	Oct 16, 2021–Jan 31, 2022	1,003	2.51	4.9	Landline and mobile telephone	Spanish	
Armenia	ECA	Upper-middle	Aug 5–Dec 12, 2021	1,000	1.59	3.9	Face-to-face (HH)[d]	Armenian	Settlements near territories disputed with Azerbaijan were not included for security reasons. The excluded area represents approximately 3 percent of the total population.
Australia	HI	High	Oct 4– Nov 14, 2021	1,000	1.66	4	Landline and mobile telephone	English	
Austria	HI	High	Oct 18–Nov 12, 2021	1,000	1.64	4	Landline and mobile telephone	German	

(table continues on next page)

Details of survey methodology for economies included in the Global Findex 2021 survey and database

Economy	Region[a]	Income group	Data collection date	Number of interviews	Design effect[b]	Margin of error[c]	Mode of interview	Languages	Exclusions and other sampling details (samples are nationally representative unless otherwise noted)
Bangladesh	SAR	Lower-middle	Feb 27–Mar 30, 2022	1,000	1.27	3.5	Face-to-face (HH)[d]	Bengali	
Belgium	HI	High	Nov 10–Dec 30, 2021	1,012	1.32	3.5	Landline and mobile telephone	French, Dutch	
Benin	SSA	Lower-middle	Jul 26–Aug 12, 2021	1,000	1.49	3.8	Face-to-face (HH)[d]	Bariba, Fon, French	
Bolivia	LAC	Lower-middle	Sep 11–Oct 20, 2021	1,000	2.14	4.5	Mobile telephone	Spanish	
Bosnia and Herzegovina	ECA	Upper-middle	Oct 2–Nov 8, 2021	1,000	1.81	4.2	Landline and mobile telephone	Bosnian	
Brazil	LAC	Upper-middle	Jul 21–Sep 10, 2021	1,002	2.39	1.5	Landline and mobile telephone	Portu-guese	
Bulgaria	ECA	Upper-middle	Sep 14–Oct 26, 2021	1,005	1.64	4	Landline and mobile telephone	Bulgarian	
Burkina Faso	SSA	Low	Aug 16–Sep 7, 2021	1,000	1.51	3.8	Face-to-face (HH)[d]	Dioula, French, Fulfulde, Moore	Some communities in the East and Sahel regions were excluded for security reasons. The areas represent 4 percent of the total population.
Cambodia	EAP	Lower-middle	Aug 28–Oct 5, 2021	1,000	1.95	4.3	Face-to-face (HH)[d]	Khmer	Koh Kong, Stueng Treng, Otdor Meanchey, and Kep provinces were excluded. These areas represent approximately 3 percent of the total population of Cambodia.
Cameroon	SSA	Lower-middle	Jun 11–Jul 4, 2021	1,000	1.49	3.8	Face-to-face (HH)[d]	French, English, Fulfulde	Some arrondissements in the Extreme North region, the Northwest region, and the South West region were excluded for security reasons. Neighborhoods with less than 50 households were also excluded from the sample. The exclusion represents 20 percent of the total population.

(table continues on next page)

Details of survey methodology for economies included in the Global Findex 2021 survey and database

Economy	Region[a]	Income group	Data collection date	Number of interviews	Design effect[b]	Margin of error[c]	Mode of interview	Languages	Exclusions and other sampling details (samples are nationally representative unless otherwise noted)
Canada	HI	High	Sep 3–Oct 26, 2021	1,007	1.39	3.6	Landline and mobile telephone	English, French	Northwest Territories, Yukon, and Nunavut (representing approximately 0.3 percent of the Canadian population) were excluded.
Chile	HI	High	Aug 20–Dec 22, 2021	1,000	1.52	3.8	Face-to-face (HH)[d]	Spanish	
China	EAP	Upper-middle	Nov 29, 2021–Jan 4, 2022	3,500	2.66	2.7	Mobile telephone	Chinese	Tibet was excluded from the sample. The excluded areas represent less than 1 percent of the total population of China.
Colombia	LAC	Upper-middle	Oct 5–Nov 23, 2021	1,000	1.5	3.8	Landline and mobile telephone	Spanish	
Congo, Rep.	SSA	Lower-middle	Jun 25–Jul 21, 2021	1,000	1.62	3.9	Face-to-face (HH)[d]	French, Kituba, Lingala	
Costa Rica	LAC	Upper-middle	Sep 23–Nov 5, 2021	1,001	1.41	3.7	Landline and mobile telephone	Spanish	
Côte d'Ivoire	SSA	Lower-middle	Oct 28–Nov 27, 2021	1,000	1.62	3.9	Face-to-face (HH)[d]	French, Dioula	
Croatia	HI	High	Sep 30–Nov 9, 2021	1,001	1.57	3.9	Landline and mobile telephone	Croatian	
Cyprus	HI	High	Oct 5– Nov 17, 2021	1,019	2.11	4.5	Landline and mobile telephone	Greek, English	
Czech Republic	HI	High	Nov 1–Dec 18, 2021	1,005	1.45	3.7	Landline and mobile telephone	Czech	
Denmark	HI	High	Sep 3–Oct 12, 2021	1,002	1.74	4.1	Mobile telephone	Danish	
Dominican Republic	LAC	Upper-middle	Aug 1–30, 2021	1,000	1.32	3.6	Face-to-face (HH)[d]	Spanish	
Ecuador	LAC	Upper-middle	Oct 5– Dec 2, 2021	1,000	1.66	4	Landline and mobile telephone	Spanish	

(table continues on next page)

Details of survey methodology for economies included in the Global Findex 2021 survey and database

Economy	Region[a]	Income group	Data collection date	Number of interviews	Design effect[b]	Margin of error[c]	Mode of interview	Languages	Exclusions and other sampling details (samples are nationally representative unless otherwise noted)
Egypt, Arab Rep.	MENA	Lower-middle	Sep 4–28, 2021	1,003	1.53	3.8	Face-to-face (HH)[d]	Arabic	Frontier governorates (Matruh, Red Sea, New Valley, North Sinai, and South Sinai) were excluded, as they are remote and represent a small proportion of the population of the country. The excluded areas represent less than 2 percent of the total population.
El Salvador	LAC	Lower-middle	Sep 22–Nov 24, 2021	1,002	1.61	3.9	Face-to-face (HH)[d]	Spanish	
Estonia	HI	High	Oct 20–Nov 21, 2021	1,001	1.32	3.6	Mobile telephone	Estonian, Russian	
Finland	HI	High	Sep 9–Nov 10, 2021	1,000	1.49	3.8	Mobile telephone	Finnish	
France	HI	High	Oct 18–Nov 15, 2021	1,000	1.61	3.9	Landline and mobile telephone	French	
Gabon	SSA	Upper-middle	Nov 4–16, 2021	1,020	2.36	4.7	Mobile telephone	French, Fang	
Georgia	ECA	Upper-middle	Jul 29–Dec 5, 2021	1,000	1.42	3.7	Face-to-face (HH)[d]	Georgian, Russian	South Ossetia and Abkhazia were not included for the safety of the interviewers. In addition, very remote mountainous villages or those with less than 100 inhabitants were also excluded. The excluded areas represent approximately 8 percent of the total population.
Germany	HI	High	Oct 18–Nov 13, 2021	1,000	2.34	4.7	Landline and mobile telephone	German	
Ghana	SSA	Lower-middle	Jul 27–Sep 11, 2021	1,000	1.48	3.8	Face-to-face (HH)[d]	English, Ewe, Twi, Dagbani, Hausa	Localities with less than 100 inhabitants were excluded from the sample. The excluded areas represent approximately 4 percent of the total population.
Greece	HI	High	Oct 1–29, 2021	1,003	2.2	4.6	Landline and mobile telephone	Greek	
Guinea	SSA	Low	Sep 4–27, 2021	1,000	1.4	3.8	Face-to-face (HH)[d]	French, Malinke, Pular, Soussou	
Honduras	LAC	Lower-middle	Sep 22–Dec 21, 2021	1,000	1.98	4.4	Face-to-face (HH)[d]	Spanish	

(table continues on next page)

Details of survey methodology for economies included in the Global Findex 2021 survey and database

Economy	Region[a]	Income group	Data collection date	Number of interviews	Design effect[b]	Margin of error[c]	Mode of interview	Languages	Exclusions and other sampling details (samples are nationally representative unless otherwise noted)
Hong Kong SAR, China	HI	High	Aug 18–Nov 9, 2021	1,003	1.18	3.4	Landline and mobile telephone	Chinese	
Hungary	HI	High	Nov 15–Dec 17, 2021	1,003	1.9	4.3	Landline and mobile telephone	Hungarian	
Iceland	HI	High	Oct 5–31, 2021	502	1.38	5.1	Landline and mobile telephone	Icelandic	
India	SAR	Lower-middle	Jul 30–Oct 18, 2021	3,000	1.34	2.1	Face-to-face (HH)[d]	Assamese, Bengali, Gujarati, Hindi, Kannada, Mala-yalam, Marathi, Odia, Punjabi, Tamil, Telugu	Excluded populations living in Northeast states and remote islands and Jammu and Kashmir. The excluded areas represent less than 10 percent of the total population.
Indonesia	EAP	Lower-middle	Jul 7–Oct 15, 2021	1,062	1.42	3.6	Face-to-face (HH)[d]	Bahasa Indonesia	
Iran, Islamic Rep.	MENA	Upper-middle	Sep 14–20, 2021	1,005	1.26	3.5	Landline and mobile telephone	Farsi	
Iraq	MENA	Upper-middle	Nov 1–Dec 9, 2021	1,012	1.66	4	Face-to-face (HH)[d]	Arabic, Kurdish	
Ireland	HI	High	Oct 18–Nov 13, 2021	1,000	1.9	4.3	Landline and mobile telephone	English	
Israel	HI	High	Aug 15–Nov 26, 2021	1,000	1.16	3.3	Face-to-face (HH)[d]	Hebrew, Arabic	The sample does not include the area of East Jerusalem. This area is included in the sample of West Bank and Gaza.
Italy	HI	High	Oct 18–Nov 13, 2021	1,000	2.51	4.9	Landline and mobile telephone	Italian	
Jamaica	LAC	Upper-middle	Sep 17–Nov 24, 2021	502	1.36	5.1	Face-to-face (HH)[d]	English	

(table continues on next page)

Details of survey methodology for economies included in the Global Findex 2021 survey and database

Economy	Region[a]	Income group	Data collection date	Number of interviews	Design effect[b]	Margin of error[c]	Mode of interview	Languages	Exclusions and other sampling details (samples are nationally representative unless otherwise noted)
Japan	HI	High	Sep 29–Dec 16, 2021	1,010	1.28	3.5	Landline and mobile telephone	Japanese	For landline random digit dialing, excluded 12 municipalities near the nuclear power plant in Fukushima. These areas were designated as not-to-call districts due to the devastation from the 2011 disasters. The exclusion represents less than 1 percent of the total population of Japan.
Jordan	MENA	Upper-middle	Nov 8–Dec 1, 2021	1,009	1.38	3.6	Mobile telephone	Arabic	
Kazakhstan	ECA	Upper-middle	Sep 3–Oct 19, 2021	1,000	1.46	3.8	Face-to-face (HH)[d]	Russian, Kazakh	
Kenya	SSA	Lower-middle	Jun 19–Jul 18, 2021	1,000	1.37	3.6	Face-to-face (HH)[d]	English, Swahili/ Kishwahili	
Korea, Rep.	HI	High	Sep 8–Oct 31, 2021	1,011	1.59	3.9	Landline and mobile telephone	Korean	
Kosovo	ECA	Upper-middle	Jul 3–Oct 4, 2021	1,000	1.55	3.9	Face-to-face (HH)[d]	Albanian, Serbian	
Kyrgyz Republic	ECA	Lower-middle	Aug 26–Oct 23, 2021	1,000	1.43	3.7	Face-to-face (HH)[d]	Kyrgyz, Russian, Uzbek	
Lao PDR	EAP	Lower-middle	Aug 30–Dec 14, 2021	1,000	1.49	3.8	Face-to-face (HH)[d]	Lao	Excluded Xaisomboun Province, Xayaboury Province, and some communes that are unreachable or have security considerations. In addition, during fieldwork Attapu and Houaphan were excluded due to COVID-19 (COVID-19 red zones). The excluded areas represent approximately 14 percent of the total population.
Latvia	HI	High	Nov 10–Dec 10, 2021	1,006	1.55	3.8	Mobile telephone	Latvian, Russian	
Lebanon	MENA	Upper-middle	Oct 26–Nov 6, 2021	1,022	1.24	3.4	Landline and mobile telephone	Arabic	
Liberia	SSA	Low	Jul 27–Sep 6, 2021	1,000	1.53	3.8	Face-to-face (HH)[d]	English, Pidgin English	
Lithuania	HI	High	Oct 20–Dec 3, 2021	1,009	1.79	4.1	Landline and mobile telephone	Lithuanian	

(table continues on next page)

Details of survey methodology for economies included in the Global Findex 2021 survey and database

Economy	Region[a]	Income group	Data collection date	Number of interviews	Design effect[b]	Margin of error[c]	Mode of interview	Languages	Exclusions and other sampling details (samples are nationally representative unless otherwise noted)
Malawi	SSA	Low	Aug 2–13, 2021	1,000	1.42	3.7	Face-to-face (HH)[d]	Chichewa, English, Tumbuka	
Malaysia	EAP	Upper-middle	Dec 17, 2021–Jan 28, 2022	1,000	1.7	4	Face-to-face (HH)[d]	Bahasa Malay, Chinese, English	Labuan and Putrajaya were excluded due to low population. The excluded areas represent approximately 1 percent of the total population.
Mali	SSA	Low	Jul 15–Aug 11, 2021	1,000	1.35	3.6	Face-to-face (HH)[d]	French, Bambara	The regions of Gao, Kidal, Mopti, and Tombouctou were excluded for security reasons. Quartiers and villages with less than 50 inhabitants were also excluded from the sample. The excluded areas represent 23 percent of the total population.
Malta	HI	High	Sep 14–Nov 8, 2021	1,000	1.41	3.7	Landline and mobile telephone	Maltese, English	
Mauritius	SSA	Upper-middle	Oct 21–Dec 13, 2021	1,000	2	4.4	Landline and mobile telephone	Creole, English, French	
Moldova	ECA	Lower-middle	Jul 12–Sep 10, 2021	1,000	1.25	3.5	Face-to-face (HH)[d]	Romanian/ Moldavian, Russian	Transnistria (Prednestrovie) excluded for safety of interviewers. The excluded area represents approximately 13 percent of the total population.
Mongolia	EAP	Lower-middle	Aug 20–Oct 13, 2021	1,000	1.49	3.8	Face-to-face (HH)[d]	Mongolian	
Morocco	MENA	Lower-middle	Oct 14–28, 2021	1,000	1.84	4.2	Mobile telephone	Moroccan Arabic	
Mozambique	SSA	Low	Oct 28–Dec 16, 2021	1,000	1.87	4.2	Face-to-face (HH)[d]	Portu-guese, Xichan-gana, Emakhuwa	Cabo Delgado province, as well as a small number of districts in other provinces, were excluded for security reasons. The excluded areas represent 11 percent of the total population.
Myanmar	EAP	Lower-middle	Oct 9–Nov 11, 2021	1,000	2.01	4.4	Mobile telephone	Myanmar, Burmese	
Namibia	SSA	Upper-middle	Aug 29–Oct 13, 2021	1,000	1.62	3.9	Face-to-face (HH)[d]	English, Oshi-vambo, Afrikaans	
Nepal	SAR	Lower-middle	Sep 10–Nov 19, 2021	1,000	1.45	3.7	Face-to-face (HH)[d]	Nepali	

(table continues on next page)

Details of survey methodology for economies included in the Global Findex 2021 survey and database

Economy	Region[a]	Income group	Data collection date	Number of interviews	Design effect[b]	Margin of error[c]	Mode of interview	Languages	Exclusions and other sampling details (samples are nationally representative unless otherwise noted)
Netherlands	HI	High	Oct 25–Nov 27, 2021	1,000	1.39	3.7	Landline and mobile telephone	Dutch	
New Zealand	HI	High	Sep 27–Nov 7, 2021	1,000	1.48	3.8	Landline and mobile telephone	English	
Nicaragua	LAC	Lower-middle	Sep 15–Nov 23, 2021	1,007	1.62	3.9	Face-to-face (HH)[d]	Spanish	
Nigeria	SSA	Lower-middle	Jul 15–Aug 20, 2021	1,000	1.91	4.3	Face-to-face (HH)[d]	English, Hausa, Igbo, Pidgin English, Yoruba	The states of Adamawa, Borno, and Yobe were excluded for safety and security reasons. These states represent 7 percent of the total population.
North Macedonia	ECA	Upper-middle	Oct 22–Dec 12, 2021	1,003	1.22	3.4	Landline and mobile telephone	Macedonian, Albanian	
Norway	HI	High	Aug 31–Oct 17, 2021	1,001	1.94	4.3	Mobile telephone	Norwegian	
Pakistan	SAR	Lower-middle	Oct 16–Dec 14, 2021	1,002	1.72	4.1	Face-to-face (HH)[d]	Urdu	Did not include Azad Jammu and Kashmir (AJK) and Gilgit-Baltistan. The excluded area represents approximately 5 percent of the total population. Gender-matched sampling was used during the final stage of selection.
Panama	LAC	Upper-middle	Oct 4–Dec 17, 2021	1,002	1.64	4	Face-to-face (HH)[d]	Spanish	
Paraguay	LAC	Upper-middle	Sep 1–Nov 11, 2021	1,000	1.37	3.6	Face-to-face (HH)[d]	Spanish, Jopara	
Peru	LAC	Upper-middle	Aug 22–Oct 21, 2021	1,000	1.34	3.6	Face-to-face (HH)[d]	Spanish	
Philippines	EAP	Lower-middle	Sep 20–Nov 15, 2021	1,000	1.82	4.2	Mobile telephone	Filipino, Cebuano, Bicol, Waray	
Poland	HI	High	Sep 11–Oct 22, 2021	1,001	1.45	3.7	Landline and mobile telephone	Polish	
Portugal	HI	High	Oct 8–Nov 8, 2021	1,002	1.74	4.1	Landline and mobile telephone	Portuguese	

(table continues on next page)

Details of survey methodology for economies included in the Global Findex 2021 survey and database

Economy	Region[a]	Income group	Data collection date	Number of interviews	Design effect[b]	Margin of error[c]	Mode of interview	Languages	Exclusions and other sampling details (samples are nationally representative unless otherwise noted)
Romania	ECA	Upper-middle	Sep 4–Oct 6, 2021	1,001	1.44	3.7	Landline and mobile telephone	Romanian	
Russian Federation	ECA	Upper-middle	Oct 4–Dec 13, 2021	2,011	1.54	2.7	Landline and mobile telephone	Russian	
Saudi Arabia	HI	High	Sep 5–20, 2021	1,019	2.02	4.4	Landline and mobile telephone	Arabic, English, Hindi, Urdu	Includes Saudis, Arab expatriates, and non-Arabs who were able to complete the interview in Arabic, English, Hindi, or Urdu.
Senegal	SSA	Lower-middle	Aug 17–Sep 9, 2021	1,000	1.49	3.8	Face-to-face (HH)[d]	French, Wolof	
Serbia	ECA	Upper-middle	Sep 29–Dec 3, 2021	1,001	1.95	4.3	Landline and mobile telephone	Serbian	
Sierra Leone	SSA	Low	Jun 16–Jul 19, 2021	1,001	1.46	3.7	Face-to-face (HH)[d]	English, Krio, Mende	
Singapore	HI	High	Nov 23, 2021–Jan 17, 2022	1,000	1.24	3.4	Face-to-face (HH)[d]	English, Chinese	Twenty-eight of 55 Planning Areas were excluded due to zero or small population size, accounting for less than 3 percent of the total population. In addition, individuals living in private condos or landed properties were excluded, representing approximately 20 percent of households in Singapore.
Slovak Republic	HI	High	Sep 28–Nov 6, 2021	1,005	1.51	3.8	Landline and mobile telephone	Hungarian, Slovak	
Slovenia	HI	High	Nov 10–Dec 8, 2021	1,000	1.97	4.4	Landline and mobile telephone	Slovene	
South Africa	SSA	Upper-middle	Aug 6–Nov 8, 2021	1,014	1.71	4	Face-to-face (HH)[d]	Afrikaans, English, Sotho, Xhosa, Zulu	

(table continues on next page)

Details of survey methodology for economies included in the Global Findex 2021 survey and database

Economy	Region[a]	Income group	Data collection date	Number of interviews	Design effect[b]	Margin of error[c]	Mode of interview	Languages	Exclusions and other sampling details (samples are nationally representative unless otherwise noted)
South Sudan	SSA	Low	Oct 13–Dec 14, 2021	1,001	1.84	4.2	Face-to-face (HH)[d]	Arabic, Bari, Dinka, English, Juba Arabic, Nuer, Zande	Some areas were excluded due to territorial dispute, security reasons, or inaccessibility. The excluded areas represent approximately 10 percent of the total population. In addition, 40 percent of the primary sampling units (PSUs) were replaced during fieldwork, primarily due to flooding.
Spain	HI	High	Oct 18–Nov 13, 2021	1,000	1.86	4.2	Landline and mobile telephone	Spanish	
Sri Lanka	SAR	Lower-middle	Nov 11–Dec 28, 2021	1,005	2.47	4.9	Mobile telephone	Sinhala, Tamil	
Sweden	HI	High	Sep 29–Nov 9, 2021	1,006	1.44	3.7	Landline and mobile telephone	Swedish	
Switzerland	HI	High	Oct 18–Nov 12, 2021	1,000	1.76	4.1	Landline and mobile telephone	German, French, Italian	
Taiwan, China	HI	High	Aug 16–Sep 14, 2021	1,000	1.88	4.3	Landline and mobile telephone	Chinese	
Tajikistan	ECA	Lower-middle	Aug 18–Oct 11, 2021	1,000	1.67	4	Face-to-face (HH)[d]	Tajik	
Tanzania	SSA	Lower-middle	Aug 2–29, 2021	1,001	1.54	3.9	Face-to-face (HH)[d]	Swahili, Kishwahili	
Thailand	EAP	Upper-middle	Oct 11–Dec 1, 2021	1,017	2.68	5.09	Mobile telephone	Thai	
Togo	SSA	Low	Sep 4–21, 2021	1,000	1.66	4	Face-to-face (HH)[d]	French, Ewe	
Tunisia	MENA	Lower-middle	Sep 24–Oct 16, 2021	1,000	1.29	3.5	Face-to-face (HH)[d]	Arabic	
Türkiye	ECA	Upper-middle	Nov 24–Dec 17, 2021	1,000	1.41	3.7	Landline and mobile telephone	Turkish	
Uganda	SSA	Low	Sep 12–Oct 5, 2021	1,000	1.46	3.7	Face-to-face (HH)[d]	Ateso, English, Luganda, Runyan-kole	Three districts in the North region were excluded for security reasons– Kotido, Moroto, and Nakapiripirit. The excluded areas represent 2 percent or less of the total population.

(table continues on next page)

Details of survey methodology for economies included in the Global Findex 2021 survey and database

Economy	Region[a]	Income group	Data collection date	Number of interviews	Design effect[b]	Margin of error[c]	Mode of interview	Languages	Exclusions and other sampling details (samples are nationally representative unless otherwise noted)
Ukraine	ECA	Lower-middle	Sep 27–Oct 14, 2021	1,001	1.88	4.3	Landline and mobile telephone	Russian, Ukrainian	
United Arab Emirates	HI	High	Oct 19–Nov 17, 2021	1,000	1.41	3.7	Mobile telephone	Arabic, English, Hindi, Urdu	Includes only Emiratis, Arab expatriates, and non-Arabs who were able to complete the interview in Arabic, English, Hindi, or Urdu.
United Kingdom	HI	High	Oct 18–Nov 12, 2021	1,000	1.47	3.8	Landline and mobile telephone	English	
United States	HI	High	Oct 5–Dec 27, 2021	1,007	1.61	3.9	Landline and mobile telephone	English, Spanish	
Uruguay	HI	High	Aug 24–Nov 20, 2021	1,000	1.29	3.5	Face-to-face (HH)[d]	Spanish	
Uzbekistan	ECA	Lower-middle	Aug 12–Oct 6, 2021	1,000	1.65	4	Face-to-face (HH)[d]	Uzbek, Russian	
Venezuela, RB	LAC	Upper-middle	Oct 4–Nov 24, 2021	1,000	1.72	4.1	Landline and mobile telephone	Spanish	
West Bank and Gaza	MENA	Lower-middle	Aug 16–Sep 22, 2021	1,000	1.3	3.5	Face-to-face (HH)[d]	Arabic	Areas with security concerns close to the Israeli borders, areas that are accessible only to special Israeli permit holders, and areas with population concentrations of less than 1,000 people were excluded. The excluded areas represent less than 2 percent of the total population. The sample includes East Jerusalem.
Zambia	SSA	Lower-middle	Aug 31–Sep 28, 2021	1,000	1.54	3.9	Face-to-face (HH)[d]	Bemba, English, Lozi, Nyanja, Tonga	
Zimbabwe	SSA	Lower-middle	Jun 26–Aug 8, 2021	1,000	1.4	3.7	Face-to-face (HH)[d]	English, Shona, Ndebele	

Source: Global Findex Database 2021.

Note: Similar to the World Development Indicators, the aggregation rules for global regions are intended to yield estimates for a consistent set of economies from one period to the next and for all indicators. World Bank abbreviations for the regions are as follows: EAP = East Asia and Pacific; ECA = Europe and Central Asia; LAC = Latin America and the Caribbean; MENA = Middle East and North Africa (referred to as MNA in Global Findex 2017); SAR = South Asia (referred to as SAS in Global Findex 2017); SSA = Sub-Saharan Africa.

a. Regions exclude high-income economies (HI) and may differ from common geographic usage.

b. The design effect calculation reflects the weights and does not incorporate the intraclass correlation coefficients because they vary by question. Design effect calculation: n*(sum of squared weights)/[(sum of weights)*(sum of weights)].

c. The margin of error is calculated around a proportion at the 95 percent confidence level. The maximum margin of error was calculated assuming a reported percentage of 50 percent and takes into account the design effect. Margin of error calculation: $\sqrt{(0.25/N)}*1.96*\sqrt{(DE)}$. Other errors that can affect survey validity include measurement error associated with the questionnaire, such as translation issues, and coverage error, where a part of the target population has a zero probability of being selected for the survey.

d. Hand-held (HH) data collection.

Account Ownership, 2021

Account ownership, by economy, 2021

Economy	Adults with an account (%)	Women with an account (%)	Poor adults with an account (%)[a]
Afghanistan	10	5	6
Albania	44	46	27
Algeria	44	31	32
Argentina	72	74	65
Armenia	55	52	45
Australia	99	100	98
Austria	100	100	100
Bangladesh	53	43	49
Belgium	99	99	98
Benin	49	40	41
Bolivia	69	63	56
Bosnia and Herzegovina	79	70	72
Brazil	84	81	82
Bulgaria	84	84	74
Burkina Faso	36	31	25
Cambodia	33	33	23
Cameroon	52	49	34
Canada	100	100	99
Chile	87	87	86
China	89	87	83
Colombia	60	56	48
Congo, Rep.	47	44	33
Costa Rica	68	61	57
Côte d'Ivoire	51	37	44
Croatia	92	90	84

(table continues on next page)

Account ownership, by economy, 2021

Economy	Adults with an account (%)	Women with an account (%)	Poor adults with an account (%)[a]
Cyprus	93	93	91
Czech Republic	95	93	95
Denmark	100	100	100
Dominican Republic	51	49	39
Ecuador	64	58	59
Egypt, Arab Rep.	27	24	20
El Salvador	36	29	23
Estonia	99	100	99
Finland	100	99	99
France	99	100	98
Gabon	66	61	59
Georgia	70	71	62
Germany	100	100	100
Ghana	68	63	55
Greece	95	93	92
Guinea	30	24	24
Honduras	38	29	27
Hong Kong SAR, China	98	98	96
Hungary	88	87	81
Iceland	100	100	100
India	78	78	78
Indonesia	52	52	47
Iran, Islamic Rep.	90	85	87
Iraq	19	15	14
Ireland	100	100	99
Israel	93	92	89
Italy	97	97	95
Jamaica	73	72	68
Japan	98	99	98
Jordan	47	34	37
Kazakhstan	81	84	82
Kenya	79	75	67
Korea, Rep.	99	99	97
Kosovo	58	47	52

(table continues on next page)

Account ownership, by economy, 2021

Economy	Adults with an account (%)	Women with an account (%)	Poor adults with an account (%)[a]
Kyrgyz Republic	45	44	44
Lao PDR	37	38	23
Latvia	97	98	94
Lebanon	21	17	13
Liberia	52	44	42
Lithuania	94	90	91
Malawi	43	38	33
Malaysia	88	88	83
Mali	44	41	38
Malta	96	95	93
Mauritius	91	89	91
Moldova	64	63	54
Mongolia	98	99	98
Morocco	44	33	34
Mozambique	49	39	34
Myanmar	48	46	33
Namibia	71	69	56
Nepal	54	50	45
Netherlands	100	99	99
New Zealand	99	99	97
Nicaragua	26	22	21
Nigeria	45	35	33
North Macedonia	85	80	78
Norway	99	100	99
Pakistan	21	13	18
Panama	45	43	32
Paraguay	54	55	48
Peru	57	53	46
Philippines	51	47	34
Poland	96	96	94
Portugal	93	90	88
Romania	69	66	57
Russian Federation	90	90	86
Saudi Arabia	74	63	67

(table continues on next page)

Account ownership, by economy, 2021

Economy	Adults with an account (%)	Women with an account (%)	Poor adults with an account (%)[a]
Senegal	56	50	48
Serbia	89	90	84
Sierra Leone	29	25	21
Singapore	98	97	96
Slovak Republic	96	94	91
Slovenia	99	98	98
South Africa	85	86	78
South Sudan	6	4	4
Spain	98	97	98
Sri Lanka	89	89	87
Sweden	100	100	99
Switzerland	99	99	99
Taiwan, China	95	94	93
Tajikistan	39	39	38
Tanzania	52	46	39
Thailand	96	93	98
Togo	50	44	39
Tunisia	37	29	32
Türkiye	74	63	61
Uganda	66	65	51
Ukraine	84	81	80
United Arab Emirates	86	87	83
United Kingdom	100	100	100
United States	95	97	91
Uruguay	74	76	63
Uzbekistan	44	39	41
Venezuela, RB	84	80	78
West Bank and Gaza	34	26	17
Zambia	49	45	33
Zimbabwe	60	54	47

Source: Global Findex Database 2021.

Note: Data for all indicators are available at http://www.worldbank.org/globalfindex.

a. Adults in the poorest 40 percent of households. Data are based on household income quintiles.

Global Findex Glossary

Account (%): The percentage of respondents who report having an account (by themselves or together with someone else) at a bank or another type of financial institution (see *financial institution account*), or report personally using a mobile money service in the past year (see *mobile money account*).

Borrowed any money (%): The percentage of respondents who report borrowing any money (by themselves or together with someone else) for any reason and from any source in the past year.

Borrowed any money using a mobile money account (%): The percentage of respondents who report borrowing any money using a mobile money account in the past year.

Borrowed for health or medical purposes (%): The percentage of respondents who report borrowing any money for health or medical purposes in the past year.

Borrowed from a formal financial institution (%): The percentage of respondents who report borrowing any money from a bank or another type of financial institution or using a credit card in the past year.

Borrowed from a savings club (%): The percentage of respondents who report borrowing any money from an informal savings club in the past year.

Borrowed from family or friends (%): The percentage of respondents who report borrowing any money from family, relatives, or friends in the past year.

Can use a mobile money account without help from anyone, including a mobile money agent (%): The percentage of respondents who report that they can use a mobile money account without the help of another person, including a mobile money agent.

Can use an account at a bank or financial institution without help if they opened one (% without an account): Among the share of respondents without an account, the percentage of respondents who report they could use an account at a bank or a financial institution without help, if they opened one.

Coming up with emergency money in 30 days: possible and not difficult or somewhat difficult (%): The percentage of respondents who say it is possible and not difficult at all or somewhat difficult to come up with 1/20 of gross national income (GNI) per capita in local currency units in 30 days.

Coming up with emergency money in seven days: possible and not difficult or somewhat difficult (%): The percentage of respondents who say it is possible and not difficult at all or somewhat difficult for them to come up with 1/20 of GNI per capita in local currency units in seven days.

Experience or continue to experience severe financial hardship as a result of the disruption caused by COVID-19: very worried (%): The percentage of respondents who are very worried that they will experience or continue to experience severe financial hardship as a result of the disruption caused by COVID-19.

Financial institution account (%): The percentage of respondents who report having an account (by themselves or together with someone else) at a bank, credit union, microfinance institution, or post office that falls under prudential regulation by a government body. [1]

First financial institution account ever was opened to receive a wage payment (%): The percentage of respondents who report opening a financial institution account for the first time to receive a wage payment.

First financial institution account ever was opened to receive money from the government (%): The percentage of respondents who report opening a financial institution account for the first time to receive money from the government.

Has access to the internet (%): The percentage of respondents who report having access to the internet.

Has an inactive account (%): The percentage of respondents who report neither a deposit into nor a withdrawal from their account in the past year. This also includes making or receiving any kind of digital payment.

Made a digital in-store merchant payment for the first time after COVID-19 started (%): The percentage of respondents who report that after COVID-19 started, they used for the first time a debit or credit card, or a mobile phone, to make a purchase in-store.

Made a digital merchant payment (%): The percentage of respondents who report using a debit or credit card, or a mobile phone, to make a purchase in-store, or to pay online for an internet purchase.

Made a digital merchant payment for the first time after COVID-19 started (%): The percentage of respondents who report that the first time they used a debit or credit card, or a mobile phone, to make a purchase in-store or to pay online for an internet purchase, happened after COVID-19 started.

Made a digital online merchant payment for an online purchase (%): The percentage of respondents who report using the internet to buy something online in the past year.

Made a digital online payment for an online purchase for the first time after COVID-19 started (%): The percentage of respondents who report that they used the internet to buy something online for the first time after COVID-19 started.

Made a digital payment (%): The percentage of respondents who report using mobile money, a debit or credit card, or a mobile phone to make a payment from an account; or who report using the internet to pay bills or to buy something online or in a store in the past year. This includes respondents who report paying bills or sending remittances directly from a financial institution account or through a mobile money account in the past year.

Made a utility payment (%): The percentage of respondents who report making regular payments for water, electricity, or trash collection in the past year.

Made a utility payment: using an account (%): The percentage of respondents who report personally making regular payments for water, electricity, or trash collection in the past year directly from a financial institution account or a mobile phone.

Made a utility payment: using an account for the first time after COVID-19 started (%): The percentage of respondents who report personally making regular payments for water, electricity, or trash collection using a financial institution account or a mobile phone for the first time after COVID-19 started.

---

1. Data on adults with a financial institution account include respondents who reported having an account at a bank or at another type of financial institution, such as a credit union, a microfinance institution, a cooperative, or the post office (if applicable). The data also include an additional 3 percent of respondents in 2021 who reported receiving wages, government transfers, a public sector pension, or payments for agricultural products into a financial institution account in the past year; paying utility bills or school fees from a financial institution account in the past year; or receiving wages, government transfers, or agricultural payments into a card in the past year. The definition does not include nonbank financial institutions such as pension funds, retirement accounts, insurance companies, or equity holdings such as stocks. As used throughout the report, financial institution refers to a formal financial institution.

Made a utility payment: using cash only (%): The percentage of respondents who report personally making regular payments for water, electricity, or trash collection in the past year using cash only.

Made digital in-store merchant payments (%): The percentage of respondents who report using a debit or credit card, or a mobile phone, to make an in-store purchase.

Made or received a digital payment (%): The percentage of respondents who report using mobile money, a debit or credit card, or a mobile phone to make a payment from an account—or report using the internet to pay bills or to buy something online or in a store—in the past year. This includes respondents who report paying bills, sending or receiving remittances, receiving payments for agricultural products, receiving government transfers, receiving wages, or receiving a public sector pension directly from or into a financial institution account or through a mobile money account in the past year.

Mobile money account (%): The percentage of respondents who report personally using a mobile money service to make payments, buy things, or to send or receive money in the past year.[2]

Most worrying financial issue: money for old age (%): The percentage of respondents whose primary financial worry is that they will not have enough money for old age.

Most worrying financial issue: money to pay for monthly expenses or bills (%): The percentage of respondents whose primary financial issue is that they will not have enough money for monthly expenses or bills.

Most worrying financial issue: paying for medical costs in case of a serious illness or accident (%): The percentage of respondents whose primary financial issue is that they will not have enough money for medical costs in the case of a serious illness or accident.

Most worrying financial issue: paying school or education fees (%): The percentage of respondents whose primary financial issue is that they will not have enough money to pay school fees.

Owns a debit or credit card (%): The percentage of respondents who report having a debit or credit card.

Owns a mobile phone (%): The percentage of respondents who report owning a mobile phone.

Received a public sector pension (%): The percentage of respondents who report personally receiving a pension from the government, military, or public sector in the past year.

Received a public sector pension: in cash only (%): The percentage of respondents who report personally receiving a pension from the government, military, or public sector in the past year in cash only.

Received a public sector pension: into an account (%): The percentage of respondents who report personally receiving a pension from the government, military, or public sector in the past year directly into a financial institution account, into a card, or through a mobile phone.

Received digital payments (%): The percentage of respondents who report using a mobile money account, a debit or credit card, or a mobile phone to receive a payment into an account in the past year. This includes respondents who report receiving remittances, receiving payments for agricultural products, receiving government transfers, receiving wages, or receiving a public sector pension directly into a financial institution account or into a mobile money account in the past year.

---

2. Data on adults with a mobile money account include respondents who reported personally using services included in the GSM Association's Mobile Money for the Unbanked (GSMA MMU) database to pay bills or to send or receive money in the past year. The data also include an additional 2 percent of respondents in 2021 who reported receiving wages, government transfers, a public sector pension, or payments for agricultural products through a mobile phone in the past year. Unlike the definition of account at a financial institution, the definition of mobile money account does not include the payment of utility bills or school fees through a mobile phone. The reason is that the phrasing of the possible answers leaves it open as to whether those payments were made using a mobile money account or an over-the-counter service.

Received government payments (%): The percentage of respondents who report personally receiving any payment from the government (government transfers, public sector pension, or public sector wages) in the past year. This includes payments for educational or medical expenses, unemployment benefits, subsidy payments, or any kind of social benefits. It also includes pension payments from the government, military, or public sector, as well as wages from employment in the government, military, or public sector.

Received government payments: in cash only (%): The percentage of respondents who report personally receiving payments from the government (government transfers, public sector pension, or public sector wages) in the past year in cash only.

Received government payments: into an account (%): The percentage of respondents who report personally receiving payments from the government (government transfers, public sector pension, or public sector wages) in the past year directly into a financial institution account, into a card, or through a mobile phone.

Received government transfer (%): The percentage of respondents who report personally receiving any transfer from the government in the past year. This includes payments for educational or medical expenses, unemployment benefits, subsidy payments, or any kind of social benefits. It does not include a pension from the government, military, or public sector; wages; or any other payments related to work.

Received government transfer or pension (%): The percentage of respondents who report personally receiving any transfer or pension from the government in the past year. This includes payments for educational or medical expenses, unemployment benefits, subsidy payments, or any kind of social benefits. It also includes payments for a pension from the government, military, or public sector.

Received government transfer or pension: cash only (%): The percentage of respondents who report personally receiving a government transfer or pension in the past year in cash only.

Received government transfer or pension: into an account (%): The percentage of respondents who report personally receiving any transfer or pension from the government in the past year into a financial institution account, into a card, or through a mobile phone.

Received government transfer: cash only (%): The percentage of respondents who report personally receiving any transfer from the government in the past year in cash only.

Received government transfer: into an account (%): The percentage of respondents who report personally receiving any transfer from the government in the past year directly into a financial institution account, into a card, or through a mobile phone.

Received payments for agricultural products: in cash only (%): The percentage of respondents who report personally receiving money from any source for the sale of agricultural products, crops, produce, or livestock in the past year in cash only.

Received payments for agricultural products: into an account (%): The percentage of respondents who report personally receiving money from any source for the sale of agricultural products, crops, produce, or livestock in the past year directly into a financial institution account, into a card, or through a mobile phone.

Received payments for the sale of agricultural products, livestock, or crops (%): The percentage of respondents who report personally receiving payments from any source for the sale of agricultural products, crops, produce, or livestock in the past year.

Received private sector wages (%): The percentage of respondents who report being employed in the private sector and receiving any money from their employer in the past year in the form of a salary or wages for doing work.

Received private sector wages: in cash only (%): The percentage of respondents who report being employed in the private sector and receiving any money from their employer in the past year in the form of a salary or wages for doing work in cash only.

Received private sector wages: into an account (%): The percentage of respondents who report being employed in the private sector and receiving any money from their employer in the past year in the form of a salary or wages for doing work, and who received that money directly into a financial institution account, into a card, or through a mobile phone.

Received public sector wages (%): The percentage of respondents who report being employed by the government, military, or public sector and receiving any money from their employer in the past year in the form of a salary or wages for doing work.

Received public sector wages: in cash only (%): The percentage of respondents who report being employed by the government, military, or public sector and receiving any money from their employer in the past year in the form of a salary or wages for doing work, and who received that money in cash only.

Received public sector wages: into an account (%): The percentage of respondents who report being employed by the government, military, or public sector and receiving any money from their employer in the past year in the form of a salary or wages for doing work, and who received that money directly into a financial institution account, into a card, or into a mobile phone.

Received wages (%): The percentage of respondents who report receiving any money from an employer in the past year in the form of a salary or wages for doing work. This does not include any money received directly from clients or customers.

Received wages into an account: paid higher-than-expected fees (%): The percentage of respondents who report paying higher fees than expected to receive a salary or wages.

Received wages: in cash only (%): The percentage of respondents who report receiving any money from an employer in the past year in the form of a salary or wages for doing work, and who received it in cash only.

Received wages: into an account (%): The percentage of respondents who report receiving any money from an employer in the past year in the form of a salary or wages for doing work, and who received it directly into a financial institution account, into a card, or through a mobile phone.

Saved any money (%): The percentage of respondents who report personally saving or setting aside any money for any reason and using any mode of saving in the past year.

Saved at a financial institution (%): The percentage of respondents who report saving or setting aside any money at a bank or another type of financial institution in the past year.

Saved at a financial institution or using a mobile money account (%): The percentage of respondents who report saving or setting aside any money at a bank or another type of financial institution or using a mobile money account to save in the past year.

Saved for old age (%): The percentage of respondents who report saving or setting aside any money in the past year for old age.

Saved money using a mobile money account (%): The percentage of respondents who report saving money using a mobile money account.

Saved using a savings club or a person outside the family (%): The percentage of respondents who report saving or setting aside any money in the past year by using an informal savings club or a person outside the family.

Sent or received domestic remittances (%): The percentage of respondents who report personally sending or receiving any of their money in the past year to or from a relative or friend living in a different area of their country.

Sent or received domestic remittances: in-person and in cash only (%): The percentage of respondents who report personally sending or receiving any of their money in the past year to or from a relative or friend living in a different area of their country and who sent or received it in-person and in cash only.

Sent or received domestic remittances: through a money transfer service (%): The percentage of respondents who report personally sending or receiving any of their money in the past year to or from a relative or friend living in a different area of their country and who sent or received it over the counter in a branch of their financial institution, through a mobile banking agent, or through a money transfer service.

Sent or received domestic remittances: using an account (%): The percentage of respondents who report personally sending or receiving any of their money in the past year to or from a relative or friend living in a different area of their country and who sent or received the money using a financial institution account or a mobile money account.

Store money using a financial institution or a mobile money account (%): The percentage of respondents who report keeping money in a financial institution account or a mobile money account.

Use a mobile phone or the internet to make payments, buy things, or to send or receive money using a financial institution account (%): The percentage of respondents who report that in the past year they used a mobile phone or the internet to make payments, buy things, or to send or receive money using a financial institution account.

Used a credit or a debit card (%): The percentage of respondents who report using their own credit or debit card in the past year.

Used a mobile phone or the internet to access a financial institution account (%): The percentage of respondents who report that in the past year they used a mobile phone or the internet to make a payment, make a purchase, or to send or receive money through their financial institution account.

Used a mobile phone or the internet to access an account (%): The percentage of respondents who report that in the past year they used a mobile phone or the internet to make a payment, make a purchase, or to send or receive money through their account.

Used a mobile phone or the internet to check account balance (%): The percentage of respondents who report using a mobile phone or the internet to check their balance for a financial institution account in the past year.

Used a mobile phone or the internet to pay bills (%): The percentage of respondents who report using a mobile phone or the internet to pay bills in the past year.

Used a mobile phone or the internet to send money (%): The percentage of respondents who report using a mobile phone or the internet to send money to a relative or friend in the past year.

Worried about not being able to pay for medical costs in case of a serious illness or accident: very worried (%): The percentage of respondents who are very worried about not being able to pay for medical costs in the case of a serious illness or accident.

Worried about not being able to pay school fees or fees for education: very worried (%): The percentage of respondents who are very worried about not being able to pay school fees or fees for education.

Worried about not having enough money for monthly expenses or bills: very worried (%): The percentage of respondents who are very worried about not having enough money to pay for monthly expenses or bills.

Worried about not having enough money for old age: very worried (%): The percentage of respondents who are very worried about not having enough money for old age.

www.ingramcontent.com/pod-product-compliance
Lightning Source LLC
Chambersburg PA
CBHW041442210326

41599CB00004B/98